Dangerous Trade

Dangerous Trade

ARMS EXPORTS, HUMAN RIGHTS, AND INTERNATIONAL REPUTATION

Jennifer L. Erickson

COLUMBIA UNIVERSITY PRESS

NEW YORK

Columbia University Press
Publishers Since 1893
New York   Chichester, West Sussex
cup.columbia.edu

Library of Congress Cataloging-in-Publication Data

Erickson, Jennifer L., author.
Dangerous trade : arms exports, human rights, and
international reputation / Jennifer L. Erickson.
pages cm
Includes bibliographical references and index.
ISBN 978-0-231-17096-3 (cloth : alk. paper)—ISBN 978-0-231-53903-6 (e-book)
1. Arms transfers—Law and legislation   2. Arms control.
3. Export controls.   4. Human rights.   I. Title.

K3924.M8E75 2015
382'.456234—dc23
2014022403

Columbia University Press books are printed on
permanent and durable acid-free paper.
This book is printed on paper with recycled content.
Printed in the United States of America

c 10 9 8 7 6 5 4 3 2 1

COVER DESIGN: FACEOUT STUDIO

References to websites (URLs) were accurate at the time of writing.
Neither the author nor Columbia University Press is responsible for URLs that
may have expired or changed since the manuscript was prepared.

To my parents

CONTENTS

ACKNOWLEDGMENTS

It is with deep gratitude and appreciation that I acknowledge the individuals whose support and feedback have made it possible for me to write this book. To my mentors at Cornell University in particular, I still cannot adequately express my thanks for their generosity of time, thorough comments, and steady support. They stretched me intellectually and gave me a research foundation on which I continue to rely. Peter Katzenstein is an unparalleled mentor, scholar, and teacher. I will always be grateful for his wisdom, knowledge, and guidance on "the long road to Ithaka" and beyond. The road has been a long one, and he has been there with me every step of the way. Christopher Way has given patient advice on statistics, invaluable commentary, and supportive conversation. Matthew Evangelista's thoughtful reading pointed me in theoretical and empirical directions that helped to shape the project from its early stages onward. I also thank Jonathan Kirshner for his sharp questions as external reader and his mentorship while I moved the project forward. This final product is incalculably better because of these individuals' tireless efforts, and I cannot imagine having completed it without them.

As I have worked to complete the book, I was fortunate to start out at the Dickey Center for International Understanding at Dartmouth College, where I encountered a wonderful intellectual community among center fellows and the faculty in the Government Department. I am also grateful to Susan Shell and the administration at Boston College for allowing me to take that postdoc year and for their continued support ever since. Tim Crawford, Dave Deese, Jerry Easter, Peter Krause, and Bob Ross gave thoughtful comments on the project, and I have been continuously impressed by the challenging questions I received from my colleagues across departmental subfields at research presentations. I also thank Shirley Gee for her helpful administrative support and Caroline Tilden and Elizabeth Wall for their excellent assistance with additional data collection. Finally, I am grateful to the Institute for Quantitative Social Science at Harvard University, which provided me with office space and library access as I completed the penultimate draft of the manuscript.

For their generous financial support, I gratefully acknowledge the Peace Studies Program, the Institute for European Studies, the Mario Einaudi Center for International Studies, and the Graduate School, all at Cornell University, as well as the Einaudi Foundation of Turin and the Deutscher Akademischer Austausch Dienst (DAAD). For providing me with institutional homes and intellectual communities during my time in the field, I thank the Stiftung Wissenschaft und Politik, in particular Markus Kaim and Oliver Tränert for arranging my affiliation, as well as the Wissenschaftszentrum Berlin and Michael Zürn for welcoming me to his research group there. I thank Mark Bromley at the Stockholm International Peace Research Institute for so quickly and graciously providing some of the institute's data for my statistical analyses before its databases went online, for offering helpful advice in the early stages of the project, and for continuing to be a valued colleague. Finally, although they wished to remain nameless, I am deeply indebted to all of the individuals I interviewed in the course of my research. The knowledge and experiences they shared with me form the backbone of this project, and I am profoundly impressed by their energy and dedication to conventional arms control.

This book is immeasurably better because of the tremendous feedback I have received on it over the years from many individuals: Rawi Abdelal, Michal Ben-Josef Hirsch, Richard Bensel, Clifford Bob, Noelle Brigden, Steve Brooks, Michael Brzoska, Joshua Busby, Jeff Checkel, Danielle Cohen, Neil Cooper, M. Patrick Cotrell, Ben de Bivort, Barbara Frey, Denise Garcia, Eugene Gholz, Kelly Greenhill, Michael Herron, Ian Hurd, Keith Krause, Ulrich Krotz, Jennifer Lind, Nic Marsh, Manjari Chatterjee Miller, Sara Moorman, Melinda Negron, TV Paul, Tsveta Petrova, Daryl Press, Daniel Sledge, Sid Tarrow, Ben Valentino, Stéfanie von Hlatky, Srdjan Vucetic, and Bill Wohlforth. I cannot thank all of them enough for finding the time and energy amid their own busy schedules to help me think and write about the project in a far better way than I could have done on my own.

Beyond this direct feedback, the conversations with and support from my friends and colleagues at Cornell, Dartmouth, and Boston College and in Berlin, Boston, and elsewhere have been both stimulating and inspiring. They have also made this process more creative and less lonely than it might otherwise have been: Peter Andreas, Phil Ayoub, Ameya Balsekar, Martin Binder, Jenny Stepp Breen, Noelle Brigden, Chia-cher Chou, Charlie Clements, Danielle Cohen, Marc DeVore, Jennifer Dixon, Molly Clark Dunigan, Daena Funahashi, Courtney Fung, Dave Glick, Owen Greene, Jennifer Hadden, Susanne Hansen, Kerstin Heidrich, Roland Hiemann, Stephanie Hofmann, Emilie Hodgin, Dave Hopkins, Julia Iverson, Jai Kwan Jung, Isaac Kamola, Daniel Kinderman, Gabi Kruks-Wisner, Serena Laws, Daniel Levine, Kristin McKie, Alison McQueen, Sara Moorman, Evelyn Krache Morris, Steve Nelson, Margarita Petrova, Tsveta Petrova, Barry Posen, Miranda Priebe, Leon Ratz, Jean-Marc Rickli, Zacc Ritter, Karthika Sasikumar, Oliver Schmidt, Anthony Seaboyer, Sylvia Sellers-Garcia, Lucia Seybert, Josh Shifrinson, Daniel Sledge, Michelle Smith, Monica Soare, Maria Sperandei, Anna Stavrianakis, Beth Tamayose, Jing Tao, Avery Udagawa, Bethany Vasecka, Lora Viola, Moritz Weiss, Rachel Whitlark, Cindy Williams, and Andrew Yeo. Special thanks go to Ben de Bivort, whose support, patience, and partnership helped keep me going during the long last legs of the writing process. All mistakes, of course, are my own, but the advice and support from all those individuals listed here and more have been invaluable to me.

I am grateful to my editor at Columbia University Press, Anne Routon, for her support and guidance, and to the staff at Columbia University Press for their ready assistance and responsiveness to my questions. I also thank my copy editor, Annie Barva, for her careful and thoughtful work in preparing the final manuscript.

Finally, to my teachers, without whom I would not have gone to graduate school in the first place—especially Susan Bloom, Michael Chambers, Paddy Dale, Dan Hoffrening, Stu Lade, and Charles Umbanhowar Sr.— I offer my sincerest thanks.

Last but never least, my parents have sent their love along with many care packages and remained always patient with me. Thank you for all that you have given me. This book is for you.

ABBREVIATIONS

AA	German Federal Foreign Office (Auswärtiges Amt)
APL	anti-personnel landmines
ATT	Arms Trade Treaty
BAE	British Aerospace/BAE Systems
CAT	Conventional Arms Transfer Talks
CCW	Convention on Certain Conventional Weapons
CDU	Christian Democratic Union (Christlich Demokratische Union Deutschlands)
CI	confidence intervals
COCOM	Coordinating Committee on Multilateral Export Controls
DOS	U.S. Department of State
ECOWAS	Economic Community of West African States
EU	European Union
GDP	gross domestic product
HRW	Human Rights Watch
IANSA	International Action Network on Small Arms
ICBL	International Campaign to Ban Landmines
IR	international relations
MCW	major conventional weapons

MIC	military-industrial complex
NATO	North Atlantic Treaty Organization
NGO	nongovernmental organization
NISAT	Norwegian Initiative on Small Arms Transfers
NRA	National Rifle Association
OAS	Organization of American States
OSCE	Organization for Security and Cooperation in Europe
P5	United Nations Security Council Permanent Members
PD-13	Presidential Directive 13
PRB	Poudrières réunies de Belgique
PTS	Political Terror Scale
SALW	small arms and light weapons
SAS	Small Arms Survey
SE	standard errors
SIPRI	Stockholm International Peace Research Institute
SPD	Social Democratic Party (Sozialdemokratische Partei Deutschlands)
TIV	trend-indicator value
UN	United Nations
UNGGE	United Nations Group of Governmental Experts
UNPOA	United Nations Programme of Action to Prevent, Combat, and Eradicate the Illicit Trade in Small Arms and Light Weapons in All Its Aspects (or just UN Programme of Action on Small Arms)

Dangerous Trade

1. *Introduction and Overview*

In April 2008, China attempted to make a routine delivery of ammunition and explosives worth $1.245 million to Zimbabwe by way of South Africa. What followed was anything but routine. The deal sparked an international incident and, in turn, highlighted the often conflicting security and humanitarian imperatives of the contemporary arms trade. A South African investigative news magazine exposed "the ship of shame," provoking media attention and criticism from all corners of the globe. Because the South African government had approved the shipment for transport from the port of Durban, it too came under fire for helping to arm the repressive Mugabe regime. Churches and civil society groups condemned the decision as amoral and of questionable legality under the South African Constitution. Dockworkers threatened to strike rather than unload the cargo.[1]

The arms arrived in Durban just as China was trying to avoid criticism over its own human rights record in the lead-up to the Beijing Olympics and as South Africa was facing further embarrassment over its appeasement of Mugabe. Reports of repression, violence, and torture in Zimbabwe following the contested March 2008 election fueled critics' charges that the weaponry would be used to crack down on the political opposition. To save face at home and abroad, South Africa reversed its decision and barred the transport by court order. Countries across Africa denied port to the ship and urged others to do the same, with the support of Western powers. China ultimately called the ship home, unable to find a port and unwilling to face the reputational damage brought on by fulfilling the deal (Baldauf and Ford 2008).

At the time of the attempted shipment, only the European Union (EU) had imposed a multilateral arms embargo on Zimbabwe. Neither China nor South Africa were party to any convention prohibiting the supply of arms to that country. In fact, there were no international legal restrictions barring the sale of conventional weapons to Zimbabwe. And yet the arms were never delivered. Instead, international and domestic uproar forced South Africa's hand and turned the ship around. Even so, efforts just months later in July to impose a United Nations (UN) arms embargo and other sanctions on Zimbabwe failed, with South Africa leading a small opposition and Russia and China exercising their veto power (MacFarquhar 2008). Opponents argued that sanctions fell outside the UN Security Council's mandate to deal only with matters of international peace and security. Supporters, however, believed that trade restrictions would help protect the domestic populace and reinforce the need for good governance to ensure regional and international security.

Conventional arms control is riddled with contradictions like these, presenting states with conflicting security, economic, and normative imperatives. Small arms and light weapons (SALW) and major conventional weapons (MCW)[2] are responsible for the vast majority of conflict deaths, frequently associated with societal instability, and commonly involved in human rights violations. Calls to control the spread of small arms, now referred to as "the real weapons of mass destruction,"[3] and major conventional arms have become widespread in the past decade. Yet conventional arms also have an enduring and legitimate place in world politics. States have long protected their right to choose their arms trade partners as a matter of self-defense, and conventional arms are recognized as essential tools of national and international security. Moreover, arms manufacturers worldwide have an economic stake in more open arms markets and considerable political influence at home. In some countries, such as the United States, domestic law also protects civilians' right to bear arms. Historically, states have therefore determined their own arms export criteria and eschewed calls for common controls that might stem the flow of weapons to unstable regions. Even today, as states debate the political utility and ethical dilemmas of selling or restricting arms to parties in the Syrian conflict, it is clear that arms remain an important currency in world politics.

Yet despite states' past reluctance and persistent concerns, the UN General Assembly passed the Arms Trade Treaty (ATT) on April 2, 2013, in a vote of 154 to 3 (figure 1.1).[4] It goes into effect on December 24, 2014. For the first time, states have agreed to worldwide, legally binding humanitarian or "responsible" arms

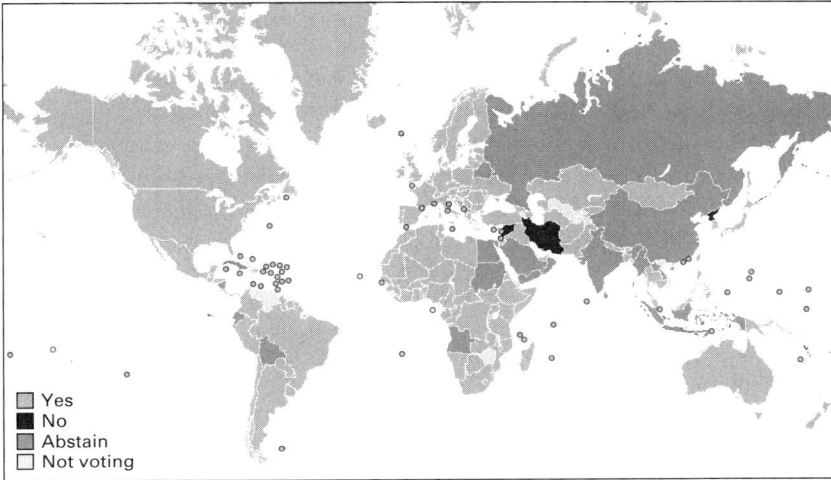

FIGURE 1.1. UN ARMS TRADE TREATY VOTE (2013).

trade standards to restrict small and major conventional arms transfers to human rights violators and conflict zones. The ATT marks the culmination of a dramatic policy reversal that began in the 1990s. Once reluctant—or even hostile—to multilateral export controls, most major arms-producing states began to endorse such standards following the Cold War. And, like South Africa, some have also faced unexpected domestic pressure to act on those commitments. Such standards promise little by way of material gain for supplier states but rather impose restrictions on their foreign-policy autonomy and defense sales—no small price to pay as many governments have faced austerity measures at home. Why, then, have major arms-exporting democracies decided to support multilateral, humanitarian arms export controls, such as the ATT? And why have some of those supportive states been more sensitive than others about appearing to implement these normative changes and policy commitments? This book is the first systematic attempt to answer these questions, with important insights for scholars and practitioners of arms trade politics, international security, and global governance.

CONTROLLING THE ARMS TRADE: THE THEORETICAL AND EMPIRICAL PUZZLES

At its core, the contemporary conventional arms trade brings together vital interests in security and foreign policy, economics, and human security, confronting states with conflicting demands as they decide their arms trade policy and partners. The creation of the ATT and related initiatives therefore presents a microcosm of the policy pressures and imperatives states face in the post–Cold War world. By taking an in-depth look into the politics of the arms trade, this book provides insights into three important theoretical questions. First, at the state level, what explains commitment to multilateral policies that were once considered impossible or out of the question, even in the absence of material or normative incentives to implement them? International negotiations are not cheap; they require time, political capital, and economic resources. Rather than "mere window dressing," the resulting agreements may impose costs and bind behavior in expected ways, risk unanticipated costs and consequences over time, and open states up to domestic legal challenges and hypocrisy costs (Goodliffe and Hawkins 2006; Greenhill 2010; Schimmelfennig 2001; Simmons 2009). If states wish to avoid costly restrictions on their behavior, what motivates them to spend resources and take risks on an agreement in the first place?

Second, at the international level, what explains how new norms gain prominence and legitimacy beyond their initial norm entrepreneurs? Scholars often highlight the importance of "norm cascades" to show how new ideas of appropriate behavior become accepted by a critical mass of states and institutionalized in international politics (Finnemore and Sikkink 1998; Florini 1996; Krook and True 2012). If norm survival hinges on such "tipping points" of state acceptance, then it is essential to dig deeper and theorize the mechanisms that create those tipping points. Why do states—especially those critical states invested in the status quo but without which new norms may flounder—respond to basic forms of social pressure, such as esteem, emulation or conformity, ridicule, and praise (Finnemore and Sikkink 1998; Johnston 2008; K. Waltz 1979)? As Martha Finnemore and Kathryn Sikkink point out, social construction interacts with actors' "instrumental rationality" to enable new norms to diffuse and take hold (1998:910–11). Delving into the motives behind norm adoption and why socialization can be a powerful influence on rational actors can therefore shed light on how norm cascades work in practice and expectations of state behavior change over time.

Finally, by examining the seeds of normative change in one issue area, scholars can gain insights into the processes that generate shifts in the broader social structure of the international system. The "responsible" arms transfer norm cascade is not an isolated phenomenon. It is part of a larger cascade of norms, in which changing ideas of security, transparency, and responsibility make their acceptance possible. New arms trade norms, in turn, can make the international environment more conducive to resolving other debates in favor of responsibility and humanitarianism. At the same time, this case shows that even once institutionalized, change can be slow to come and require a great deal of work by governmental and nongovernmental actors in domestic politics. How and why the system does—and does not—change sits at the heart of international relations (IR) theory, which must meet head on both the material and normative imperatives and constraints confronted by international actors as they shape and are shaped by the system.

"Responsible" arms export control is an ideal case with which to investigate these persistent theoretical questions: states anticipate that new controls will bring heavy material costs without material gains but sign on nevertheless, highlighting new norms in their formal policies but not in their export practice. I argue that top arms supplier states have strategically adopted popular policies out of social concern for their international reputations rather than out of any existing practice or norm internalization. I then show that states' varied concerns for compliance can be traced primarily to the threat of reputational damage from "irresponsible" arms transfers in domestic politics. These findings are valuable for the theoretical insights they provide into states' commitment to and compliance with international policy initiatives, as well as into the sources and processes of normative change. They also offer practical lessons for the ATT as it goes into effect. Indeed, the difficulty of achieving conventional arms control makes it an important empirical puzzle in its own right, with consequences for state and human security.

The deck is stacked against conventional arms control (Gray 1992). Conventional arms are the only category of weapon (legally) used since the Cold War and have, until recently, appeared immune from multilateral controls. The major arms-producing states confront not only the responsibility for restricting trade in the interest of peace and security elsewhere, but also domestic economic and security pressures to export to keep their defense industries afloat. As one French government official notes, conventional weapons have been the "last area of freedom" in arms control (interview 60108220; see appendix B for an explanation of the interviews and interview identification codes). Although extensive diplomatic and technical efforts have been made to ban the production, use, and spread of nuclear, chemical, and biological weapons, conventional arms have gone largely untouched by the international community. The rare attempts to create conventional arms control in the twentieth century buckled under the weight of states' sovereignty, foreign-policy, and economic interests.

Certainly, most states have long required permits for the import and export of arms from their borders, but such controls have been a distinctly national prerogative, attached to economic and military security. The arms trade has often served both as a tool of foreign and economic policy and as a symbol of national self-sufficiency and strength (Cahn et al. 1977; Eyre and Suchman 1996; Kolodziej 1979; Moravcsik 1991). UN Charter Article 51 establishes states' right to provide for their own defense as a fundamental principle of national sovereignty and has been upheld as justification for states to transfer arms as they choose. The sanctity of national sovereignty for the production and transfer of arms was also enshrined from the outset of European integration.[5] Conventional arms transfers can signal friendship and effectuate alliance between states by demonstrating trust, establishing a security relationship, and enhancing interoperability for joint military operations. Sending arms abroad also can be a less costly form of support than sending troops. Finally, conventional weapons can showcase the technological modernity and military strength of the states that import and export them.

At home, governments commonly perceive arms exports as necessary to sustain their domestic defense industry, employment, balance of trade, and national economic well-being. With defense budgets rarely sufficient to maintain production lines, sales abroad can keep the assembly line moving and facilitate economies of scale. The intimate relationship that results between the state and the defense industry also encourages exports and export promotion in response to industry preferences.[6] Politicians and constituents who rely on jobs and other benefits tied to defense-based local economies reinforce political support. More generally, publics often back defense industry interests in response to perceived threats to national security.

These sovereignty, security, and economic concerns have not disappeared over time. In some cases, they have been exacerbated by changes in world politics: the decline in defense spending following the end of the Cold War; the beginning of the war on terror; austerity measures imposed in the wake of the global financial crisis; and advent of the Arab Spring. Since the late 1990s, however, numerous multilateral initiatives have established controls on the licit and illicit trade of small and major conventional arms (see appendix A for a list of the key talks and agreements from 1919 to 2014), including the EU Code of Conduct on Arms Exports, the Economic Community of West African States (ECOWAS) Moratorium, the UN Programme of Action on Small Arms (UNPOA), and the ATT. Even so, as I show in chapter 3, states have not made dramatic changes in their arms export practice, suggesting that standard explanations for international commitments rooted in material gain and normative obligation may be limited. What, then, accounts for top arms-exporting democracies' commitment to new arms trade norms, and why are some more concerned about avoiding the appearance of norm violations than others?

OVERVIEW OF THE ARGUMENT: SOCIAL REPUTATION IN INTERNATIONAL AND DOMESTIC POLITICS

The incentives for major exporters to make a dramatic and potentially costly policy shift in favor of "responsible" arms transfer standards are not immediately clear. States expect new policies (if implemented) to generate high material costs without material gain. Existing practice does not reflect an established normative commitment. Defense industry lobbies were initially opposed or inattentive. Public opinion has been largely indifferent. Explanations that rely on material interests, normative obligation, or domestic politics thus come up short. I argue instead that states strategically adopt policies in line with new norms out of concern for their international reputations. Here. maintaining a good reputation with other international actors serves as a *social* incentive, which can deliver social benefits. Yet policy adoption motivated by such instrumental image building may not lead to compliance, if noncompliance is difficult for other international actors to observe. In fact, supportive states differ in their concern for compliance. I point to domestic politics as the source of this variation, where some states face conditions that make reputational damage from arms trade scandal at home more likely.

In cases of popular policy initiatives, states may commit to new policies as a means to establish, improve, or preserve their international social reputation. Simply defined, a reputation is a collective judgment of an actor's character or the esteem in which that actor is held (*Oxford English Dictionary* 1989). In response to their social environments, states may strategically choose policies to build a reputation among other international actors in line with their self-images as "responsible" or "humanitarian" international citizens. States care about their reputation not only for the material benefits it can bring, but also—and sometimes primarily—for its social benefits, such as national self-esteem or international standing and legitimacy. I use interviews, speeches, and other documents to assess states' concern for reputation in what could be seen as a competition "to remain equal" with their peers (Bailey 1971:19). Such social reputational concerns may also pertain to human rights, climate change, development aid, peacekeeping participation, and other diplomatically popular but otherwise costly initiatives.

Concern for international reputation may pressure states to commit to new policies, but without international accountability mechanisms, those policies' ability to inspire compliance may be limited. States may avoid implementing costly commitments when noncompliance is likely to go unpunished and norm internalization is weak. Under the right conditions, however, domestic politics can provide incentives for states to avoid the appearance of "irresponsible" arms transfers. In democracies especially, arms trade scandals can capture public attention and harm a government's reputation among its constituents. For those democracies in which transparency measures make more information available and nongovernmental organizations (NGOs) are able to take advantage of that information to spotlight "irresponsible" exports in the media, scandal becomes more likely. Those governments become more sensitive to the threat of scandal and impose greater export restraint in cases of clear-cut, severe norm violations to avoid reputational damage at home.

Governments thus attempt to shape the perceptions that other actors have of them (i.e., their reputations) in line with their national identity and values. They do this because of the social benefits a good reputation can bring. When their reputation is threatened—for example, by scandal or NGO shaming—governments may adjust their policies or practice to counter negative claims. In this way, policy support as a means to enhance, maintain, or repair reputation is a rational strategy to obtain social ends. Accounting for states as both strategic and social actors, social reputation can therefore be a powerful if often over-looked and undertheorized force in foreign-policy making. It can provide an explanation for a range of state and NGO behavior, including why states invest in agreements whose provisions place costly restrictions on their basic security and economic decision making.

THE IMPORTANCE OF ARMS EXPORT CONTROLS

Conventional arms are the building blocks of armed forces around the world. In 2011, world military expenditures were estimated at $1.738 trillion and 2.5 percent of global gross domestic product (GDP) (Stockholm International Peace Research Institute [SIPRI] 2012:147). In the same year, according to the Congressional Research Service, the value of conventional arms transfer agreements (i.e., orders for future delivery) amounted to approximately $85.3 billion, with more than 83 percent going to agreements with developing countries (Grimmett and Kerr 2012). For top arms-producing states, typically located in the developed world,[7] arms transfers have long been seen as an important tool of foreign influence and military power, a source of national security and employment, and key to defense industry survival. Governments have used arms transfers to achieve foreign-policy goals, sway other governments' policy preferences, and sustain production lines, employment, and defense industry health at home. For these countries, arms export promotion—not restraint—has long been the rule in practice, and policy changes rarely attract public attention.

For individuals in many recipient states, however, arms export decisions made elsewhere can directly affect daily life. Arms transfers can destabilize fragmented countries, prolong conflict and make it more deadly, and increase the difficulty of postconflict reconstruction.[8] Conventional arms are the most commonly used tools of war, causing the vast majority of conflict-related deaths. Experts estimate that 128 armed conflicts since 1989 have directly or indirectly caused at least 250,000 deaths annually, and an additional 300,000 nonconflict deaths per year have been perpetrated with firearms (Amnesty International 2010). These numbers are disproportionately made up of women and children, who are more likely to be internally displaced and suffer higher rates of mortality and health problems stemming from conflict (Southall and O'Hare 2002). Even in the rare cases where arms are not the primary tools of conflict, they may still play a prominent role. Although machetes are commonly considered the main instrument of killing in the 1994 Rwandan genocide, foreign arms sales fueled the conflict (Goose and Smyth 1994). Mass killings in some communes were carried out by firearms and were made more widespread and deadly by firearms in others (Verwimp 2006). After conflict, the widespread availability of arms puts pressure on weak governance structures and slows economic development (Musah 2002; Stohl and Grillot 2009).

Both small and major conventional arms are also associated with worse human rights performance in some recipient states.[7] Lerna Yanik observes that between 1999 and 2003—after humanitarian export controls had taken a prominent place on the international agenda—"almost half of the global arms trade ended up in the hands of countries with poor human rights records" (2006:363). This relationship is, of course, complex. Governments can use arms directly to repress popular dissent (Klare 1984) or indirectly to strengthen the role of the military in society (Maniruzzaman 1992; Musah 2002), with adverse consequences for human rights. Amnesty International (2010) estimates that 60 percent of documented human rights violations involve the use of small arms and light weapons. Major conventional weapons may also allow repressive governments to increase the scale of oppression: recall the iconic images of tanks rolling into Tiananmen Square in 1989 or reports of the Turkish government's use of military aircraft to attack Kurdish villages in the mid-1990s. Conflict and human rights violations can also come hand in hand: governments involved in internal conflict are significantly more likely to engage in repressive practices in the interest of maintaining security and order (Blanton 1999).

Examples abound of both legal and illicit arms transfers fueling conflict and human rights violations. In addition, the vast majority of weapons sold illicitly started as legally manufactured and sold weapons but were diverted later to the black market (Marsh 2002). Thus, even if some states adopt national restrictions on weapons exports to areas of instability and repressive governments, the realities of a global market are that recipients denied weapons from one supplier can likely find them from another for the right price. As a result, starting in the 1980s, some "affected" states, NGOs, and experts began to advocate for common "responsible" export criteria rooted in human rights and conflict prevention. As I explain more fully later, their efforts, together with key political events in the 1990s, have put conventional arms control on the international agenda. Once ignored, SALW have joined major conventional weapons as targets of multilateral humanitarian export restrictions.

In 1998, the EU adopted the Code of Conduct on Arms Exports to restrict arms transfers to human rights violators and conflict zones, and in 2006, after years of discussion, the UN began formally working toward an ATT. The ATT, which goes into effect in December 2014, internationalizes and expands those standards promoted by "affected" states and pioneered by the EU. It explicitly prohibits the transfer of small and major conventional arms that "would be used in the commission of genocide, crimes against humanity, grave breaches of the Geneva Conventions of 1949, attacks directed against civilian objects or civilians protected as such, or other war crimes as defined by international agreements" (Art. 6, sec. 3).[10] It also includes criteria requiring states to deny arms in cases of an "overriding risk" that they might undermine peace and security or facilitate human rights violations; to consider the risk that arms will be used to facilitate "serious acts of violence against women and children"; and to take measures to prevent diversion to the black market (Art. 7, 11). Yet the ATT's secretariat will have no enforcement authority. State parties are instead charged with ensuring their own implementation and enforcement of treaty provisions. Thus, alongside ATT supporters' hope and enthusiasm, difficult questions and concerns exist about its potential effectiveness—a point for which this book has important implications.

METHODS AND CASE SELECTION

The question of *why* major arms supplier states have supported "responsible" arms transfer standards requires an in-depth examination of domestic and international politics. It also relies on knowing *how well* those standards reflect states' arms export practice in order to evaluate explanations that expect compliance to accompany or even precede policy commitment. I use qualitative historical and interview data with case study methods alongside quantitative arms export data to demonstrate broad normative changes in the international community and explain major exporters' response to those changes. This multimethod approach enables a close analysis of potential explanations and mechanisms, while avoiding the assumption that the rationale for states' commitment will be reflected in their compliant practice.[11]

HISTORICAL AND STATISTICAL TRENDS

I begin by examining historical and statistical trends to provide a broad overview of arms export policies and practices over time. Historical cases of failed arms export controls in the twentieth century reveal deep political resistance to multilateral commitments. Although many sources of resistance remain, I identify a confluence of events in the 1990s that charged the normative environment surrounding the international arms trade and set the stage for a dramatic policy shift. This historical overview both sets up the central puzzle and puts in perspective the magnitude and importance of the change in major exporters' policy after the end of the Cold War.

Quantitative data complement the historical analysis to show the relationship between states' policy and practice. An analysis of small and major conventional arms export deliveries between 1981 and 2010 asks whether and when top supplier states reduce transfers to human rights violators in line with new policies.[12] This analysis is particularly valuable because it accommodates a larger population of cases to illustrate trends in arms trade behavior over time. It also shows whether and how arms export practice maps onto changing policy and helps to weigh explanations that expect states' practice to reflect their commitment. Normative explanations are more viable if states exhibit "responsible" arms exports in practice as well as in policy. Alternatively, if states expect material gain from new multilateral initiatives, then practice should come to reflect policy, or vice versa, if those initiatives simply codify existing practice. Yet by uncoupling policy and practice, the analysis also serves as a reminder that commitment and compliance need not come hand in hand. Explanations of states' policy choices in light of such a policy–practice gap are therefore necessary.

The statistical analyses forge new ground in arms trade research. First, contrary to existing quantitative analyses (e.g., Blanton 2005), it widens the focus beyond U.S. exports. Although the United States is certainly important, as the dominant supplier it may not reflect global trends. This book looks at arms exports from twenty-two top supplier states, including the United States. Second, it treats SALW and MCW transfers separately to reflect their historically separate policy treatment, rather than aggregating them or excluding small arms. Finally, it uses statistics to test how norms codified in state policy affect state practice and to investigate "claims that norms influence behavior" (Klotz and Lynch 2007:18). As Emilie Hafner-Burton and James Ron note, statistical analyses are often more skeptical about the prospects for behavioral change than case studies, in part because the latter deal more frequently with norm creation and the former with norm implementation (2009:369, 385). As a result, this study takes advantage of the complementary strengths of quantitative and qualitative research to assess norm creation *and* norm implementation, state policy *and* state practice.

BIG STATES WITH BIG STAKES

Case study process tracing and interview data move beyond the broad trends provided by the historical and statistical analyses by examining in-depth states'

TABLE 1.1. SELECTED CASES:
FIVE MAJOR ARMS-EXPORTING DEMOCRACIES

Supplier	SALW Supplier	MCW Supplier	Democracy?	Support for Transfer Controls, 1998–2014*
Belgium	Top 5	Top 20	Yes	Yes
France	Top 20	Top 5	Yes	Yes
Germany	Top 5	Top 5	Yes	Yes
United Kingdom	Top 20	Top 5	Yes	Yes
United States**	Top 5	Top 5	Yes	No/Yes

*This support is primarily for the 1998 EU Code of Conduct (EU members only); the 2001 UNPOA and its review conferences, which debated but did not approve including transfer controls; and the formal ATT process, which began in 2006.

**Only the United States voted no on the 2006 UN General Assembly resolution to initiate the ATT process. It was also an opposition state in the UN small arms conferences between 2001 and 2008.

Note: Russia, a top-five supplier of both SALW and MCW, is not included here because it is not fully democratic. Italy, although a top-five SALW supplier and a democracy, has also been excluded because its policies and practices generally reflect those of the other European cases. China did not become a top-five MCW supplier (at the expense of the United Kingdom) until 2012 and is not democratic.

support for "responsible" export policies, their varying concern about compliance, and the role of social reputation. Case studies "compensate for less range by gains in depth" (Eckstein 1975:122; see also George and Bennett 2005). By analyzing the political dynamics of arms transfer policy in five major exporting democracies (table 1.1), I explore states' motivations behind their commitment or opposition to new policies as well as their concerns for compliance.

Case selection is nonrandom, based on two key characteristics thought to influence the likelihood of states' support for multilateral humanitarian export standards.[13] First, I select "big" exporters of small or major conventional arms (both in two of the country cases). According to the Small Arms Survey (SAS) and SIPRI, the chosen cases are historically top suppliers, including at the time they chose to support major multilateral initiatives, such as the EU Code of Conduct and the ATT. Yet, unlike states less invested in global arms markets, these states have clear economic incentives *not* to endorse external controls. Moreover, whereas states adversely affected by "irresponsible" arms exports may have a direct interest in new controls, major exporter states are rarely also affected states. Instead, they have a large material stake in blocking new controls.

Indeed, with the mixed exception of the United States, big exporters consistently opposed multilateral standards in the past. Most exporters' support of recent initiatives is therefore not only crucial if new export controls are ultimately to help reduce arms supplies to troubled areas—making them "critical states" in the norm cascade—but also the most puzzling.

Second, among the major exporters, I have selected full democracies. Many scholars find that democracies in particular have a common commitment to human rights rules and norms and international law more broadly (Burley 1992; Simmons 1998). As such, they are "most likely cases" for supporting new export criteria. Indeed, if democratic suppliers were *not* signing on, the chances of nondemocratic suppliers doing so would presumably be slim to none. Yet the meaningful variation in the principal outcome—state support—is also among democracies: the United States was the most vocal opponent of UN arms export initiatives and the only "no" vote on the ATT until 2009, when it reversed its position. In contrast, nondemocratic major exporters (e.g., Russia and later China) have taken a backseat, abstaining from voting rather than blocking popular initiatives. On the compliance side, democracies are also more vulnerable to domestic pressures to implement new policies (Simmons 2009). I therefore hold regime type constant under the assumption that democracies are the most susceptible to pressures to support and implement new policies.

Using interviews with key players in the policy-making process (government, defense industry, and NGO representatives), NGC and news reports, speeches, and government documents, I examine how new standards gain acceptance in domestic and international political debates.[14] This process-tracing approach enables me to identify the causal mechanisms connecting the independent variables to the outcome in question (George and Bennett 2005). The interviews address governments' reasoning behind their policy and practice as well as advocates' strategies for influencing government decision making. In addition, I examine public opinion, the positions of key advocacy groups, and the timing of advocacy-group support or opposition to determine the role of domestic pressures. In conjunction with the statistical trends, the qualitative analysis can therefore help parse between the explanations and ultimately provide substantive support for the reputational argument.

PLAN OF THE BOOK

Chapter 2 provides the theoretical framework for the book and makes a two-part argument about reputation as a social mechanism. First, it introduces a social logic of reputation in *international* affairs. I argue that states may commit to popular policies as a means to maintain their reputations as "responsible" members of the international community and acquire the social benefits such a reputation can bring. Yet where international accountability measures are weak, states may collect social reputational gains without engaging in costly implementation. Second, the chapter looks to reputation in *domestic* politics to fill this accountability gap. I contend that variation in governments' concern for compliance stems from variation in their perception that grossly noncompliant exports will come to light and damage their domestic reputations. More specifically, when domestic NGOs with expertise and access to arms trade reports can spotlight "irresponsible" export decisions in the media, governments' domestic reputations and legitimacy may come under fire. These conditions can push governments to make a public effort to adhere more closely to new standards—at least in clear-cut cases of norm violations—to avoid reputational damage brought on by scandal at home.

Chapter 3 analyzes the "business as usual" of conventional arms exports. It provides an overview of the twentieth century's failed multilateral attempts to regulate the global arms trade, highlighting both entrenched norms of sovereignty and the dramatic shift presented by the success of contemporary policy initiatives. I then identify key events in the 1990s that explain the origins of new "responsible" arms export norms. Finally, I investigate how these changes in policy expectations map onto small and major conventional arms export trends between 1981 and 2010. I find that although some change has occurred at the margins, state practice has been largely inattentive to recipients' human rights records over time. This policy–practice gap casts doubt on explanations that rely on normative obligation or material incentives to explain policy commitment. Instead, it shows that states have supported new initiatives *in spite* of their underlying export preferences, not because of them.

Building on the trends outlined in chapter 3, the remainder of the book examines major democratic exporters' response to new arms export norms. In chapter 4, I explain why these states have put aside past opposition to multilateral arms export controls in favor of "responsible" arms trade initiatives. I find that states' concern for their reputations as "good international citizens" propels them to support and promote socially appropriate policies they might not otherwise. For states deeply embedded in international institutions as a part of their national identity and values, the choice of policies to improve, reinforce, or mend their social reputation is a strategic one. Even if practice is slow to change, states' broader socialization into the international community and desire to be recognized by their peers push them to adopt new policies, particularly following the success of other popular initiatives. This initial instrumental commitment nevertheless opens the door for NGOs to use naming and shaming, rhetorical entrapment, and hypocrisy costs to encourage compliance and norm internalization down the road.

Chapter 5 turns to domestic reputation to explain variation in states' concern for compliance with new rules and norms. Although public attention to arms export policies is typically low, news of extremely "irresponsible" arms transfers can generate scandal in domestic politics. Scandals can damage governments' reputations at home, leading to loss of legitimacy and other political costs, particularly in democracies. Interviews suggest that governments that perceive a greater threat of public condemnation for "bad" export deals may exercise greater caution in choosing their import partners. I argue that governments are more sensitive to scandal when arms export information is publicly available and civil society actors are willing to mine that information to spotlight potentially controversial export deals. As a result, the growth of transparency measures and NGO watchdogs in some states may prompt greater concerns about avoiding exports at least in the most clear-cut cases of noncompliance. This finding is especially important for the ATT, which has no formal enforcement mechanisms of its own, as it seeks to motivate implementation among state parties.

In the final chapter, I examine the theoretical arguments in the context of three examples of non-European exporters: Brazil, Israel, and South Africa. I conclude with policy implications that provide reasons for both pessimism and optimism for the prospects of the new ATT. On the one hand, I show that arms transfer practice is hard to change and continues to defy states' policy commitments. Even in states that value international laws and norms, change takes place at the margins, where the reputational costs of "irresponsible" policy and practice are most threatening. On the other hand, states once hostile to shared export controls are now leading the international community on new initiatives. Small arms alone have gone from being overlooked and ignored to being a prominent policy concern on the global agenda. Although norm internalization may require more time, states have demonstrated increasingly widespread acceptance of new policies. In turn, policy commitments in international fora combined with domestic accountability can begin a dynamic in which supplier states implement policies designed to enhance security and human rights outside their own borders and around the world.

2. "Responsible" Arms Transfer Policy and the Politics of Social Reputation

Major conventional arms–exporting states now widely support the Arms Trade Treaty and other multilateral arms export initiatives. Why they have done so— in the absence of material gain or norm socialization—not only presents an important empirical puzzle but also addresses several enduring questions for IR theory: Why do states commit to international agreements, especially those that may impose high implementation costs without material benefits in return? What explains norm adoption by "critical" but skeptical states? How does social change take place in the international system? This chapter outlines a theoretical argument about social reputation in international and domestic politics to give fresh insights into these questions through the lens of "responsible" arms export controls.

In this case, states confront both enduring material pressures to avoid multilateral commitments and increasing normative pressures from other states and NGOs to make those commitments. How states reconcile these conflicting pressures and why provide a window into their motivations and priorities in international politics as well as into how broader normative change can occur. In recent years, most top arms supplier states have conformed to normative pressures to commit to humanitarian arms export initiatives. At the same time, they have worried that their support will entail costs for their sovereignty and national security as well as harm their defense industries and domestic economy. Even as states have adopted policies in line with new norms, norm internalization has not caught up with state practice, and compliance is mixed at best. But if norm adoption is instrumental, as it appears to be, what do states hope to get out of it? Without the promise of material gain, why expend time and resources on multilateral initiatives intended to impose costly restrictions on decision making and risk domestic legal challenges and hypocrisy costs if compliance is weak?

This chapter proposes a theory of state behavior that highlights the importance of social reputation to explain states' commitment to and varied compliance with "responsible" arms export norms. Beyond the arms trade, the theory seeks to contribute to research on international security, norm development, and global governance. I begin with a brief overview of the argument and then review existing IR approaches to reputation. These approaches focus on the economic and military benefits that a reputation for credibility can provide, but they do not acknowledge reputation more broadly as a social concept.[1]

First, I argue that states care about their reputations for not only material but also social reasons attached to their self-image, legitimacy, and standing in international politics. States may strategically commit to new policies out of concern for their international reputations and the social benefits (or costs) that a good (or bad) reputation can bring. Second, I introduce concern for domestic reputation as a source of variation in states' compliance. Compliance efforts will be stronger in democracies where export transparency and civil society activity are high, making leaders more vulnerable to reputational damage from scandalous arms deals. Finally, I suggest that alternative explanations have difficulty accommodating cases in which there are gaps between commitment and compliance. Where the international normative environment has changed but norm internalization is slow to emerge, social reputation may provide a more satisfying explanation for states' policy and practice.

THE ARGUMENT IN BRIEF

Major arms supplier states see neither security nor economic gain to be had from committing to responsible arms trade initiatives. Quite the opposite, in fact: they have long avoided multilateral export controls because of their high costs to security, foreign-policy autonomy, and economic well-being. Instead, states support new arms export initiatives as a means to maintain, repair, or better their reputations as responsible citizens of the international community on the "right side" of conventional arms control. They may strategically support popular norms and policies in order to receive the social benefits a good reputation can bring, such as a positive self-image and increased international legitimacy. Here, norm adoption is instrumental, done to reap *social* benefits and avoid *social* costs. Yet without international enforcement and accountability mechanisms to trigger compliance-related reputational concerns, states may avoid costly policy implementation. Where international politics does not offer compliance incentives, the task may fall to domestic politics. In particular, democracies with arms export transparency and NGO activity at home may improve efforts to implement their formal policy commitments in practice in order to protect their domestic reputation from the damage of scandal.

The argument proceeds in two parts. First, states deeply embedded in the international community and its institutions may formally *commit* to popular multilateral initiatives out of social concern for their reputation among their peers. As the international normative environment has increasingly linked arms transfers to human rights, so too have the related standards by which states collectively judge their legitimacy and standing. Major exporters have pursued arms transfer restraints to conform to new policy expectations in this changed normative environment out of a desire to uphold or improve their international reputation. Their policy commitment seeks to signal that they possess the qualities of good international citizens, supporting peace and human rights. These states respond to social incentives and benefit not in the form of material profit, but rather in the form of social recognition in a deliberate strategy to confirm their self-images and contribute to their external social influence. Unlike other IR approaches, the approach taken here acknowledges an important social dimension to reputation. It does not view reputation solely as a means to material ends based on a catalog of states' past actions. Instead, it recognizes a role for reputation both as an end in and of itself, having an internal "feel-good" effect on state identity, and as a means to additional social benefits in the international community.

This social reputational dynamic can explain why otherwise skeptical states with significant material stakes in the status quo may nevertheless support new norms and policies. Indeed, the most skeptical states in the case examined here—top exporters of small and major conventional arms—are also the most critical for enabling new norms to reduce arms availability to human rights violators. These states' largely supportive response to the norm cascade is both instrumental and social. Yet although their policies are available for all to see, their arms trade practices are more easily hidden from international scrutiny. States can therefore reap the reputational rewards of adopting "responsible" policies without necessarily paying the costs of equally "responsible" implementation. Such a gap between commitment and compliance can easily go unpunished in international politics, where transparency is poor and agreements—such as the ATT—lack enforcement capabilities.

The second part of the argument introduces a role for domestic reputation, often overlooked by other IR approaches to reputation, in explaining variation in states' concern for *compliance* with new rules and norms. It finds that governments faced with scandal or threat of scandal are more likely to seek improvements to their export practice (not "just" to policy) out of concern for their domestic reputation. Where arms trade practice remains relatively unmonitored at home, the risks of scandal and its effect on the reputation of a state and its leaders are low. However, policy makers in democracies with an active civil society and domestic transparency measures are more sensitive to threats of arms trade scandal. In response, they may attempt to conform more closely to export standards—at least in clear-cut cases of norm violations—rather than suffer the reputational costs of scandal.

Scandals link reputation to domestic politics by highlighting the violation of fundamental societal values. Although arms trade scandals rarely swing elections, they nevertheless erode the image and legitimacy of leaders in the eyes of their constituents and provide an opening for presumptive leaders to win support in their place. This dynamic is most viable in democracies, where transparency and accountability are valued norms of governance and where civil society can mobilize to take governments to task when behavior contravenes stated policies, domestic values, and national identity. Scandals are, in a sense, an extreme and widespread consequence of shaming, hypocrisy costs, or rhetorical entrapment. Without any formal enforcement capacity, the ATT's long-term effectiveness may lean heavily on such civil society engagement and developments in transparency to tap into states' domestic reputational concerns and motivate some compliance. Policy commitment may serve an international audience, but compliant practice—at least for some states—may serve a domestic one.

REPUTATION IN INTERNATIONAL RELATIONS

Reputation is a prevalent but often undertheorized concept in IR. The *Oxford English Dictionary* (1989) defines reputation as 'the common or general estimate of a person with respect to character or other qualities; the relative estimation or esteem in which a person or thing is held."[2] But why does reputation matter? According to most IR scholars, reputation is valuable because it informs predictions of states' future behavior, whether as a credible military ally or opponent or as a credible partner in multilateral cooperation. A reputation for credibility, in turn, is a means to increase states' military power or economic gain. These motivations, however, fail to capture the reputational benefits accrued from supporting "responsible" arms transfer policy, which are not primarily material but social and focus on the esteem component of reputation. In this

TABLE 2.1. REPUTATION IN INTERNATIONAL POLITICS

	Image and social status	Credible threat	Credible cooperation
Why does reputation matter?	Affirm positive self-image in line with views of national identity and social influence	Effective threat making; crisis decision making with limited information	Ability to enter into profitable cooperative arrangements
What is the purpose of reputation?	Attain and maintain social standing, legitimacy, and influence in international and national politics	Predict behavior; signal resolve to follow through with threats	Predict behavior; provide information about own reliability as a partner; regime maintenance
What reputation is desirable?	Good international citizen, transparent and accountable	Action, resolve, toughness	Reliable, cooperative, compliant
How do states build their reputations?	Policies in line with societal and international norms	Follow through on threats	Comply with international agreements and regimes
Target audience	Domestic and international	International	International
Other fields of research	Sociology, anthropology, social psychology, international law	Game theory	Game theory, economics, corporate management, international law

section, I outline the standard uses of reputation in IR before I discuss reputation as a social concept. For an overview of the three IR approaches to reputation, see table 2.1. I test the first approach in the chapters to come.

Jonathan Mercer defines reputation as "a judgment of someone's character (or disposition) that is then used to predict or explain future behavior" (1996:6). To form a reputation, he continues, it is necessary for an observer of an actor's behavior to use "character-based attributions" to explain its present behavior and attach these judgments to expectations of future behavior (6, 36). IR scholarship typically emphasizes the second part of Mercer's definition: reputation's ability to serve as a tool to predict future behavior. Broadly speaking, certain reputations help states get what they want, whether acquiescence to threats or profitable cooperative arrangements. The ability to extract these material gains hinges on the belief that past or present behavior is indicative of likely future behavior. In this sense, reputation is primarily a proxy for past action. This version is often used in international security and political economy research. Although not to be discounted, it is less useful in explaining states' commitment to "responsible" arms trade initiatives, which also stems from reputational concerns but is geared toward social—not military or economic—advantage.

CREDIBLE THREATS

From a security standpoint, states or leaders seek to build a reputation for making credible threats. From this perspective, threat making and deterrence work because states believe that opponents who demonstrated resolve in the past will demonstrate resolve in the future. States want to stand firm against coercive pressure, and they want their own threats taken seriously. As a result, Thomas Schelling argues, the interdependence of a state's worldwide commitments makes its reputation for action—not its status, honor, or worth—"one of the few things worth fighting over" (1966:124).[3] Reputation also supplements information about an opponent's likely actions and relative power in order to "assess their strategies in crisis situations" (Crescenzi 2007:385; see also Axelrod 1984 and Crescenzi, Kathman, and Long 2007).

In short, states worry about their reputation because they believe it affects their ability to make credible—and therefore effective—threats. Past behavior serves as information to make more accurate predictions about other states' behavior in a military crisis, revealing their "type" to be strong or weak (Hugh-Jones and Zultan 2012; Walter 2009). Although Mercer (1996) maintains that the content of a state's reputation also depends on its relationship with the observer state, the value of its reputation is still the same: a tool to enhance military credibility.[4] Daryl Press's (2005) critique goes further, arguing that states do not actually take their adversaries' past behavior into account when making decisions during a military crisis. Nevertheless, he notes that states often do seek to protect their own reputations—a puzzling finding for this variant of reputation, whose rationale depends on reputation mattering because of the material outcome it can provide.

Because this use of reputation is threat oriented, it makes at best only a distant connection to arms transfer control policy. Certainly, if a state uses weapons supplies as a coercive tool—requiring another state to comply with its demands or face a cessation of its arms supplies—such threats will be effective only if the recipient believes the supplier state will indeed cut off arms. This use of reputation may relate to the threat and effectiveness of arms embargoes, but it does not address supplier states' willingness to adopt humanitarian export constraints.

CREDIBLE COOPERATION

For scholars of international political economy, reputation is again about credibility and information, but for cooperative ends rather than for conflict. Compliance with current agreements can serve as an indicator of likely future compliance. Because states cooperate to improve their economic welfare, having a reputation for reliability can "[make] it easier for a government to enter into advantageous international agreements; tarnishing that reputation imposes costs by making agreements more difficult to reach" (Keohane 1984:105–6; see also Guzman 2002; Larson 1997; Sartori 2002; Tomz 2007). Concerned about their reputations as precedent for an unspecified number of future rounds of cooperation, states will keep their commitments, even without specific threats of retaliation for noncompliance (Guzman 2002; Keohane 1984). In deciding whether to enter an agreement with another state, states also determine whether their potential partner can be trusted on the basis of "[its] reputation for fulfilling commitments, the public record of [its] reliability" (Larson 1997:710; see also Ahn, Esarey, and Scholz 2009; Guzman 2002; Sartori 2002; Tomz 2007).[5] Here again, a state's behavior reveals information about its type to other actors, forming a reputation to help potential partners decide if its commitments to cooperate are credible.

Even for J. C. Sharman, who explicitly seeks to offer a "social" version of reputation in international political economy (2006:6), states' concern for reputation is driven by a profit motive (107). He argues that states act to protect their reputations out of fear of being shunned by investors (10). A reputation for credibility thus matters for the material costs and benefits it provides. But whether investors use reputation in this way is not always clear.[6] Moreover, states expect neither enhanced military power nor economic profits from "responsible" arms export controls. In fact, profit incentives may work against them. Restraints shrink available arms markets and reduce profit opportunities. Cutting off arms supplies may also make a government less economically competitive against suppliers with fewer scruples and brand it as an unreliable partner. In a competitive buyer's market, commitments to rule out or drop certain categories of customers do not sit well with companies' bottom lines. Instead, to understand why states support such costly standards, it is useful to look to the social benefits and pressures created by reputation.

SOCIAL REPUTATION AND CONVENTIONAL ARMS TRANSFERS POLICY

The version of reputation I develop here emphasizes reputation as a judgment of states' character and not simply as the sum total of their past actions. As such, it differs in a number of respects from the variants just outlined. First, it recognizes the importance of reputation as a policy *end*, not solely as a means to achieve other policies. States attach social value to their reputations and may commit to policies as a means to enhance their reputations. Second, it considers a role for domestic reputation linked to compliance. Governments' concern for reputation can have tangible domestic effects when conditions are ripe for scandal brought on by a gap between professed policies and irresponsible practice, revealed in the public domain. Finally, it creates an opening to consider a more eclectic theoretical view of international politics. States are strategic actors operating in a social setting where norms and institutions affect the behaviors that are collectively valued and that build reputation. States adopt policies to enhance their reputation in the international community; they apply rational strategies to achieve social goals.[7] Reputation is therefore a concept that can apply to both rationalist and constructivist research and serve to find an area of common ground between the two.

In a new normative environment linking arms transfers to human rights, states face social pressures at the international level to commit to responsible arms transfer controls. As a group, democracies are the most likely to respond to these pressures: their domestic obligations to the rule of law and other democratic values can translate to international politics (Doyle 1986; Simmons 1998; Slaughter 1995). In addition, democracies are subject to greater internal and external pressure to conform to international norms related to peace, human rights, and international law (Burley 1992; Simmons 1998). Nondemocracies can also face external social pressure to conform to norms,[8] but without the added expectations attached to democratic values and the rule of law. After all, the ATT has been overwhelmingly supported by democracies and nondemocracies alike. Moreover, skeptical states such as Russia and China have kept a low profile and refrained from blocking ATT progress, despite their distaste for its sovereignty costs and the domestic human rights standards it seeks to enforce. Reputational concerns may therefore keep dissenting states from publicly voicing opposition. Nevertheless, in general, social reputation tends to be a more powerful commitment incentive among democracies due to shared values and the social pressures to conform to them.

At the domestic level, the link between reputation, scandal, and compliance is confined to democracies. Although corruption can occur anywhere, scandals need democracy, where political power is subject to popular accountability and sanctioned by strict rules of legal process (Markovits and Silverstein 1988). Scandals also rely on democratic expectations of transparency and free media to flourish in the public eye. Later in the chapter, I describe the conditions that make some democracies more sensitive to the threat of arms trade scandal and the reputational damage it can inflict. However, the vulnerability of more scandal-prone governments to reputational damage may be tempered by the structure of executive responsibility.[9] The effects of scandal may be more potent where executive responsibility affects the whole party in power and is not dependent on drawing a clear link to a single leader at the top. Because of the difficulty of directly implicating a single executive for irresponsible state action in this case, leaders in presidential systems may be less concerned about reputational damage from arms trade scandal. In contrast, in parliamentary systems, the party in power can suffer collectively in response to scandal and may be more likely to adjust its behavior accordingly. I detail both the international and domestic reputation arguments in the following sections.

REPUTATION AMONG STATES

REPUTATION AS A SOCIAL INCENTIVE

At the international level, states may strive to maintain or improve their reputation by adopting policies in line with rules and norms of the international community and its institutions in order to signal their "good international citizenship." In the traditions of constructivism and the English School, I observe that international politics can foster social standards and encourage social behavior on the part of states. And, like Ian Hurd (2007) and Alastair Iain Johnston (2008), I argue that states are rational actors within a social context. When material incentives to cooperate or comply are absent—or material costs are present—social incentives can nevertheless motivate leaders to commit to popular initiatives. States' concern for reputation and how others in the international community view them can prompt support for policies they might otherwise oppose.[10] States care about their reputations, first, as a positive reinforcer for their self-image and identity. A good reputation has a feel-good effect on state identity. Second, states care about their reputations because of the implications for their legitimacy and social standing, particularly within international institutions, which can set behavioral expectations and advertise states' policy commitments. Moreover, reputation not only is important to states in the abstract but is also connected to and carried by its individual diplomats and elites meeting in international fora as representatives of their countries.[11]

Many states that once shunned multilateral conventional arms export standards now support them because they want to be viewed as conforming to international norms. In contemporary politics, "good" or "responsible" international citizenship broadly refers to a state's active commitment to human, social, and economic rights or other collective goods (Lebovic and Voeten 2006; Wheeler and Dunne 1998), which states can signal through their policy choices.[12] The value of a good reputation attached to conventional arms control is not derived from anticipated increases in procurement or overseas sales. As I show in chapter 4, industry has been slow to back government initiatives to the extent that it has at all, and benefits directly connected to increased power and economic gain are negligible to nonexistent. Nor do states appear to possess deeply internalized normative convictions about new policies. Rather, it requires a broader understanding of reputation, connected to social standing and recognition, to explain states' willingness to support "responsible" arms transfer standards.

International relations research typically describes social status as a tool of small or weak states to gain political influence in global politics that is not available to them through traditional military or market power (Ingebritsen 2006). Yet social goals can also be sought by more powerful states embedded in the international community (Johnston 2008). International embeddedness both reduces states' insulation from international rules and enhances their desire for social standing. A good international reputation typically requires states to participate in rules, norms, and responsibilities recognized as legitimate by international society (Chayes and Chayes 1995; Franck 1990; Wendt 1999; Wheeler and Dunne 1998).[13] States seek both "conformity and esteem" in international politics, stemming from social pressure and a desire for legitimation from their peers (Finnemore and Sikkink 1998:903). Even where norms are not internalized, states may therefore be socialized to conform to expectations in order to gain recognition and prestige while avoiding shame and social opprobrium (J. Busby 2008; Johnston 2008; Zarakol 2011).

As a judgment on states' policies and actions, reputation is wrapped up with states' internal or self-images as well as with how they are perceived by other international actors. The term *image* can refer both to how a state sees itself (i.e., its national self-image[14]) and to how it wants others to see it (i.e., the external image it projects from its policies and practice[15]). It is this latter external image that shapes a state's *reputation*, which is a judgment by others of the images that a state projects, intentional or otherwise. Although states cannot control this collective judgment—reputation is, after all, relational and defined by others—they can seek to shape it through their publicly observable behavior (Jervis 1970; Klotz 1995; O'Neill 2006). Image management is essentially the point of public diplomacy and "nation-branding" campaigns. As actors try to "control the impression" other actors have of them, they play a social part to their audience over time that reinforces an acquired value system, whether their behavior is sincere or not (Boulding 1956; Goffman 1959).[16] Figure 2.1 captures this relational component of reputation and the role of image in shaping it. In this sense, reputation serves as feedback to a state from others in the international community about the image it projects.

Reputation contains two interwoven dynamics that make it a persuasive social incentive among states tightly bound to the international community. As Axel Honneth (1995) argues, social recognition brings self-respect and a confirmation of equal status as well as esteem and increased standing in a community of shared values. First, states and their leaders seek to confirm their equal status

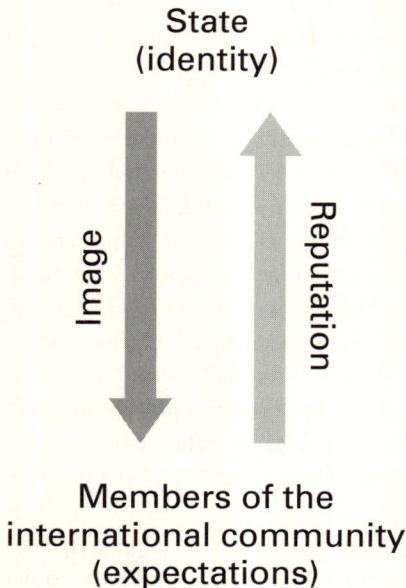

FIGURE 2.1. RELATIONSHIP BETWEEN REPUTATION AND IMAGE.
Source: Based on Whetten 1997.

and with it their identities as good international citizens. A good reputation confers and reinforces a positive self-image. States keep up with evolving norms of appropriate behavior in part to be recognized as legitimate and equal members of the international community (Abdelal et al. 2009; Wendt 2004; Zarakol 2011). Normative obligation is "a necessary reciprocal incident of membership in the community" (Franck 1988:753) and helps define its "boundaries and distinctive practices" (Abdelal et al. 2009:21; see also Chayes and Chayes 1995; Franck 1990; Henkin 1968; Wendt 1999). By conforming to international expectations, states can develop reputations that align more closely with their identities and can be recognized by their peers as equals with the capacity and right to act in international affairs.[17]

Second, states may seek not only to be recognized as equals but also to distinguish themselves among their peers. Policy leadership and a good reputation can bring increased social standing or prestige.[18] This aspect of reputation refers to a state's position in a social hierarchy of "respect, deference and social influence," valuable as both a means to gain influence and an end in itself (Ridgeway and Walker 1995:281–82; see also D. Bromley 1993; Huberman, Loch, and Önçüler 2004).[19] Social hierarchy does not replace the formal anarchy of the international system. Rather, it suggests that some states informally enjoy a more favored and influential position than others, which can stem from hard or soft power.[20] States, wishing to improve their reputations, may therefore seek to outperform their peers, particularly with respect to policies on issues close to their self-image (Tesser and Campbell 1980). In this case, some states may adopt "more responsible" policies than prescribed by community norms in order to set themselves apart from other states and enhance their legitimacy, esteem, and prestige.

States' concern for reputation thus illuminates a search for recognition of their equal status as "good" members of the international community and an effort to increase their standing in that community. Within a group, social status and esteem can be valued for their own sake and sought independently of—or even in place of—material gain (Huberman, Loch, and Önçüler 2004). Alexander Wendt, for example, asserts that among a state's interests is a "need to feel good about itself, for respect or status" (1999:236; see also Chayes and Chayes 1995; Finnemore and Sikkink 1998; Lebow 2008). More fundamentally, states' concern for reputation points to a need for social approval within the framework of positively valued identity characteristics of a particular group (Finnemore and Sikkink 1998; Shannon 2000; Tajfel and Turner 1986). In turn, external validation from a state's peers can serve to confirm and even shape its understanding of its own identity.[21] Identity is grounded both in an actor's internal or self-understanding and in an external interpretation of that identity by other actors (Wendt 1999:224).[22] This external interpretation of identity can be and is reflected in a state's reputation and helps explain why reputation functions as a social concept.

INTERNATIONAL INSTITUTIONS AS A SOCIAL SETTING

Reputation is more easily formed in the context of international institutions. Institutions help legitimate rules and norms, leading to actors' perceptions that they should be obeyed and forming the basis for expectations of appropriate behavior and good international citizenship (Hurd 2007). Institutions also provide a setting for regular and intensive interaction among diplomats, in which peers' judgments take on greater meaning and socialize states into policy expectations.[23] Finally, participation in international institutions can force states to publicly declare their positions, making their policy choices more observable to other actors and therefore subject to social appraisal. As a result, reputation can be more easily assessed and assigned.[24] In some cases, institutions may also make peer-review processes and other monitoring mechanisms available to examine state performance.

Institutions introduce an opportunity for states to strategically choose policies to maintain, enhance, or repair their reputations. "Indeed," Johnston notes, "there is no point engaging in [behavior] for reputational purposes unless [that behavior] is observable to others" (2008:7; see also O'Neill 2006). UN General Assembly votes, for example, put states' policy positions on public display. Even where consensus rules may mask individual policy choices from public view, diplomats in the room are nevertheless aware of who dissents from the norm.[25] As I discuss in chapter 4, multilateral fora on issues related to the conventional arms trade have proliferated in the past decade, providing a community of diplomats who interact regularly and in the process have established policy expectations and the ability to assess whether those expectations are met. For small arms specifically, they have also created institutionalized reviews of states' policies and aid giving through national reporting to the UN and published assessments of those reports.[26]

Especially within international institutions, leaders who "value their social standing in international society seek to avoid negative social judgments" and choose policies, behavior, and their justifications for both accordingly (Shannon 2000:294; see also Chayes and Chayes 1995; Johnston 2008; Lumsdaine 1993). Members in a society ostracize, criticize, and punish norm violators just as they reward norm followers, in turn either revoking or granting reputational benefits (O'Neill 1999:197). In this way, reputation becomes a constraint on a state's actions. States typically prefer to "avoid the social pressures of remaining aloof from a multilateral agreement to which most of their peers have already committed themselves" (Simmons 2009:13). Not only have "responsible" arms transfer controls become a means to enhance reputation, but *not* adopting them is also seen as having potential reputational costs. Policy opposition may carry social stigma, as the United States discovered when it sought to weaken consensus-driven small arms agreements and cast the sole "no" vote on the ATT initiative until late 2009.

Such forms of social control are recognized as important for the functioning of the less formally codified international community.[27] A good reputation reinforces a state's positive self-image and helps it wield social influence and moral authority by improving its standing and legitimacy. However extensive a state's hard power, social influence can be a cheaper and subtler resource to bring fellow states' preferences in line with its own. Indeed, the ability to leverage soft power—"the ability to get what you want through attraction rather than coercion or payments" (Nye 2004:x)—is based on a positive image abroad and suggests that relying solely on military power can be inefficient and counterproductive. States are also "motivated by a desire to avoid the sense of shame or social disgrace that commonly befalls those who widely break accepted rules" (Young 1992:177; see also Zarakol 2011). A damaged reputation can lessen a state's influence or "political capital" in international politics and its ability to achieve its policy agenda in international institutions (American Political Science Association 2009:7, 12).

This relationship between reputation and influence points to social influence as an additional instrumental motivation behind states' concern for reputation. Indeed, social reputational concerns illustrate the intimate connection between social norms and strategic behavior. States and their leaders are often motivated by a combination of material and social interests as well as normative expectations.[28] Nevertheless, states are limited in how flexible they can be with their reputation-building policy choices, without which their influence also cannot grow. States must adopt and promote policies that reflect the reputation they wish to promote and maintain (Chong 1992; Ingebritsen 2006), while also counteracting any negative images that may serve to undermine their reputation and related influence.[29] As Dennis Chong observes, "By not acting on [his or her] self-professed values, each person's reputation would be diminished in the eyes of the others" (1992:191). The importance of consistency between values and policy[30] is multiplied when states take a leadership role to promote a policy on the international agenda (J. Busby 2008; Wheeler and Dunne 1998). In these circumstances, states stake their reputations not only on their own policy and behavior but also on their success in spreading similar policies elsewhere.

LIMITATIONS OF SOCIAL REPUTATION
AS A CONSTRAINT ON STATES' BEHAVIOR

Despite the strong social (and material) incentives that can drive states' reputational concerns, reputation's ability to shape states' behavior can have two main limitations. First, it may operate more strongly within rather than across issue areas.[31] Just as individuals or states are often said to have multiple identities, so too can they have multiple, compartmentalized reputations (D. Bromley 1993:44; R. Fisher 1981:130). When it comes to the consequences of reputation for states' credibility, multiple reputations is a matter of practicality: states must work together over a wide range of issues. To assume that disreputable behavior in one area spoils the credibility of cooperation in all would be inconvenient, costly, and problematic. Nor do states have reason to believe that this would be the case; the value and content of and interest in cooperative behavior also vary across issues (Downs and Jones 2002).[32] However, when states' attention is turned to social concerns for "good international citizenship," the benefits gained from containing a reputation to one area may be less relevant. In such cases, states perceive their policy choices as contributing to a broader reputation with implications for their legitimacy and standing rather than to separate reputations with implications for their credibility in other issue areas.

Second, reputation's ability to influence state behavior is limited when states' policies are observable to other actors but their practices are not. Even when policy is observable and subject to reputational judgment, practice may not be. Transparency measures play a significant role in generating compliance with international norms and treaties (Chayes and Chayes 1995:135; Norman and Trachtman 2005). Because reputation is assessed from *observed* policy and practice, where transparency is limited, scrutiny of practice must also be limited. Low levels of public information on compliance restrict the evaluative capacity of an issue for states' reputations and allow for more superficial norm adoption (Guzman 2002; Norman and Trachtman 2005). In the absence of international accountability mechanisms, governments can therefore look forward to the kudos brought on by adopting popular policies, without having to worry about paying high implementation costs—or being punished by other international actors if they do not. Thus, a state may sign on to an agreement with little intention of adhering to its obligations, "especially if it believes that its violations might not be detected" (Henkin 1968:34). Although some might dismiss such behavior as "cheap talk" or "mere window dressing,"[33] social reputational concerns can explain why states bother to commit to invest in such commitments at all. States are willing to risk potential—but by no means certain—hypocrisy costs or rhetorical entrapment in the future to receive what they see as certain social benefits (and to avoid social costs) in the present. Moreover, where either norms or behavior are ambiguous, a state may more easily deny accusations of noncompliance to reduce its reputational damage (Guzman 2002:1863).

The social reputation argument therefore suggests that a convergence of practice and policy—although conceivable without public scrutiny of state practice[34]—is less likely without more comprehensive and widespread transparency and accountability measures. Costly rules, standards, and norms may be adopted into policies not for their inherent value but (at least initially) for the value of the reputation to which they contribute. For the conventional arms trade, international monitoring and evaluation of export practices are largely absent, even where trade information is available. Indeed, despite a distinctive shift in arms transfer policy among most major exporters in response to evolving international norms, changes in export practice are slow in coming, as I show in chapter 3.[35] States' underlying arms export preferences have remained relatively stable even as policies have adapted to new norms not for their material benefits but rather for their social reputational gains in the international community.

REPUTATION IN DOMESTIC POLITICS

SCANDAL AND REPUTATIONAL DAMAGE

Multilateral conventional arms transfer policies are typically represented by states' ministries of foreign affairs, which take a direct interest in their international reputations. Policy implementation, however, is carried out by multiple government agencies and leaves the most politically sensitive cases to top decision makers more responsive to domestic audiences. Yet domestic constituencies are typically uninterested in arms transfers, a complex issue followed only by a small set of specialists, NGOs, and the defense industry. For politicians, arms export controls bring few electoral benefits and restricting defense markets has been seen—rightly or wrongly—as costly to employment and national security. Looking to public pressure to explain changes in export control policy can therefore be difficult. Nevertheless, as some scholars point out, the adoption of international rules into domestic politics is often key to enhancing compliance (Keohane 1998; Koh 1998; Simmons 2009).

Without public interest or legally binding treaties to open up a role for enforcement by domestic courts (Simmons 2009; Smith-Cannoy 2012), domestic strategies to provoke compliance are limited. Whether the ATT (legally binding on state parties) will introduce a genuine source of domestic enforcement remains to be seen; mobilizing the public to push compliance—in the courts or otherwise—tends to be difficult. In this section, I argue that it is primarily with the onset or threat of scandal that governments seek some changes in arms trade practices for domestic political gain—or for salvation.[36] Scandals emerge when arms deals are publicly revealed that violate fundamental national values and threaten governments' reputations at home. When values and norms are expressed in multilateral regimes, violations become easier for domestic actors to identify and spotlight in the public sphere. International law thus can "formally restate social values and norms" (Lutz and Sikkink 2000:657) and legitimate domestic groups' calls for behavioral change (Simmons 2009). When rules and their violations are clear-cut, civil society can engage in "naming and shaming," as well as rhetorical entrapment to create a public crisis of reputation (i.e., scandal) for leaders in power.

Scandals work with reputation to generate compliance in two ways. First, severe scandal *outbreak* can push politicians to improve practice and repair reputational damage. Second, an increased *threat* of scandal can cause decision makers to choose arms trade partners more carefully in order to avoid scandal. As arms trade transparency measures make more information publicly available, and as civil society actors are willing and able to make use of that information, export decisions become more susceptible to scrutiny. Policy makers, in turn, become more sensitive to scandal and concerned about compliance, at least in extreme cases of clear norm violations. As such, scandals are domestic political phenomena with (depending on the issue) important implications for states' foreign policy and practice.

A scandal entails public knowledge of "a departure or lapse from the normative standards that guide behavior in public office" (Williams 1998:7).[37] It is not "merely" corruption but rather a public revealing of corruption in which a politician, party, or government faces a crisis of reputation.[38] Yet an action need not be illegal to bring on scandal. As Suzanne Garment observes, "An act that affronts the moral sensibilities or pretensions of its audience may cause a scandal even if it is in reality no sin" (1992:14). What makes for a scandal thus varies across cultures, societies, and political systems,[39] and a government's and leader's practices are judged against the shared values of the society of which they are a part. A favorite popular example is the ubiquity of sex scandals in American politics compared to many European publics' less perturbed reactions to similar reports in their own national politics.

When it comes to the arms trade, major supplier states have varied in their historic susceptibility to scandal due to differences in their relationships with the arms trade, views of the arms trade as a tool of foreign policy, and the interplay of both of these factors with societal values and government structures. Some states appear somewhat more prone to arms trade scandals, such as Belgium, occasionally Germany, and increasingly Great Britain. However, pub-

lic responses to similar events in other states—for example, France and the
United States—have been more subdued. Even so, as governments agree to
common export standards linking arms transfers to peace and human rights,
the societal values associated with governments' conduct of the arms trade appear to be converging over time.

Arms trade scandals rarely topple governments or decide elections.[40] This is
not surprising: voters are unlikely to punish scandalized incumbents in elections, whether because they benefit from the politician's position of power or
because other issues are simply more important to them (Dobratz and Whitfield 1992; Mancuso 1998). Nevertheless, scandals are costly. They boost opposition strength and detract from the government's domestic legitimacy. Leaders
may be perceived as less trustworthy by the public and lose legislative influence.[41] Scandals may even set off questions about the exercise of government
itself (Bowler and Karp 2004; Mancuso 1998). These consequences stem from
tarnished reputations and reduced political capital for those deemed responsible for the government's irresponsible decisions.[42]

In democracies, where leaders are subject to the scrutiny of the public and
open press, the likelihood of scandals and their detrimental effects escalate in
tandem (Markovits and Silverstein 1988; J. Thompson 2000; Williams 1998). As
transparency of government practice improves, this dynamic becomes ever more
salient. By nature, a scandal occurs when norm-violating government practices
come into public view. If there appears to be an upswing in scandals in American politics in recent years, says Paul Apostolidis, "it's not that politicians are
behaving more badly. We're just learning about it more often" (qtd. in Kleinfield 2008). Transparency measures increase public information about where a
country's arms exports are going and open up its decisions to public opprobrium. If domestic actors are willing and able to spotlight "irresponsible" arms
exports in the media, the result may be heightened "scandal sensitivity," which
can pressure governments to choose their trade partners more carefully in order
to avoid reputational damage.

Governments' desire to avoid the reputational fallout of scandal in domestic
politics is also motivated by a desire for a positive image. In general, a positive
image is maintained by the promotion of conformity to domestic norms and
values, whether conformity is real or perceived.[43] As Matthew Hirshberg notes,
"A positive national self-image is crucial to continued public acquiescence and
support for government, and thus to the smooth, on-going functioning of the
state" (1993:78). The social control that comes from government legitimacy greatly
reduces the costs of governing and, in cases of established democratic regimes in
particular, can be essential to it.

In contrast, behavior that deviates from closely held internal definitions of
identity and values results in cognitive dissonance (Shannon 2000) and may

force a society to confront the relationship between its policies and its actions. In violating deeply rooted conceptions of identity—"we are a good/responsible/ethical member of the international community"—practice that appears irresponsible in the public sphere can lead to scandal. Governments may initially adopt and promote "responsible" arms export standards without much attention from their constituents. However, if governments are caught circumventing or violating those standards, NGOs, media, and the public will be more likely to pay attention. Scandals call public attention to discrepancies between states' values and identity and their actions. Because governments care about their reputations, the rhetorical entrapment and hypocrisy costs generated by the need to reconcile policy rhetoric and implementation may cause them to comply with policies in which they may have had no interest otherwise (J. Busby 2008; Greenhill 2010; Schimmelfennig 2001).

Scandals therefore have two main effects on compliance. First, when scandals erupt, governments will take highly visible action to counteract negative reports, especially when high-level leaders are directly implicated in the scandal-causing decision. Chong states, "We will defend our reputations vigorously when it is [sic] at risk and be more self-serving when reasonably assured that no one is looking" (1992:187). Second, when the *threat* of scandal is heightened, governments will act with at least some greater diligence to meet standards dictated by national policy, domestic values, and the international community (Chong 1992). It is, as Oran Young observes, "the prospect of being found out [that] is often just as important, and sometimes more important, to the potential violator than the prospect of becoming the target of more or less severe sanctions of a conventional or material sort" (1992:176–77).

As I show in chapter 5, improvements in arms trade transparency and the presence of active domestic NGOs together can make leaders more sensitive to the possibility of scandals. More information about states' arms export activities enables cases of noncompliance to be identified. For "naming and shaming" and rhetorical entrapment strategies to work, however, there must not only be information about discrepancies between policy and practice but also actors willing to advertise and condemn those discrepancies (Chong 1992:190). In the post–Cold War era, arms control NGOs—to the surprise of many, including perhaps the NGOs themselves—have emerged prominently in this role.

DOMESTIC NGOS, TRANSPARENCY, AND ACCOUNTABILITY

Changes in international expectations regarding conventional arms export policy have been facilitated—but not necessarily led—by NGOs. As Denise Garcia points out, "the influence of NGOs is more manifest" in the case of landmines than in the case of small arms, where states have been much more integral to the process of norm diffusion (2006:25). Government sponsorship can be crucial for convincing other states to join new initiatives (Koh 1998), and in the case of conventional weapons, big-state leadership especially has been key to growing support among other major suppliers. Even so, as I show in chapter 3, NGOs helped put small arms on the agenda, often in partnership with affected states. NGOs and epistemic communities used technical expertise, field experience, and empirical research to establish connections between problems in the developing world and the spread of small and major conventional arms (D. Garcia 2006). In many countries, NGOs have since then been invited to participate in discussions as consultants and even delegation members.

Partnerships between NGOs and "like-minded states" have become more common, even in the once highly secretive and statist area of conventional arms control.[44] Largely as a result of the landmine campaign, officials commonly describe a fundamental shift in their efforts to open up to NGOs (D. Garcia 2006; Hampson and Reid 2003; Malone 2002). Democratic states especially have found political value at home in working closely with civil society actors to signal their public accountability and transparency and to legitimatize their policies. Even in countries where NGO–government links have traditionally been weak, such as France, officials have made efforts in recent years to reach out to NGOs for consultations and information exchanges about conventional arms policy.

While partnering with many states on international policy promotion, NGOs have also sought to maintain sufficient distance to critique government policies and practices.[45] Even where international laws and norms are weak, civil society can help serve "the function of much-needed enforcement mechanisms" (Hafner-Burton and Tsutsui 2005:1402). This is where NGOs have perhaps been the most influential on arms export controls. By highlighting specific cases of "irresponsible" arms exports in the media, NGOs publicize the gap between governments' policy and practice—and, more fundamentally, between their self-image as responsible states and their irresponsible practices. Such influence suggests that shaming may work when states violate fundamental notions of *domestic* values tied to national identity.[46] And because arms trade transparency has improved since the end of the Cold War, with initiatives such as the UN Register of Conventional Arms, the Wassenaar Arrangement on Export Controls for Conventional Arms and Dual-Use Goods and Technologies, the EU Code of Conduct, and national reporting, NGO whistle-blowing has become both easier and more influential.

Robert Keohane observes, "Without transparency, the transnational norm entrepreneurs cannot undertake their key task of exposing the inconsistency between norms accepted within the domestic society (as well as transnationally), on the one hand, and state practice, on the other" (1998:710). As I describe in chapter 3, the movement toward arms trade transparency has occurred alongside an international movement toward transparency more broadly.[47] Defined as "the ease with which the public can monitor government behavior with respect to the commitment" in question (Broz 2002:864), transparency has become an expected tool of government and corporate accountability.[48] Although transparency norms have evolved separately from new export standards, they have nevertheless helped promote those standards and, in some cases, compliance with them. Nevertheless, simply revealing information does not ensure accountability; the information must also be in a form that is accessible and understandable to the public (Fung et al. 2004). In the case of arms transfers, NGOs often do the legwork to transform hundreds of pages of national reports and registers into information that the media and public can digest.

Transparency enhances a public's potential knowledge of a government's wrongdoing and the "clarity of responsibility" in policy making (Powell and Whitten 1993). The threat of publicizing a government's severe wrongdoings creates an incentive for it to alter its behavior—at least at the margins—to avoid audience costs or bad publicity.[49] Transparency thus wields a double-edged sword for governments: democracies especially strive to improve transparency as a signal of good governance (Besley 2006; Best 2005).[50] Yet transparency also provides ammunition for NGOs to call governments to task on "bad" arms deals that have the potential to resonate with the media and public. And as more information is available about government practices, the possibility of rhetorical entrapment and scandal becomes greater.

In response to growing transparency and NGO engagement, governments may be motivated to make changes in their behavior in order to avoid or deal with the costs of scandal. Joshua Busby notes, "Advocates can shape the general image and reputation of decision-makers through praise and shame, making them 'look good' or 'look bad'" (2007:251). The media, in turn, provide the critical means by which "political and public attention [is focused] on particular incidents" (Tanner 2001:159; see also Apodaca 2007).[51] In doing so, the media makes transparency a functional tool of accountability whereby information is disseminated to the public (Besley 2006; Fung, Graham, and Weil 2007). In essence, the media collectivize awareness of scandalous acts in the public sphere (Tanner 2001). "After all," observes Anthony King, "a scandal by definition is not a scandal until knowledge of it becomes public" (1984:2). NGOs have therefore purposefully engaged in "a new kind of media oriented politics" (Dezalay and Garth 2006:232; see also Simmons 2009) as a means to raise public attention and increase costs to governments for behaving "badly"—that is, contrary to their public commitments.[52]

In fact, governments contend that the anticipation of NGO criticism spread by the media has been behind their move to better scrutinize and justify arms export decisions. In a parallel example, Mark Duggan and Steven Levitt (2000) find that match rigging in Japanese sumo wrestling drops when media attention increases in anticipation of corruption, in order to avoid future scandal. Scandal even occasionally encourages policy change. NGOs have had a hand in creating and sustaining arms trade scandals in recent years by drawing media attention to flagrant noncompliant behavior in hopes of improving future compliance. States with transparency and active civil society groups are more susceptible to scandal and tarnished reputations that are due to clearly "irresponsible" export decisions. In this manner, NGOs are a direct conduit between reputation and practice in domestic politics, exploiting governments' interest in avoiding rampant bad press at home. Unlike the alternative explanations outlined next, this perspective avoids depending on a close alignment between commitment and compliance and can explain changing practices in a subset of cases where reputational incentives are strong.

ALTERNATIVE EXPLANATIONS AND THE NEED FOR ANALYTICAL ECLECTICISM

Research explaining major suppliers' support for "responsible" arms export controls is lacking, but suitable prepackaged explanations are also hard to come by. The alternative explanations outlined here are based primarily on the assumptions and arguments of IR theories and how they conceive of states' interests in relation to their commitment to international rules and norms. The theoretical expectations for state policy and practice are summarized in table 2.2. Yet standard IR theories often rely on commitment and compliance working hand in hand in their explanations of states' policy choices. In cases like this one, where commitment and compliance are largely divorced, I argue that these explanations are restricted in their ability to account for states' behavior.

REALISM: ARMS TRANSFERS AND NATIONAL SECURITY

Major suppliers' support for new arms export controls presents a challenge for realism. For states to support humanitarian export policies, they must either anticipate net material gains from new controls or see them as simply codifying their existing practice (Downs, Rocke, and Barsoom 1996; Goldsmith and Posner 2005; Morrow 2007). Commitment must therefore come with compliance,

TABLE 2.2. SUMMARY OF THEORETICAL EXPECTATIONS

	Social reputation	Realism	Neoliberalism	Domestic preferences	Constructivism
Policy commitment	Commit to maintain/improve international reputation	States will not commit (because not in material interest)	States will not commit (because not in material interest)	Commit if public pressure/industry lobbying in favor	Commitment because of socialization into international norms
Practice compliance	Compliance varies, can be partial, depends on reputational concerns	Compliance unlikely without commitment (for material gain)	Compliance unlikely without commitment (for material gain) or enforcement	Compliance if in industry's material interest	Compliance because of socialization into international norms

so that states can receive the benefits they seek from an agreement or because the agreement happens to reflect what they are already doing. For example, if major exporters support multilateral export controls to improve national security by reducing the need for external intervention (or at least the costs of it), they can accrue these benefits only by stopping supplies to problematic recipients in practice.

Yet the potential benefits of multilateral export controls are easily trumped by their direct, high costs to state sovereignty and national security, as the historical record shows. In an anarchical international system, states must prioritize basic security needs, in part by avoiding dependence on others (K. Waltz 1979). As long as arms transfers are considered necessary to maintain a viable national defense industry, states will prevent external restrictions for fear of weakening their defense capabilities.[53] Any material benefits that might come from new export controls would be significantly outweighed by the costs to states' security. By restraining exports, "responsible" arms transfer controls might undermine states' foreign-policy autonomy, their defense industries, and, by extension, their material positions in the international system.[54] Overall, humanitarian export policies thus fail to serve state interest, defined by the preservation and enhancement of material power capabilities.[55] Confronted by the high costs to material power created by export controls unrelated to national security, commitment to—and certainly compliance with—such policies would be unexpected.

From a realist perspective, then, the states with *low* export dependence (such as the United States) at least might not oppose new export controls. Similarly, the states most involved in external interventions (again, such as the United States[56]) might even support them. In addition, supportive policy makers will link humanitarian controls to material power interests and capabilities, whether as a reduction of intervention costs or as backing for the defense industry. It is not that states necessarily lack the moral interests behind humanitarian export controls, but that moral interests are "less tangible, and policy, for better or worse, tends to be made in response to relatively tangible rational objectives" (Donnelly 1986:616). Without evidence of coercion from a powerful supporter or a pure "coincidence of interest" (Goldsmith and Posner 2005) to motivate states' commitment (and compliance), realism may be more useful to identify the puzzle of shared humanitarian export controls rather than to serve as its explanation.

NEOLIBERALISM: ARMS TRANSFERS AND ECONOMIC GAIN

In order to commit to and comply with international regimes, states, from a neoliberal perspective, must derive some mutual economic gain from cooperation

(Keohane 1984) or solve a costly collective-action problem (Simmons 1998). In short, self-interested states must deem cooperation to be in their material interest. Without the promise of such benefits, regime formation is difficult to explain. If the material benefits from trading arms outweigh the benefits of restricting arms sales, states will be more likely to oppose a restrictive regime. Supportive states may therefore be those that have already adopted unilateral restrictions and wish to "level the playing field" to their economic advantage (never mind explaining the prior adoption of unilateral standards). Yet if those rare arms exporters with existing national humanitarian standards—such as the United States or Germany—were initially reluctant to agree to similar standards on a larger scale, then the "level playing field" argument loses traction.

Once a regime is established, compliance hinges primarily on states' desire to receive the resulting benefits now and in the future (Keohane 1984; Simmons 1998) and secondarily on the form of the agreement. Without compliance, the benefits from present-day cooperation—and potential economic payoffs from related future agreements—will not materialize. In this sense, compliance should reflect the material motivations that should be behind states' willingness to cooperate; compliance should again follow commitment. Some neoliberals nevertheless point out that, absent strong enforcement and monitoring mechanisms, a regime will have trouble inducing compliance (Fortna 2003; Hafner-Burton 2005; Hafner-Burton and Tsutsui 2005). Arms export controls have become institutionalized in most regions, and their numbers are growing internationally. However, because most are not subject to any costly enforcement, their effect on state activity may be minimal.[57]

DOMESTIC LIBERALISM: DEFENSE INDUSTRY INTERESTS

Liberal theories of domestic interests explore the influence of societal actors as they shape states' broader interests and preferences (Milner 1997; Moravcsik 1997). The state is not so much an actor in world politics in its own right but rather a "representative institution constantly subject to capture and recapture, construction and reconstruction by coalitions of social actors" and their interests (Moravcsik 1997:518). In some cases—such as the landmine ban—domestic public pressure may drive states' policy commitments. In the case of arms transfers, many experts' primary expectation—and the conventional wisdom—is that policies will reflect the powerful, well-funded, and well-networked voice of the arms industry (Hartung 1996; Moravcsik 1992).[58] I explore both of these possible explanations—public pressure and defense industry preferences—later in the case studies.

The concept of the military-industrial complex (MIC) encapsulates the close relationship between government and the defense industry and industry's influence in government decision making.[59] Government policies, financial aid for foreign sales, and export decisions commonly reflect industrial interests designed to keep companies in business (Hartung 1996; Moravcsik 1992). According to this perspective, governments should take their policy cues from the defense industry. If industry perceives material benefits from new export controls—perhaps to level the playing field or to pursue profitable coproduction arrangements abroad—it will push policy makers to commit to them. If, however, industry perceives an economic incentive (or even need) to exploit foreign markets to survive, governments will seek *less* restrictive policies.

The substance and timing of defense industry policies in this case is key: if industry has either ignored the issue or *followed* the lead of supportive governments, this explanation is less plausible. An alternative societal-level explanation might look to evidence of a groundswell of public pressure on governments to generate policy commitment. Yet I find in the case study chapters ahead that public or industry pressure in advance of states' commitment decisions is missing. Without such domestic-level pressures, domestic liberalism struggles to explain governments' policy support. This is not to argue that domestic politics do not play a role. Indeed, as I have argued, domestic politics can prove essential for compliance. It then becomes a question of whether states' practice simply reflects societal interests according to domestic liberalism or whether it anticipates and reacts to them based on their international commitments for more complex reasons.

CONSTRUCTIVISM: ARMS TRANSFERS AND INTERNATIONAL NORMS

For constructivists, interests are not determined solely by material power or societal demands but are instead constructed through social interactions in domestic and international politics.[60] In light of the increasing integration of established international norms of human rights and state responsibility[61] into arms trade agreements, states' interests themselves should come to embrace and internalize these changes. Even in the absence of formal institutions, hard law, or coercive measures, normative obligations established in shared customs should affect not only states' policy but also their compliance with that policy (Checkel 2001; Finnemore and Toope 2001). Here again commitment and compliance come together.

Norms create prescriptions for behavior "that predispose states to act in certain ways" (Wendt 1999:234; see also Finnemore 1996a, 1996b).[62] Constructivism therefore expects that states' export policy and practice will reflect new humanitarian standards. For example, Garcia (2011) argues that support for humanitarian arms control policy stems from other-oriented moral progress in international politics that has transformed states' interests. Precisely to whom these expectations apply, however, divides constructivists. A *broad* form of constructivism expects norms to shape the behavior of all states in similar ways. Interests are socialized by international institutions and governed by the logic of appropriateness, thus predicting "similar behavior from dissimilar actors because rules and norms may make similar behavioral claims on dissimilar actors" (Finnemore 1996b:30; see also Koh 1998). All states—regardless of regime type, power, or position—should be similarly affected by the spread of arms transfer norms. A more *narrow* approach (also related to the English School) would limit the influence of norms to a subsystemic group of states with shared values and beliefs (Bull 1977; Klotz 1995). This approach points to democracies as the group of states most likely to be susceptible to human rights norms[63] due to a shared community of values, an internal commitment to human rights, and greater openness to societal influence and accountability (Burley 1992; Henkin 1968; Risse-Kappen 1995b; Slaughter 1995).

However, these expectations may be overly optimistic in this case. As Andrew Hurrell points out, the real test of the strength of international rules and norms is their ability to bind states "despite countervailing self-interest" (1993:53). If the empirical evidence reveals gaps between states' policy and practice or between their public and private policy preferences, states' normative commitment to new policies must be questioned. Noncompliance that reflects states' material interests rather than normative obligations would especially call into question constructivist explanations. Of course, it may simply be too early in the "responsible" arms transfer norm life cycle to impose strong expectations on state practice. If states become increasingly compliant over time, it may suggest that norms are becoming accepted and valued for their own sake—though their initial adoption would still have resulted from instrumental, not normative, motivations.[64]

The chapters ahead explore and explain the policies and practice of top conventional arms exporters. First, historical and statistical patterns of arms trade practice set the stage for a more in-depth analysis of international and domestic material and social pressures to account for major exporters' dramatic change in arms trade policy. Most of the alternative explanations have difficulty accounting for commitment without compliance, suggesting the need for a more analytically eclectic explanation to understand the policy–practice gap.[65] Although scholars often acknowledge the role that mechanisms and motivations associated with both rationalist and constructivist theories can play in determining the decisions of political actors, the task of combining them in practice is often left incomplete. Yet, as I show, it is the combination of normative change, social incentives, and state interest—channeled through concern for social reputation—that can explain states' commitment to "responsible" arms export policies and their poor (but potentially improving) compliance.

The social reputation argument combines rational and social motivations for states' policy and practice for a more complete analytical account of state behavior. It views states as rational actors responding to social incentives within a changed international normative environment. Particularly in the context of international institutions, policy expectations can shift and, with them, states' motivations to support those policies. In the case of conventional arms transfers, states have faced contradictory material and social interests. I argue that their commitment to "responsible" export standards stems from social pressure at the international level. That pressure, however, does not necessarily transform their private preferences.[66]

Compliance with new standards presents costly trade-offs for states seeking to maintain a viable defense industry and flexible foreign policy. Without international accountability, states may balance these trade-offs by engaging in less-restrictive practices without harming their international reputations. Yet as arms trade transparency improves and civil society activism spreads, democracies especially may face domestic consequences for clear-cut cases of poor compliance and so may choose to reform practice at the margins to avoid negative public attention. In contrast, if states have internalized new norms or seek material benefits from new policies, their practice should more fully reflect those norms and policies. The book next explores historical and statistical trends in conventional arms export policy and practice. It assesses the normative status quo and challenges in creating multilateral policy success in the twentieth century, the sources behind international normative shifts in the 1990s, and the influence of human rights on major exporters' practice. In doing so, it surveys not only the policy landscape over time but also demonstrates the gap between commitment and compliance, leading to the case studies to explain these findings in greater depth and the need for the social reputational argument.

3. History and Contemporary Trends in Conventional Arms Export Controls

States' support for the Arms Trade Treaty and "responsible" arms export controls belies long-standing expectations. Conventional weapons play a vital role in national and international security and present a hard case for international commitment. Until the late 1990s, conventional arms sales remained the prerogative of national foreign and economic policy. Whether arms were used to influence allies or to support domestic economic interests, recipients' human rights were not considered, conflict was a concern for only a handful of suppliers,[1] and material interests dominated export decision making. For the most part, states pushed away multilateral efforts to impose controls on major conventional arms sales and divorced national policy from any restrictive international standards or obligations. Small arms were absent entirely from the international agenda. Even initial post–Cold War optimism for a transfer control regime[2] quickly faded "in the face of desperate competition between supplier states for a share of the . . . dwindling international market" (Spear 1994:99). With the often close relationship of governments and defense industries, along with deep concerns for state sovereignty and security, such a stalemate was hardly surprising—nor have these relationships and concerns disappeared over time.

Since the late 1990s, however, material pressures to export have increasingly had to coexist with normative pressures to control. Conventional arms transfers have been found to undermine human rights, governance, social and economic development, domestic and international stability, and postconflict reconstruction. By 2006, states had reached numerous regional and international agreements reflecting these concerns and voted to begin a formal process at the UN to create an ATT (see appendix A for the history of related agreements).[3] Many suppliers had also adopted national "responsible" arms transfer controls, focused in particular on their import partners' human rights practices. These initiatives culminated in the UN Arms Trade Treaty, which lays out the first-ever legally binding global humanitarian standards for small and major conventional arms exports. In 2013, a total of 154 member states voted to approve the ATT, with only Iran, North Korea, and Syria opposing it. Most major supplier states—including the United States, France, Germany, and the United Kingdom—once considered external export restrictions too costly but now count themselves among supporters of multilateral humanitarian export controls.

How did this policy transformation come to pass, what makes it so dramatic, and how well does it reflect states' existing arms export practice? This chapter analyzes the changing contours of the international normative environment for conventional arms exports in three main parts. In essence, it charts the "business as usual" of the global arms trade over time. In the first section, I provide an overview of the twentieth century's failed multilateral attempts to control arms exports. This section highlights the entrenched norms of sovereignty and material stakes that states perceive in maintaining control over their arms exports as well as the absence of human rights from the discussion. Second, I identify the key events in the 1990s that explain the origins of new "responsible" arms export norms, a dramatic shift that once seemed improbable given enduring national material interests and exporter preferences. Finally, I investigate how these changes in international normative expectations map onto broad trends in small and major conventional arms export practice between 1981 and 2010. I find that state practice does not reflect humanitarian policy changes. This casts doubt on explanations that rely on either normative obligation or material incentives to explain states' policy commitments. States have supported new initiatives *in spite* of their underlying export preferences, not because of them. Changes in policy can come without changes in practice if states can receive the social reputational benefits of commitment without engaging in costly implementation. By examining the historical continuities and broad shifts in how states collectively engage in arms export policy and practice, the chapter sets the stage for the more in-depth analysis of major exporters' specific policy choices within this international environment.

ASSESSING GLOBAL ARMS EXPORT TRENDS

This chapter examines four key periods in the twentieth-century global arms trade: (1) the League of Nations and interwar years; (2) the Cold War; (3) the early 1990s; and (4) the road to the ATT. Attempts to create shared arms trade regulations prior to the late 1990s were notorious failures. Yet although the contemporary historical record on arms export *policy* is well established, the lack of available data on states' arms export *practice* (i.e., policy implementation, in this case arms deliveries) has been a roadblock for cross-national analyses until recent decades. Until the 1990s, a norm of secrecy ruled interstate arms deal making, and information was restricted to news reports and publicly released (or leaked) intelligence reports.[4] Major conventional weapons data are generally more comprehensive than small arms data, though small arms data have improved greatly in the past decade. MCW are easier to track, invited greater policy attention until the late 1990s, and, if publicly known, could provide greater prestige and deterrent value than SALW. But even if public records may underestimate arms transfers, it is important to examine export practice alongside export policy in order to evaluate explanations for why policies might change and to what effect.

Although public attention to conventional arms in the United States during the late 1970s brought some more information on MCW there, this trend did not spread elsewhere quickly. A 1979 U.S. government report summarized the problem: "Virtually all nations consider arms sale statistics highly sensitive. Most insist that publication of such information would harm their relationships with purchasing countries. . . . Only the United States publishes country-by-country details of its arms export transactions. In fact, it appears that few nations actually maintain a central repository of detailed information. Many major suppliers could not, even if they were willing, supply the sort of detailed data that the United States makes available" (U.S. Senate 1979:7).[5] As a result, a statistical analysis of trends in export practice cannot extend as far back in time as a historical overview of export policy. Fortunately, data have improved as records have been declassified. And although SALW data are rough in the 1980s, they provide useful insights into this period—when the arms trade was not a prominent issue and human rights considerations were not on the table—as a baseline for assessing later changes in policy and practice.

Since the end of the Cold War, growing arms trade transparency and international research institutes' long-term efforts have vastly improved the quality and availability of arms export data. The UN Register of Conventional Arms went into effect in 1992, replacing secrecy with a norm of transparency in international, regional, and national politics (Laurance, Wagenmakers, and Wulf 2005:233). Suppliers in particular "have come to accept that almost total secrecy surrounding the arms trade is counterproductive" (Anthony 1997:29–30). Although some exporters still have poor records of reporting,[6] transparency has otherwise advanced across the board, especially among established democracies. The reporting improvements now sought in the United States and Europe are meant primarily to increase the level of detail about individual export decisions and do not affect the aggregate annual export–import data used here. Most major suppliers contribute regularly to the UN Register, and the level of detail, especially from European suppliers, is increasingly meticulous. Export information tends to be more regularly and widely submitted than import information (Durch 2000; Lebovic 2006), although reporting in general continues to grow. According to the UN Office of Disarmament Affairs (2012), the number of countries submitting reports rose from 95 in 1992 to a high of 126 in 2011, with 173 countries participating at least once by 2011. The Wassenaar Arrangement and the EU also have arms trade transparency provisions, which increase the volume of reporting.

These transparency initiatives began with MCW exports. Research institutes and governments typically overlooked small arms transfers until the mid-1990s, so SALW data collection relies on general and trade-specific news reports, UN Comtrade (customs) data, and other sources, where government reports are not available.[7] The absence of attention to small arms has changed as they have become a significant policy issue in their own right. By 1999, twenty-two states had begun to include small arms in their export reports (Haug et al. 2002). In 2003, Wassenaar decided to include small arms on its list of strategic goods used for intergovernmental transparency. The UN also formally expanded the UN Register in 2003 to include voluntary reporting on small arms transfers. In 2004, only 4 percent of reports submitted to the register included information about small arms transfers. By 2010 and 2011, that number had risen to 66 percent (UN Office of Disarmament Affairs 2012). Despite these limitations, the importance of SALW on the international agenda in recent years and their prominent role in human rights violations make it both valuable and necessary to examine them alongside MCW transfers.

In order to map the relationship between trends in arms export policy and practice in this chapter, I build an original arms trade data set covering as thoroughly as possible SALW and MCW transfers from 22 top supplier states (20 of which voted in favor of the ATT in 2013) to 189 potential importer states from 1981 to 2010. This means that the data are *dyadic* (e.g., exporter state to importer state) and annual.[8] A "dyad-year" therefore refers to exporter–importer pairings in a particular year. Thus, the United States (exporter) and Colombia (importer) dyad or pairing includes thirty dyad-years, covering each year from 1981 to 2010 in the data set.

Details about the data set are provided in appendix B, including exporters covered, variable coding, and control-variable selection. No other data set covers cross-national data for both SALW and MCW transfers.[9] The UN defines small arms as "those weapons designed for personal use" and light weapons as "those designed for use by several persons serving as a crew" (UN 1997:11). SALW therefore include, for example, revolvers, machine guns, rifles, and ammunition and explosives (UN 1997:11–12).[10] SIPRI defines and codes MCW as large weapons with a military purpose in one of nine categories: aircraft, armored vehicles, artillery, sensors, air-defense systems, missiles, ships, engines, or "others" fulfilling certain qualifications (2007:428–29).[11] Scholars have linked both SALW and MCW to human rights violations, but the EU Code of Conduct and the ATT are the only multilateral export control initiatives to encompass both.

This chapter uses the Arms Trade Data Set to assess conventional arms transfer practice from the 1980s to the present day[12] through (1) basic cross-tabulations with recipient human rights, (2) regression analyses, and (3) moving-windows (or moving-regression) analyses. I use a measure of recipient countries' human rights provided by the Political Terror Scale, which scores countries' physical integrity rights annually based on U.S. Department of State (DOS) and Amnesty International reports (Gibney and Dalton 1996). If policy and practice coincide, Cold War patterns should reveal arms exports as a tool of foreign policy and national security that is indifferent to recipients' human rights records.[13] Given the difficulties with acquiring arms trade data before the 1990s, however, readers should be wary about drawing firm conclusions from earlier data. Following the end of the Cold War, arms transfers motivated by economic gain and industry survival became the dominant trend. Supplier states would have been unlikely to limit arms transfers to human rights violators; in fact, such states might present too valuable a market to avoid ruling them out summarily. By the late 1990s, the shift to "responsible" arms transfer policy called exporters' attention to their import partners' human rights records. Policy attention also expanded to include small arms on their own and in conjunction with MCW. If states' practice reflects their policy commitments, human rights should become increasingly important factors in states' export practice during this current period—especially among ATT supporters. Although states are still faced with economic pressures to export arms, new political pressures simultaneously push them—at least on paper—to become more discerning in their export decision making.

CONVENTIONAL ARMS TRANSFERS IN THE TWENTIETH CENTURY

States have carefully protected their sovereign right to decide their arms trade partners without reference to international obligations or external restrictions.

The decades before World War I have been referred to as having "the fewest restraints and regulations on the arms trade in modern history" (Krause and MacDonald 1993:712).[14] Yet even in the twentieth century the rare attempts to create multilateral arms trade controls consistently failed. The historic absence of multilateral controls strongly reflects this norm of noninterference. And, except for the United States briefly in the late 1970s, humanitarian arms export controls did not hit the policy agenda until the late 1990s. Arms export decision making has been constrained only by states' national law and policy, which until recently have excluded human rights considerations.

Prior to contemporary "responsible" arms export initiatives, the conventional arms trade took the international spotlight on just three occasions, each partly in response to domestic outrage within major powers about unrestricted arms transfers. Unlike contemporary efforts, these failed predecessor initiatives did not seek regulations based on humanitarian principles, nor were "affected" states among their champions. Rather, they set out to limit arms transfers to specified "unstable" regions, with great powers seeing an opportunity to manipulate allies', enemies', and colonies' (or even their own) access to arms markets in line with their geopolitical and industrial interests. Time and again, absent any sustained social pressure or real change in international policy expectations, states' material concerns for sovereignty, national security, and economic interests won out over cooperative restraint with little contest.

POST–WORLD WAR I AND THE LEAGUE OF NATIONS

Global arms transfer controls first came onto the agenda after World War I under the aegis of the League of Nations. The initial attempt—the St. Germain Convention for the Control of the Trade in Arms and Ammunition—was signed in 1919 as part of the postwar settlement. It was motivated primarily by the European powers' desires to keep weapons from falling into the hands of "problem actors" in areas of colonial influence, but the public's "moral criticism of the role of arms traders in fomenting the First World War was also prominent in the backdrop to negotiations" (Bromley, Cooper, and Holtom 2012:1032). The St. Germain Convention was meant to implement Article 23(d) of the League of Nations Covenant, entrusting the league with "the general supervision of the trade in arms and ammunition with the countries in which the control of this traffic is necessary in the common interest." It required government licensing (already practiced by Great Britain), arms export reporting to the league, and arms sales restrictions to nonsignatories, parts of the Ottoman Empire, and Africa. In 1920, diplomats from France, Italy, Japan, and Great Britain agreed informally to implement the convention's provisions in Africa and the Middle East (Stone 2000:218).

Objections to the St. Germain Convention, however, quickly grew. Perhaps most important for setting off the dominoes of opposition, the United States refused to bind itself for three key reasons: a ban on sales to nonsignatories could harm its domestic arms industry; it felt that "the zones to which the Convention was to apply were drawn so that the result would have been almost exclusively to protect the interests of the surviving European colonial powers and even to interfere with U.S. policy in Latin America"; and, quite simply, it objected to giving power to the League of Nations (SIPRI 1971:92; see also Stone 2000). Following the United States, other arms-producing states also declined to participate, fearing that their industries would be disadvantaged by unequal trade restrictions. In the end, foreign-policy autonomy and industrial interests trumped export controls with little debate.

The League of Nations abandoned the St. Germain Convention in favor of the weaker Geneva Arms Traffic Convention in 1925. This version was tailored to address U.S. concerns and sought only arms export publicity through the league, allowing states to supervise and sanction their own transfers (SIPRI 1971; Stone 2000). In his opening remarks, negotiation conference president Carton de Wiart emphasized that the new convention's aim was not to restrict the arms trade. Rather, it was "to obviate the possible threat of illicit and dangerous traffic to compromise the good name of such legitimate trade or should hamper the success of the best efforts to create an atmosphere of peace and good will between nations" (League of Nations 1925:122). Not surprisingly, the focus on illicit trade, rather than on what producing states determined to be their legal trade, was much more palatable to producing states than handing over power to the League of Nations.[15] Nevertheless, this initiative also failed. This time, the failure was due mainly to nonproducing states (including smaller European states), which saw licensing and publicity as "intolerable infringements on sovereignty and security" that would put them "at the mercy of producers" (Stone 2000:222, 223). These states derailed the initiative by introducing unacceptably high sovereignty costs for the producing states as well, linking export publicity to production publicity and attempting to impose production restrictions (Stone 2000).

The final attempt to regulate conventional arms production and trade in the interwar years was led by the United States in the League of Nations Disarmament Conference in 1934. The U.S. change of heart was motivated by the Senate Nye Committee's investigations into the U.S. private munitions industry—dubbed "the merchants of death" in the popular press—and concerns about unregulated arms transfers to Latin America (Anderson 1992; Bromley, Cooper, and Holtom 2012).[16] The conference's proposal was unusual in a number of respects: it included arms for nonmilitary use, such as sporting rifles; it created a permanent supervisory body; and it did not single out some regions for higher restrictions (Bromley, Cooper, and Holtom 2012:1033). Although there were disagreements over specific measures, there was general agreement "that the *private* manufacture of arms should be subjected to government license and that there should be national responsibility for the manufacture of, and trade in, arms" (Krause and MacDonald 1993:719, emphasis added).

Once again, controlling production by nongovernmental actors was a much lower hurdle than controlling government production or licensing. But by the time the conference adopted the draft articles in 1935, it was already too late. The deteriorating security environment in Europe and Italy's invasion of Ethiopia turned states' attention to national rearmament and precluded "any possibility of an international agreement" (Bromley, Cooper, and Holtom 2012:1033; see also Anderson 1992). Thus, although the interwar years left a lasting legacy of governments agreeing to give themselves licensing authority over arms exported from their borders, international controls were elusive, and human rights were not an issue. The fate of the interwar initiatives depended on what quickly became clear was the impossible task of aligning the major powers' material interests and security priorities—made even more impossible when recipient states gained "meaningful agency" at the negotiating table (Bromley, Cooper, and Holtom 2012:1034). These obstacles have persisted, consistently undermining attempts at restraint throughout the twentieth century—to the extent that such attempts have even been made. That is, until the ATT.

THE COLD WAR AND SUPERPOWER FOREIGN POLICY

Disarmament and the arms trade took a backseat during the formation of the United Nations after World War II. The UN Charter established states' right to self-defense but has "never been viewed as affecting law on the regulation of weapons" (Anderson 1992:765 n. 82). During the Cold War, arms sales were seen as "foreign policy writ large" (Pierre 1982:3). Transfers were dependent not on importers' internal characteristics, but rather on their East–West ideological orientation and the maintenance of regional power balances. The United States and the Soviet Union in particular used transfers to gain influence among client states in the developing world and to push their foreign-policy preferences.[17] The two superpowers were the supersuppliers, setting the tone for the global arms trade. In general, decision makers regarded conventional arms as a valuable political tool to be distributed strategically and not to be hindered unnecessarily.[18]

Conflicts were an opportunity to sell, "if only to pre-empt transfers by the other side" (Catrina 1988:333; see also SIPRI 1971).

Controls were not entirely absent in this period, but they directly reflected these strategic concerns, codifying Cold War politics and supporting the bipolar system. The Western allies secretly established the Coordinating Committee for Multilateral Export Controls (COCOM) in 1949 as an informal agreement to embargo the exports of weapons and dual-use technologies to the Eastern bloc. Although intrabloc and third-party arms transfers went unregulated, COCOM was intended to ensure that sensitive strategic technologies did not benefit Soviet adversaries. The agreement was thought to be relatively effective, if not always enthusiastically implemented by some participating states.[19] Countries that did not follow COCOM rules could be blacklisted by the United States, which used the agreement largely as a tool of economic statecraft to serve its hegemonic interests (L. Martin 1992; Mastanduno 1992).[20]

In 1950, the United States, the United Kingdom, and France also agreed to a more formal agreement, the Tripartite Declaration, to regulate and coordinate arms sales to the Middle East, "tying arms transfers to promises of non-aggression by the recipient states" (Anderson 1992:766; see also Bromley, Cooper, and Holtom 2012; Pierre 1997). The intention was to enable Middle Eastern states to resist Soviet aggression, to maintain a balance between Israel and the Arab states, and to serve as a forerunner to a Middle East security network that would improve the West's strategic position (Slonin 1987). In reality, the Tripartite Declaration served as a "forum for discussion . . . rather than as an agreement that imposed mandatory obligations on the parties" (Bromley, Cooper, and Holtom 2012:1034; see also Slonin 1987). Indeed, France violated it from the start with secret arms sales to Israel made with the blessing of the United States (Rubenberg 1989). However, later public increases in French arms sales to Israel sowed discord among the declaration's members, and Soviet–Czechoslovakian arms sales to Egypt in 1955 and the Suez Crisis in 1956 caused its collapse. Ultimately, the Tripartite Declaration was unable to withstand Cold War politics and the overriding pressure on both sides to use arms to influence global affairs. Even within a small group of Western allies with shared security concerns, export controls remained elusive.

It was not until the late 1970s that arms export regulations returned to the global agenda,[21] thanks to U.S. public outcry in the wake of weariness over involvement in Vietnam and the lead-up to the 1976 U.S. presidential elections. In a campaign speech, Jimmy Carter argued that the United States could not be both "the world's leading champion of peace and the world's leading supplier of the weapons of war" (Carter 1976). For the first time, policy makers linked arms transfers to concerns for recipient human rights.[22] Leslie Gelb criticized arms export practice under Nixon and Ford, stating that "the character of the regime was overlooked in view of the overriding importance of stopping communism" (1976–1977:14). Michael Stohl, David Carleton, and Steven Johnson's (1984) findings that states with higher levels of human rights violations received more economic and military assistance under Nixon and Ford support Gelb's criticisms. Once in office, the Carter administration sought to promote U.S. and global export restraint through unilateral policy changes and multilateral negotiations. Both approaches, however, became casualties of Cold War politics.

First, Presidential Directive 13 (PD-13) set unilateral guidelines to limit the spread of U.S. weapons and indicated "that human rights violations would be an important consideration in the [arms sales] decision-making process" (Brzoska and Ohlson 1987:57). The directive was a radical change in policy for any major arms supplier. It introduced human rights into national-level arms export policy and imposed unilateral restraint to set an example for other suppliers. In practice, however, it was considered a failure from the start.[23] The policy itself "did not set out clear priorities and contained significant inconsistencies and contradictions," which allowed the administration flexibility in application and gave opponents to it in the U.S. bureaucracy and defense industry the means to slow its implementation (Spear 1995:177).

As a result, human rights considerations—when applied at all—were applied only in countries deemed not vital to U.S. national-security interests, with arms exports commonly used as a tool of foreign policy elsewhere (Brzoska and Ohlson 1987; Pierre 1982; Spear 1995). This practice of case-by-case flexibility to support "indispensable" nations, criticized Stanley Hoffmann at the time, made "[the Carter] administration look not so different at all from that of the previous one" (1977–1978:19–20). For the most part, quantitative evidence confirms this disconnect between policy and practice. Human rights were not a significant determinant of levels of U.S. military aid during the Carter administration (Stohl, Carleton, and Johnson 1984:222; see also Apodaca and Stohl 1999; Forsythe 1987).[24] Moreover, the same economic and security concerns that overrode human rights considerations in U.S. arms export practice during the Carter years ensured that human rights as an arms trade policy issue did not diffuse to other countries and would not even return to U.S. national arms export policy until 1995.

Second, President Carter sought to bring multilateral export restraints to the international agenda. Although not incorporating human rights considerations, between 1977 and 1978 Carter sought to negotiate multilateral transfer limitations to complement U.S. unilateral restraints articulated in PD-13. The Conventional Arms Transfer (CAT) talks were intended to be the first attempt to negotiate global restraints since the interwar years. However, when the United States approached European producer states about participating, they declined the invitation, not wanting to commit to trade limitations until it was clear that the Soviet Union would do so first (Spear 1995). As a result, the talks focused entirely on engaging the Soviet Union and fell apart before an agreement was reached (Pierre 1982:286). Whereas League of Nations talks at least had widespread major-power participation, the CAT talks could not even get West European producers to the table.

The collapse of the talks was due to disagreements both within the Carter administration and between U.S. and Soviet policies over limits on transfers to "critical regions" (Catrina 1988:130–31; Durch 2000; Hartung 1993; Pierre 1982; Wentz 1987–1988). U.S. bureaucrats disagreed about the role of arms transfers in foreign policy and whether the United States should be discussing arms transfers to sensitive regions at all, a disagreement that undermined the U.S. ability to negotiate as talks progressed (Pierre 1982; Spear 1995). Moreover, the Joint Chiefs of Staff were concerned that the United States "would be tied down in extended global negotiations with the Soviets whilst they and the European suppliers took advantage of PD-13's unilateral restraints" (Spear 1995:119). For their part, the Soviets were "incredulous and angry at the American unwillingness to hear what they had to say about the regions of concern to them" (Pierre 1982:288). The United States, however, felt that including East Asia and the Middle East, as the Soviets wanted, would be unacceptable. It privately informed the Soviet delegation that it would walk out of the fourth round of talks in December 1978 if the Soviet Union followed through on its proposal (Spear 1995). As a result, the December meeting kept any specific regions off the table and never got a chance to put them back on as détente waned, the Soviets invaded Afghanistan, and the United States prioritized relations with China over discussions about arms transfer restrictions to East Asia. Not surprisingly, politics had once again gotten in the way of arms trade cooperation, with the superpowers unwilling to limit arms sales to strategic regions.

With the inauguration of Ronald Reagan in 1981, the arms trade policies that the United States had attempted to promote under the Carter administration came to a clear end. The CAT talks had already died out, and Reagan immediately rejected PD-13 in favor of an explicit return to "the use of arms sales to counter the Soviet challenge" (Wentz 1987–1988:352). In general, the Reagan administration had little interest in limiting arms exports (Pierre 1982:63). Human rights, too, were once again absent from the discussion. The administration "refused to consider reducing security assistance or sales because of human rights considerations," given the clear and present danger from the Soviet sphere (Forsythe 1987:385). Consistent with Reagan's stated policy priorities emphasizing national security and deemphasizing human rights, Clair Apodaca and Michael Stohl (1999) find no statistically significant link between human rights and U.S. military aid allocation throughout the two Reagan administrations.[25]

The link between conventional arms transfers and human rights globally is more difficult to assess in this period. When it comes to major conventional arms, for which data availability is better, the Arms Trade Data Set reveals a picture that does not single out good human rights for reward or poor human rights for punishment during the Cold War. Figure 3.1 illustrates the results from simple cross-tabulations, which find that about 11 percent of dyad-years whose importers had records of "very bad" human rights received MCW transfers (in contrast, 89 percent did not receive MCW transfers). Clearly, only a minority of the worst human rights performers received MCW, but that portion is relatively high compared to the 7 percent of dyad-years whose importers had the best human rights records and received MCW transfers (93 percent did not). Regression analyses also reveal a strong positive relationship between poor

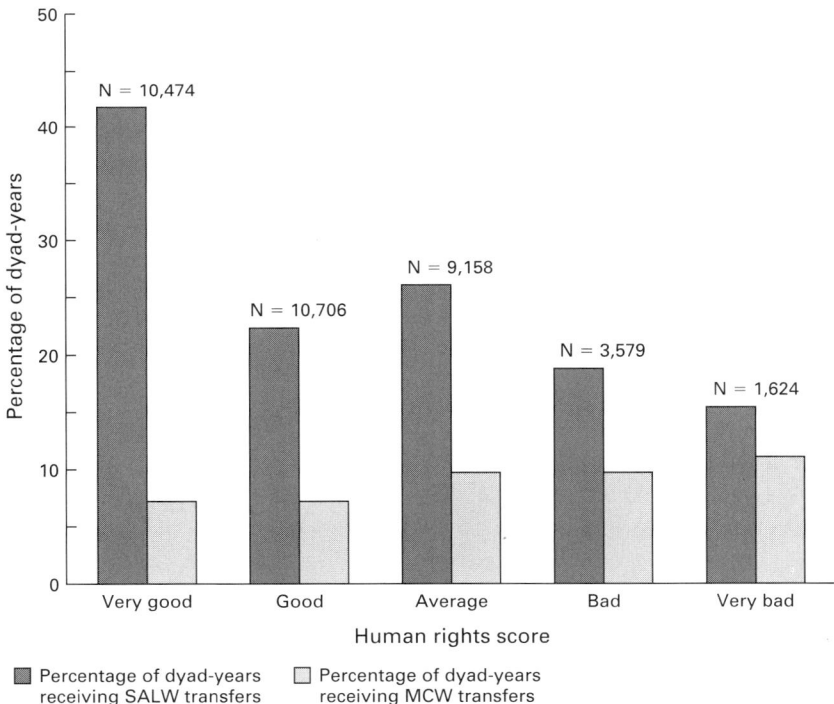

FIGURE 3.1. HUMAN RIGHTS AND ARMS TRANSFERS, 1981–1991.
Note: Each bar shows the percentage of dyad-years within that category of human rights score for which there is a record of a SALW or MCW transfer (as opposed to the percentage of dyad-years within that score for which there is no record of a SALW or MCW transfer). I use PTS-DOS data for cross-tabulations because of their broader geographic coverage.

human rights and MCW transfers (see tables C.1 and C.2 in appendix C).[26] In other words, as might be expected, countries with poor human rights were more likely on average to receive MCW than countries with the best human rights during the 1980s.

Small arms transfer data are scarce in this period, complicating the ability to draw confident conclusions about export trends. Just less than 16 percent of dyad-years whose importers had "very bad" human rights records received small arms transfers during the 1980s (figure 3.1). Although likely an underestimate, this percentage is somewhat higher than the figure for MCW but far lower than the percentage receiving SALW for any of the other human rights scores. In contrast, almost 42 percent of dyad-years whose importers had "very good" human rights records received small arms. Similarly, results from the regression analyses (tables C.3 and C.4 in appendix C) show a significantly negative relationship between poor human rights and SALW transfers—that is, poor human rights performers were less likely to get SALW—during the last decade of the Cold War.

Rather than any concerted effort by governments to wield small arms transfers as a tool to punish human rights violations, however, these regression results seem likely to be an artifact of poor SALW reporting. Countries may have received small arms even though there is no record of the transfer because attention to, tracking, and reporting of small arms were almost nonexistent during the Cold War. Alternative explanations for this finding are less compelling. Arms export controls were not on the table, human rights had been set aside after a brief flurry of interest limited to the United States in the 1970s, and small arms had yet to be recognized at all on the international agenda. Instead, Cold War politics and security drove arms trade policy, new producers were entering the market, and European producers worked at export promotion (at least with allies and friends). This focus on export promotion and the economic—rather than strategic—imperatives behind the arms trade would expand with the end of the Cold War and the contraction of the arms market that was to come.

THE END OF THE COLD WAR AND ECONOMIC IMPERATIVES

The end of the Cold War meant significant changes for the international arms trade, including changes for supplier–recipient relationships, justifications for arms transfers, and efforts to control those exports. Even so, the end of the Cold War did not mark a clear turning point in favor of arms export control, despite some initial optimistic expectations.[27] On the one hand, the end of the bipolar global system reduced states' need to use arms to buy allies and influence the balance of power, in theory opening up space for multilateral agreement. On the other hand, the disappearance of shared threats to the international system meant drastically reduced defense budgets and demand for arms. Producers struggled to remain afloat and sought to export to whatever markets were available, making multilateral controls seem impractical and even damaging for economic and military security if production lines could not be sustained.

Even during the Cold War, secondary suppliers—chiefly in Europe, although production capacity spread in the 1980s—were left "to sell arms primarily for commercial purposes" (Harkavy 1994:20; see also Catrina 1988 and Durch 2000).[28] Although claims of the economic benefits of arms transfers have been debated,[29] smaller domestic markets for defense goods led at least to the perception—if not also the reality—that exports were necessary to maintain a viable domestic defense industry (Brzoska and Ohlson 1987; Catrina 1988; Durch 2000). For the top-tier producers as well as for small and medium suppliers, the end of the Cold War intensified and broadened states' economic motivations to promote arms exports while simultaneously reducing the political utility of such exports.[30] Arms availability and production capacity were more widespread than ever before. Secondhand goods were in high supply, and companies overproduced new arms in their struggle to adjust to the new security environment. Demand shrank in both domestic and international defense markets. Sales declined globally, but exports were considered even more necessary for defense industry survival.[31] The global arms market presented an industry in decline, in terms of both production orders and the value of goods exported.[32]

It was in this economically strained arms market that the final failed attempt to create multilateral arms export controls took place, motivated by Gulf War revelations of destabilizing covert arms sales by Western suppliers to Iraq during the 1980s. In March 1991, Canada proposed a world summit with the goal of establishing shared controls by 1995 to deal with the potential risks of unrestrained arms transfers (Phythian 2000b). In May, a more skeptical United States announced an initiative to control arms sales only to the Middle East, calling on major suppliers to "develop guidelines for restraints on destabilizing transfers to that region" (Pierre 1997:376). France responded with a proposal to phase down quantities of arms in each region to the lowest levels possible. The United Kingdom expressed interest in a discussion about controls as well as an arms sales register, and the Soviet Union suggested a UN Security Council Permanent-5 (P5, China, France, the Soviet Union, the United Kingdom, and the United States) meeting on the issue. At the first meeting in July 1991, the P5 agreed to talks with the goal of setting guidelines for conventional arms transfers.[33] Additional rounds of talks took place in September 1991 and May 1992, with the P5 drafting guidelines to consider recipients' "legitimate" defense needs as well as whether a transfer would increase regional tensions or exacerbate existing conflicts (Davis 2002; Pierre 1997).

The window of opportunity for reaching an agreement closed soon thereafter, however. The draft guidelines from the September 1991 meeting "simply restated principles on which there was already broad conceptual agreement," and by May 1992 disagreements began to surface (Pierre 1997:378). In echoes of discussions past, questions about what should constitute "destabilizing" weapons sales, whether and how to provide advance notice of sales, and whether the talks were meant to address only the Middle East or to extend globally proved to be fundamental differences. The formal collapse of the talks came when China decided to boycott in response to U.S. and French arms sales to Taiwan in September 1992 (Pierre 1997:379). Indeed, although all of the P5 in theory supported export restrictions on some scale, export promotion—and, in some cases still, broader domestic and foreign-policy interests—dominated the post–Cold War era. Even a group as small as the P5 was unable to reach agreement, with competing material interests among the major powers trumping temporary political incentives to cooperate.[34]

The only concrete outcome from this post–Cold War momentum was the UN Register of Conventional Arms, also a response to Gulf War arms sale revelations. Considered a confidence-building measure at its inception, the register was meant to provide arms trade transparency as a means to prevent "the excessive and destabilizing accumulation" of major conventional weapons.[35] In addition, COCOM's replacement—the 1996 Wassenaar Arrangement—was created solely as a transparency regime without the political support to undertake export controls. Later, when paired with new commitments to humanitarian export policies, these transparency agreements would have some domestic consequences for arms export decision making, as I argue in chapter 5. In the meantime, however, transparency provided information about exports without any expectations or obligations about how those exports should be conducted.

During this period, the percentage of dyad-years in which MCW exports to any importers took place was down compared to the percentage during the Cold War, regardless of human rights performance (figure 3.2). In each category of human rights score, the percentage receiving MCW was well less than 10 percent, with the highest for recipients with "bad" human rights, at just more than 8 percent receiving MCW (and 92 percent not receiving MCW). This is likely due to a downturn in the market for large expensive weapons after the Cold War. However, the percentage of exporters sending small arms to poor human rights performers is higher in this period, with almost 30 percent of dyad-years with "bad" recipient human rights and just more than 19 dyad-years with "very bad" recipient human rights receiving SALW. Even if the export of small arms is underreported, these figures suggest a trend toward supply not restraint.

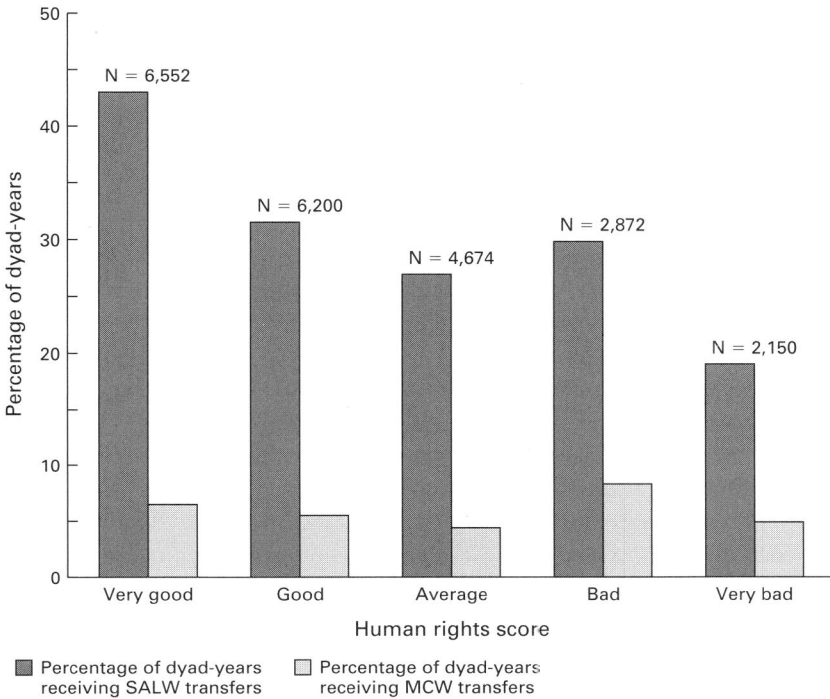

FIGURE 3.2. HUMAN RIGHTS AND ARMS TRANSFERS, 1992–1997.

The regression results tell a more complex story (tables C.1–C.4 in appendix C). To the extent that human rights were a significant factor for states' arms export practice at all during the early post–Cold War years, the trend was to provide *more* arms—not less—to poor human rights performers. For both MCW and SALW, "bad" human rights are significantly positive. In other words, recipients with "bad" human rights records were more likely to receive SALW and more MCW than the best human rights performers. "Very bad" human rights are insignificant for both types of weapons transfers. This means that supplier states did not seem to reward or punish the worst human rights performance; performance simply did not factor significantly into their export decision making. Thus, for both MCW and SALW transfers, it is important to note that state practice during these years did not foreshadow the policy changes that were to begin later in the decade. With declining demand and a tough buyer's market, many supplier states did not want further restrictions on their ability to export arms. Material interests ultimately continued to drive arms export policy and practice, with the major suppliers dominating discussions and fending off interference from external rules and expectations. The conditions for normative change had not quite arrived.

NORMATIVE CHANGE: PUTTING "RESPONSIBLE" ARMS EXPORT CONTROLS ON THE AGENDA

Yet amid the market competition of the early 1990s, the conditions for change in the international normative environment for the conventional arms trade began to appear. By the late 1990s, denying conventional arms transfers to human rights violators and conflict zones reemerged as a matter of state responsibility. By the end of the decade, this new phase was clear: the EU agreed to its politically binding Code of Conduct on Arms Exports in 1998, and in 1999 the U.S. Congress passed legislation requiring the president to start work on an international arms sales code of conduct that would include criteria to limit sales to human rights violators. This phase has not been short-lived, either. Although the 2001 UNPOA was a politically binding national-level measure to curb illicit small arms sales, its negotiation process galvanized supportive states and NGOs to pursue legally binding "responsible" export controls.[36] This momentum culminated in the Arms Trade Treaty, completing what diplomats in previous eras were unable to do: the establishment of legally binding global humanitarian standards to regulate the international trade in small and major conventional arms.[37] The ATT was approved by a wide margin of 154–3 at the UN General Assembly in April 2013. Representatives from sixty-seven states lined up at UN headquarters to sign when it opened for signature on June 3, 2013.[38] It goes into effect on December 2014.

By the end of the 1990s, human rights, governance, development, and conflict were no longer either peripheral concerns or reasons to justify weapons transfers but rather fundamental grounds to exercise restraint. This shift was in part related to a broader post–Cold War trend that put human rights and humanitarian issues in the global spotlight. Whether it was an outcome of a genuinely new movement by states to infuse ethics into their foreign policies can be debated (Dunne and Wheeler 2001; K. Smith 2001; Wheeler and Dunne 1998).[39] However, the increased prominence of these issues is undeniable, as is the newfound attention to norms of international behavior to accompany them. In the pursuit of these political agendas, direct and indirect connections to the arms trade have been made, linking an issue once the sole domain of hard security to a broader economic, social, and human security problematic.

Instead of categorizing all arms exports as good, bad, or necessary, as past rhetoric and advocacy had, the international community adopted a more nuanced approach. States began to identify a practical and symbolic foreign-policy utility in the selective denial of arms based on a recipient's internal policies and practices. In contrast to the realpolitik of past arms trade rationale, the trend since the late 1990s has introduced "an other-directed or morally based philosophy of restraint [emphasizing] the character and behavior of recipient governments toward their own people and within their security complex" (Durch 2000:152). Supplier states found themselves faced with both continued economic pressures to sell arms and new political pressures to adopt more discerning policies as a reflection on themselves as "responsible" members of the international community. Instead of seeking to reduce arms exports across the board, new policies laid out criteria obliging states to regulate their arms exports to certain types of arms importers, including states with severe human rights violations.

The normative shift that brought about these policy initiatives was not the result of a single shock to the system or critical juncture. Four key developments in the 1990s pushed the need for arms trade restraints into the spotlight and generated a new normative environment for the conventional arms trade. The emergence of "responsible" arms transfers benefited from states' acceptance of other international norms related to human rights and humanitarianism, but it was the confluence of these developments that drew international attention to these issues in the context of export controls for conventional arms and, for the first time, small arms specifically.[40] The accompanying shift in policy expectations motivated many exporting states to make dramatic changes regarding their own arms export policies. As I show in chapter 4, major suppliers' concern for reputation in the context of this changed international normative environment pushed their widespread support for "responsible" conventional arms export policies.

The first development that heightened the awareness of the need for arms trade restraints was that the 1991 Gulf War put many Coalition soldiers face to face with weapons sold to Iraq by their own countries during the 1980s. This blowback experience taught major suppliers a cautionary lesson for future arms exports in the interest of their own military security. The primary result was the creation of the UN Register of Conventional Arms and the development of arms trade transparency norms in the hope of providing an early-warning mechanism of excessive arms buildups (Goldring 1994–1995; Laurance, Wagenmakers, and Wulf 2005). The Gulf War experience also triggered numerous domestic scandals for secretive sales of arms and defense technology to Iraq, which had revealed states' poor control over their arms trade and the destabilizing consequences of exporting arms to a volatile authoritarian regime. The Arms to Iraq scandal in the United Kingdom in particular spurred early policy change and critical norm leadership by a major arms producer (Erickson 2013a). Thus, although the P5 talks failed after the war, most supplier states did improve transparency in its political aftermath and were impressed by the risks and costs of an unregulated global arms market.

Second, civil and ethnic conflicts following the Cold War—especially high-profile conflicts in Rwanda and the former Yugoslavia—highlighted problems associated with small arms proliferation and the need for multilateral export controls to prevent arms buildup in conflict zones and unstable regions.[41] Policy makers relied increasingly on arms embargoes to address this need, sparking a vigorous debate on the utility and effectiveness of arms embargoes.[42] Where arms supplies helped to fuel genocide, some states also faced backlash at home for their export decisions (see chapter 5 on domestic backlash). These conflicts as well as the peacekeeping and reconstruction efforts to follow pushed small arms to the forefront of the international agenda (Karp 1994; Klare 1994–1995; Sislin and Pearson 2001). Rather than major conventional weapons, the main tools of these internal conflicts were SALW, sold or given away without regulation as political currency during the Cold War. Research and reports from NGOs and academics spread, pointing not only to small arms' contribution to exacerbating conflict and insecurity, but also to their role in undermining development, human rights, and governance.[43]

States adversely affected by small arms proliferation also began to push the issue within the UN and regional organizations. Colombia introduced UN resolutions in 1988 and 1991, prompting a string of research missions, reports, recommendations, and guidelines.[44] The UN established the Group of Governmental Experts on Small Arms in late 1995. The group's 1997 report "worked as a cornerstone in profiling the array of problems associated with small-arms availability" and prompted the initial decision to convene an international conference on small arms trafficking (D. Garcia 2006:46). A growing coalition of like-minded states was forming, extending beyond affected states to include Canada, Norway, and Japan. Once ignored, small arms were poised to become the focal point of the international arms control agenda.

Third, the International Campaign to Ban Landmines (ICBL) and the 1997 Ottawa Mine Ban Treaty broadened the scope of the international security dialogue to include human security and introduced the possibility of humanitarian arms control (Eavis 1999; D. Garcia 2006; Lumpe 1999a). The widespread acceptance of the Ottawa Treaty legitimized the pursuit of arms control based on its relationship to societal security, individual well-being, and humanitarian obligations. Although a ban on anti-personnel landmines (APL) is not wrapped up in the same degree of political complexity as controlling broad categories of conventional weapons,[45] its momentum helped galvanize more comprehensive conventional arms control efforts, including extensive support for small arms control and the ATT process at the UN (Human Rights Watch [HRW] 1999; Lumpe 1999a; McRae 2001; Renner 1997).

The marriage between traditional security and human security begun by the landmine campaign has given new, multifaceted dimensions to arms control and has created a growing consensus on "good" conventional arms policy linked to humanitarian values. This normative shift was especially critical in convincing nonaffected states to endorse humanitarian or "responsible" export policies. Based on their experience with the Ottawa Treaty, as I show in chapter 4, states realized the reputational benefits of being seen on the "right side" of multilateral arms control, a perspective that has carried over into various regional and international initiatives on small arms and conventional arms more broadly.

Fourth and finally, related to the ICBL's success, the growing role of NGO advocacy in international affairs contributed to the emergence of arms transfer controls on the political agenda. NGO research provided a knowledge base to back up political claims behind the need to control the arms trade (D. Garcia 2006). NGOs have also pushed and partnered with states to advance export controls in national and international politics. By campaigning for and supporting governments' domestic and foreign-policy efforts to pursue new arms trade regulations, they have played a key (although not necessarily lead) role in developing and promoting the arms export control agenda (D. Garcia 2006). In addition, they have increasingly been able to use improved arms trade transparency to better hold states accountable to their policy commitments, as I discuss in chapter 5. These commitments—to the values of human rights, peace, and stability as well as more narrowly to the conduct of the arms trade—have become clearer as national legislation and multilateral agreements have emerged since 1998. In turn, the arms trade has become a reflection of states' values, their associations with other states, and how well they respect and promote the norms of the international community (Misol 2004).

The link between arms transfers and a "moral" or "responsible" foreign policy is not a new one, of course. The 1976 U.S. presidential campaign made the most explicit connection, with Carter charging that unrestricted arms transfers were contrary to U.S. principles and morally bankrupt (Pierre 1982:45). Yet Carter failed to substantively affect the practices of even his own administration, and his effort remained a unilateral initiative, criticized as inconsistent and divorced from reality (Hoffmann 1977–1978; Kearns 1980). In contrast, the current trend has not been a short-lived political debate in one country, but rather an ongoing worldwide discussion with both domestic and international dimensions and concrete policy results. Within a single decade, the normative environment for the global arms trade has changed noticeably, from noninterference on behalf of national material interests to "responsibility" and humanitarianism. States have broken with the past to sign on to multilateral standards and incorporated new norms into national policy. They have done so despite the considerable costs of adopting new policies that seem to promise no material gains, limits to their foreign-policy flexibility, and market restrictions amid domestic budget crises and financial downturn. But is this break with the past a norm success story? The answer is not yet clear.

MAPPING COMMITMENT AND COMPLIANCE: GLOBAL TRENDS IN ARMS EXPORT PRACTICE

The forces behind this macrolevel normative shift are clear, but why have major arms supplier states gone along with it and agreed to bear its costs? Scholars often expect states to sign on to multilateral initiatives in anticipation of material benefits, out of a sense of normative obligation, or simply because of the low cost of codifying existing practice.[46] As a result, all three of these explanations expect states' practice to mirror their commitments. If multilateral commitments are a means to achieve material gains or reflect states' acceptance of new norms, then ATT supporters should engage in weak implementation at least. If multilateral agreements codify existing practice, then ATT supporters' export practice should foreshadow changes in policy. A failure to find a correlation between ATT supporters' policy and their practice would deal a significant blow to each of these three arguments. In contrast, the social reputation argument, in which states make international commitments for their social benefits, does not require policy and practice to go hand in hand. States may adapt their public policies to the social expectations of a new normative environment without internalizing those norms or implementing them in practice. Social reputational motivations may be especially clear-cut in cases like this one: where the implementation of costly commitments is often unmonitored and unlikely to be punished if broken, allowing states to garner social gain without paying material costs.

As a first cut at untangling these potential explanations, it is therefore useful to examine arms export practice alongside these new policy initiatives to know whether and when ATT supporters began to decrease or eliminate arms transfers to human rights violators, if at all. Yet although research institutes have for decades tracked the annual value and quantity of major conventional arms transfers[47] and more recently of small arms transfers,[48] little is known about states' patterns of arms export practice in light of new "responsible" arms export policies.[49] Major arms exporters first articulated humanitarian arms trade norms only after 1997. As I discussed earlier, major suppliers faced a downturn in the 1990s arms market, leading to competition for buyers and an aversion to multilateral regulations. Arms export practice in the 1990s at best seemed disinterested in recipients' human rights (tables C.1–C.4 in appendix C). These findings cast initial doubt on the viability of expectations that practice will precede changes in policy to ensure low-cost commitment by participating states. Determining whether states anticipate material gains to offset the costs of adopting "responsible" export controls, however, will require an examination of more recent quantitative data as well as qualitative evidence provided in the case studies.

Normative theories are not surprised by states' policy commitment but also expect that states' practice will reflect their commitment out of a normative obligation to it. The existing literature, however, is mixed when it comes to finding a role for human rights in the contemporary arms trade. Whereas Shannon Lindsey Blanton (2000, 2005) argues that U.S. foreign military sales (the commercial subset of U.S. arms transfers) came to reflect human rights concerns during the 1990s,[50] others (e.g., Erickson forthcoming) find no such significant connection between human rights and U.S. arms transfers over time. More broadly, Lerna Yanik (2006) observes that between 1999 and 2003 top exporters continued to transfer MCW to poor human rights performers despite the exporters' emerging commitments to "responsible" export policy initiatives. One study (Erickson 2013b) finds that recipients with bad human rights tended to receive more MCW from top EU arms supplier states in the lead-up to the EU's adoption of humanitarian criteria in its Code of Conduct in 1998 and no significant relationship after 1998. However, this analysis is limited in that it does not include small arms and ends in 2004, making it unhelpful in considering the effects of global commitments to the ATT in the years to come.

Figure 3.3 shows cross-tabulation results covering 1998 to 2010 for all twenty-two exporters in the Arms Trade Data Set. Clearly, poor human rights did not seem to slow the frequency of arms sales in this period any more than they had in the past. For MCW transfers, just more than 9 percent of dyad-years in which importers had "bad" human rights received MCW (about 91 percent of dyad-years with "bad" human rights did not receive MCW), and approximately 5 percent of dyads in which importers had "very bad" human rights received MCW (about 95 percent did not). On their own, these percentages may seem low, but they are not markedly different from the 1990s (figure 3.2), when approximately 8 percent and 5 percent of dyad-years received MCW in each human rights category respectively. In the case of SALW, poor human rights performers appear to receive arms with slightly greater frequency after 1997. Approximately 42 percent of dyad-years in which the importers had "bad" human rights received SALW, compared to 30 percent in the 1990s. Of dyad-years with "very bad" human rights, about 23 percent received SALW, just up from 19 percent in the 1990s.

Yet regression analyses covering 1998–2010 show poor human rights to be either positively associated with receiving more MCW or simply insignificant (tables C.1, C.2). Importantly, there is no evidence to suggest that ATT supporters have come to collectively limit their supply of MCW to poor human rights per-

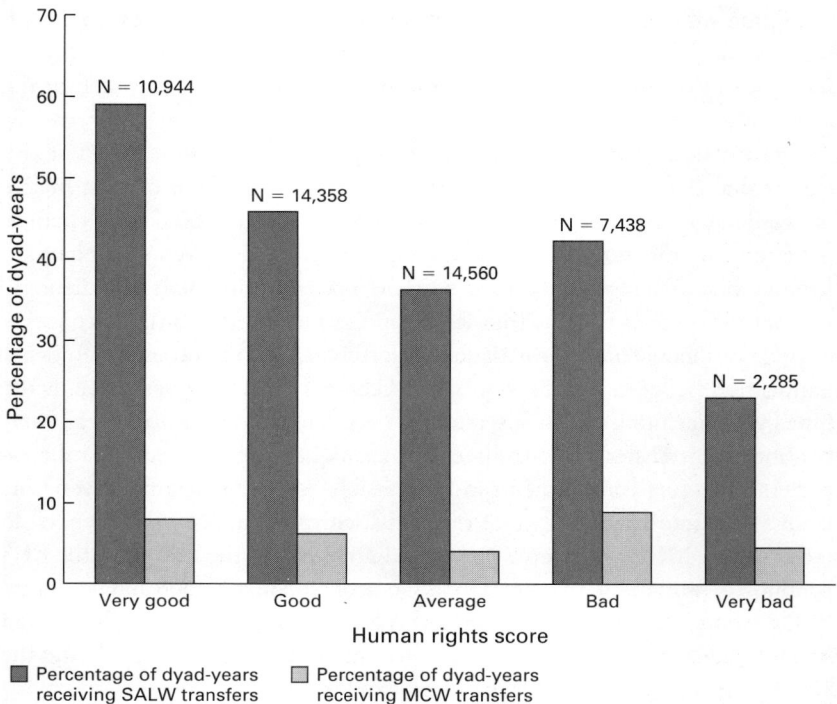

FIGURE 3.3. HUMAN RIGHTS AND ARMS TRANSFERS, 1998–2010.

formers in this period or before it (table C.2). The results for SALW transfers, however, do show critical changes in export practice (tables C.3, C.4). For the full set of supplier states as well as for the subset of ATT supporters, both "bad" and "very bad" human rights produce significantly negative coefficients. This suggests that the worst human rights performers were in fact less likely to receive SALW in the "responsible" arms trade era. Where there is preliminary evidence for change in the direction of new norms and policies, it has been with small arms, regarding which international discussions since the late 1990s have been the most intense. Of course, these findings cannot indicate causation, which I explore in the case studies in chapters 4 and 5. However, this initial look at the data across SALW and MCW transfers presents mixed results about states' arms export practice that calls for a more nuanced analysis.

By aggregating the years for important periods in arms trade policy, these regression results offer new insights into states' arms trade practice. Even so, this approach is less adept at estimating more carefully whether new policy initiatives might flow from changes in practice or vice versa. Timing also matters for assessing alternative explanations, which anticipate policy change either to precede or to follow changes in practice. For a more fine-grained approach, I therefore apply moving-windows (or moving-regression) analyses to the same regression models to explore ATT supporter states' arms export practice over time (for this type of analysis, see Beck 1983 and Swanson 1998).[51] This technique maps temporal trends in arms transfer practice in relation to recipients' human rights records during the three periods of arms export policy outlined in this chapter: Cold War security politics, the post–Cold War economic imperative, and new "responsible" or humanitarian arms trade initiatives. As a result, this approach can better recognize and pinpoint any changes in behavior, which in reality would probably not make abrupt alterations from year to year. Rather, as moving-windows analyses are equipped to show, practice would likely evolve gradually (Swanson 1998), either in anticipation of new policy commitments or as standards become more widespread and commonly accepted by states and actors within them. Certainly, the ATT may need to be around a long time for norms to take hold and change state practice, but if this turns out to be the case, then contemporary state commitment to the ATT cannot be satisfactorily explained by normative perspectives.

Figure 3.4 shows the moving-window coefficients and their 95 percent confidence intervals (CI) for the relationship between recipients' "bad" and "very bad" human rights and ATT supporters' MCW exports. The general rule is that the moving-windows coefficients are significant for the years at which their upper and lower 95 percent CI fall fully above (positive) or below (negative) the zero line. This means that in the case of MCW transfers "bad" human rights are significantly positive for all years except 1984. Countries with bad human rights are consistently more likely to receive MCW transfers from ATT supporter states than countries with the best human rights records. Outside of the Cold War years, however, "very bad" human rights are consistently insignificant from the battle for arms markets in the 1990s to more recent "responsible" export controls. This suggests that ATT supporters have been at best indifferent about their MCW import partners' human rights records, with no discernable changes in practice before or after the emergence of "responsible" export norms and the ATT. In fact, discussions about "responsible" export criteria with regard to MCW have been much slower to take hold in international fora. Although the 1998 EU Code of Conduct focused on major conventional weapons, UN initiatives only formally expanded from small arms to include MCW in 2006. As a result, MCW exports may be more resistant to the influence of new standards, with security and economic concerns—rather than new norms—continuing to drive who gets MCW.

Although the aggregate regression results for SALW suggest that major exporters were beginning to limit their supplies of small arms to the worst

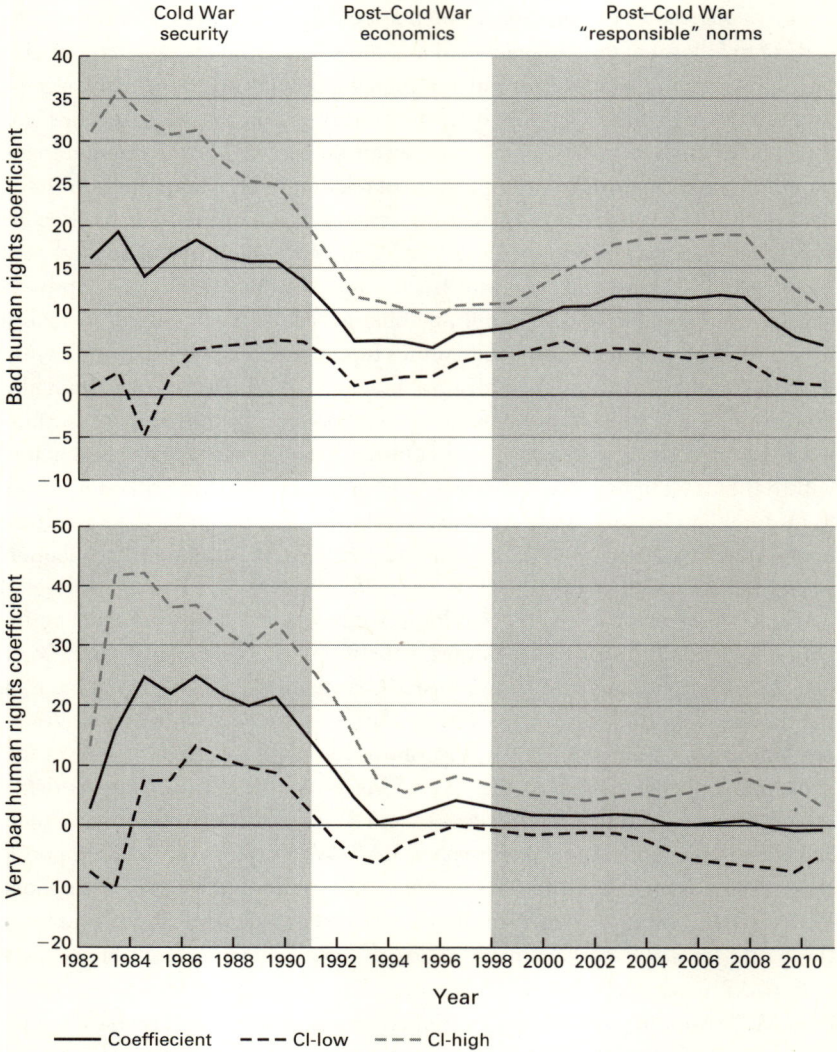

FIGURE 3.4. HUMAN RIGHTS AND MCW TRANSFERS BY ATT
SUPPORTERS.

human rights performers after 1997, these results do not carry over into the more
time-sensitive moving-windows results. Instead, the SALW results (figure 3.5)
for the most part show a picture similar to those for MCW. Leaving aside the
1980s, for which incomplete data make speculation about the results difficult at
best, we can conclude that ATT supporters have seemed either to reward or

Cold War
security

Post–Cold War
economics

Post–Cold War
"responsible" norms

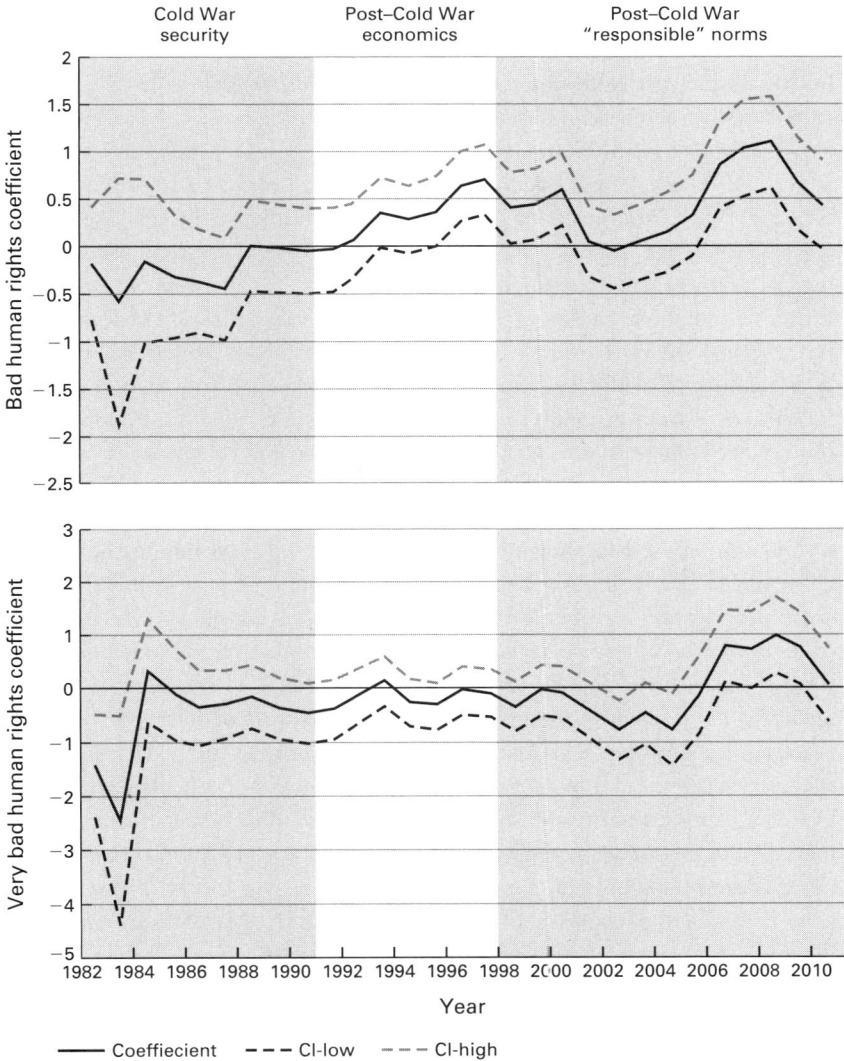

FIGURE 3.5. HUMAN RIGHTS AND SALW TRANSFERS BY ATT
SUPPORTERS.

simply to ignore recipients' poor human rights. In the case of "bad" human
rights, the results are significantly positive from 1996 to 2000. Recipients with
"bad" human rights were *more* likely to receive SALW, even as the UN Group
of Governmental Experts on Small Arms was being held and plans were being
made for the UN small arms meeting in 2001. These recipients were also more

likely to receive SALW from 2006 to 2009, the years in which the UN began its formal process to create the ATT. Rather than practice preceding—or even following—policy, these results show a clear disconnect between the two in the case of SALW and bad human rights.

The results for SALW transfers and "very bad" human rights show a similar pattern. Although there is evidence of a brief significantly negative relationship in 2002 and 2004, with recipients having "very bad" human rights *less* likely to receive SALW—perhaps in response to the global spotlight on small arms following the first UN small arms meeting in 2001—this behavior was not sustained. Indeed, to conclude that new norms were producing significant lasting effects on reducing SALW transfers to recipients with "very bad" human rights would be premature. As with "bad" human rights, between 2006 and 2009, the results for the "very bad" recipients are significantly positive, meaning that the worst human rights performers were more likely to become recipients of SALW.[52] Rather than closing as states have pledged their commitment to an ATT and its principles, the policy–practice gap appears to have widened in recent years.[53]

Yet although results showing *consistent* reward for poor human rights over all or most years would not be surprising, behavioral *change* in this direction during this period is difficult to explain, especially when no similar change is evident for MCW transfers. Falling after September 11, 2001, and before the start of the global financial crisis in 2008 and the Arab Spring in 2011, this change coincides with no significant international event or collection of events that might encourage more liberal SALW export practice from ATT supporter states. Nevertheless, it is possible that this finding reveals a collective adaptation by major exporters to the continued war on terror and its new security environment, led by export heavyweight the United States. In particular, U.S. decisions to lift arms embargoes and export arms in order to win friends in the war on terror and to address balance-of-power concerns in the Middle East have been identified as a return to a Cold War–like arms trade.[54] In response, other exporters may have seen a need to keep up in a competitive arms market as well as an opportunity to liberalize their practices despite new policy initiatives.[55] Moreover, SALW transfers to Iraq, Afghanistan, and friendly states are more likely to be accepted as counterterrorism and security necessities by domestic publics that might otherwise be skeptical of transfers to poor human rights performers.

What is clear is that there is a disconnect between global policy discussions, rules, and norms and how states actually decide to conduct their arms trade in practice. The ATT, EU Code of Conduct, and other initiatives neither codify existing practice nor reflect a closely held commitment to new norms. Thus, although new policies represent a significant normative shift in the international system, that shift is incomplete and practice has remained for the most part consistent from the last decade of the Cold War to the present day. This consistency is not necessarily surprising. Norm internalization can take decades to complete and is never guaranteed. Even so, the discrepancy between policy and practice provides initial evidence against material or normative explanations for states' multilateral commitments in the case of the arms trade. It also raises important questions about how to ensure that states' practice follows their policy.

By outlining major historical trends in arms transfer policy and practice, this chapter seeks to make three major contributions. First, it highlights persistent political difficulties in creating conventional arms transfer controls. On the rare occasion that the arms trade has found a spot on the international agenda, sovereignty, security, and economic concerns have consistently undermined attempts impose regulations. Until the late 1990s, multilateral arms control discussions instead served as a means for major exporters to protect their foreign-policy interests and arms markets, leaving human rights out of the conversation. The historical hurdles to reach an arms trade treaty were high, and the ATT's overwhelming success in the UN General Assembly in 2013 could not have been predicted fifteen years earlier.

Second, the chapter outlines four key factors in the 1990s that explain the dramatic change in the international normative environment for the arms trade: Arms to Iraq scandals following the 1991 Gulf War; high-profile civil and ethnic conflicts following the Cold War; the ICBL and the 1997 Ottawa Mine Ban Treaty; and the growing role of NGO advocacy in international affairs. Together, these factors demonstrated contemporary problems in conventional arms proliferation and generated the normative shift toward "responsible" arms transfers. The success of the landmine treaty in particular, I argue in chapter 4, changed the social cost–benefit calculus performed by major exporters, who have found themselves facing changed expectations about conventional arms trade policies.

Finally, the chapter examines states' arms export practice in light of these policy trends. It demonstrates that human rights have rarely been a significant consideration in small and major conventional arms export decision making. Practice rarely reflects policy. Human rights are largely insignificant for MCW transfers, which have long been wrapped up in exporters' security, economics, and foreign-policy considerations. Yet even where policy discussions have been the most concentrated—small arms—the disconnect with practice is evident. Although, small arms exports showed a glimmer of emerging compliance from 1998 to 2010, the effect disappears when the analysis is broken down over time. In fact, in recent years the worst human rights violators have been *more* likely to receive small arms. Arms exports have long been free of international regulations and obligations, and these trends indicate that changes in line with new criteria are no guarantee. Perhaps concerns for human rights will become more important over time as policy expectations become more firmly entrenched in domestic and international politics. Or perhaps practice will remain unchanged if monitoring and enforcement mechanisms to raise the social and material costs of noncompliance continue to be elusive.[56]

The statistical analyses also provide essential insights into whether materialist and normative theories have it right or other explanations are in order. Not only has state practice not preceded changes in state policy, it has not followed policy, either. Clearly, commitment and compliance need not go hand in hand, as normative or materialist explanations would expect. In the end, the statistical analysis helps to rule out possible explanations for major democratic exporters' support for humanitarian arms export restrictions. It is clear that states are not committing to new policies because these policies reflect existing practices and that they are not changing practice out of a deep normative commitment to new policies. The policy–practice gap remains wide. As a result, states' commitment to legally binding standards becomes more puzzling. Why bother to sign on to such policies if they are not going to be implemented?

Given the statistical findings, the social reputation approach's skepticism of the power of new norms to alter state behavior substantively in the absence of the means to impose reputational costs on noncompliance is well placed. In the case of the arms trade, international transparency measures are unconnected to "responsible" export commitments, allowing suppliers to continue with business as usual, knowing their decisions will rarely be subject to scrutiny. However, as I argue in chapter 5, where oversight in domestic politics can substitute for international monitoring, transfers may be relatively more restricted in cases of clear and severe cases of norm violations. Such cases are better able to capture media attention, rouse public ire, and threaten reputational damage at home. This means, however, that changes in practice may be concentrated at the margins among democratic exporters but minimal otherwise.

In the remaining chapters, I explore in-depth case study evidence in order to understand why major arms supplier states have signed on to initiatives such as the ATT and EU Code of Conduct. By examining historical and statistical trends, this chapter makes clear that states' perceptions of material gains and normative commitments are likely weak in this case. Alongside the core social reputational approach, I also assess domestic liberal expectations that policy commitments are intended to serve the material interests of influential domestic groups as well as arguments that the ATT has followed the path of the landmine treaty, responding to public and NGO pressure. Yet in the absence of these incentives, domestic political explanations also fail to convince. Instead, I argue that states' concern for reputation at home and abroad in order to achieve social gains and avoid social losses is key to understanding their commitment to costly new "responsible" arms export standards and the compliance gap.

4. *Explaining Commitment*

INTERNATIONAL REPUTATION AND

"RESPONSIBLE" ARMS TRANSFER POLICY

When states gathered at the July 2001 United Nations small arms conference, they anticipated neither an easy solution to the problem of regulating the global small arms market nor the widespread backing the initiative would receive. As chapter 3 shows, political and economic obstacles had always defeated multilateral conventional arms controls in the past, and practice is slow to change. Even so, organizers hoped to build on antilandmine momentum and other developments in the 1990s to negotiate a treaty covering legal and illicit small arms sales. Among the major democratic exporters, support at the 2001 conference was expected. The EU had already in 1998 adopted common arms export standards, and the United States had had a hand in promoting the conference. Proponents were therefore caught off-guard both by the largely positive reception to the conference overall and by the prominent U.S. rejection of its goals at its opening.[1] Because the conference was constrained by consensus rules, the result was merely the nonbinding UNPOA, focused solely on national standards to control the illicit small arms market. Follow-on conferences were unable to do more. Despite being considered a failure by many,[2] however, the UN small arms process catalyzed state support to create international arms export regulations and ultimately led to the ATT. The ATT does what the UNPOA could not and more: it specifies binding humanitarian criteria to regulate the legal arms trade and applies those criteria to major conventional weapons transfers as well as to small arms and light weapons transfers.

This chapter explains why five of the world's top arms-exporting democracies— Belgium, France, Germany, the United Kingdom, and the United States[3]—have supported new "responsible" arms export initiatives. Unlike states adversely affected by conventional arms proliferation or those with little stake in the global arms market, these states have significant economic incentives *not* to support new standards. Indeed, conventional wisdom suggests that major arms producers would strongly oppose any measures imposing constraints on their trade to protect economic and industrial interests. For most states, the freedom to trade arms as they choose is perceived as a matter of not only foreign-policy autonomy but also economic necessity and national security. Previous attempts in the 1920s and 1930s, 1970s, and early 1990s all failed as a result of these deep-seated concerns. During and after the Cold War, European suppliers' focus on export promotion to support industrial interests would seem to make them the prime candidates to oppose new standards. Only the United States, with its larger domestic defense market, would be freer to adopt multilateral controls without suffering sky-rocketing costs or a decline in quality.

Yet to assume that a similar logic applies to current policy developments would be mistaken and misleading. Once-reluctant European states have been among the most eager to demonstrate support for shared "responsible" arms transfer criteria, which the United States vocally resisted until it too changed course in 2009. As I showed in chapter 3, this shift was not preceded by and has not been followed by collective changes in arms export practice, calling into question explanations that rely on the low cost of commitment, material gain, or normative obligation. What changed, I argue here, was not industry interest or influence but rather the social pressures and expectations associated with "responsible" arms export standards in the context of the international institutions negotiating them. Democratic suppliers especially have faced growing pressures to back "responsible" arms transfer policies as arms trade norms have evolved since the end of the Cold War, highlighting new roles for human rights, human security, and humanitarian law. States have responded by supporting these policies as a means to signal their "good international citizenship," committed to human, social, and economic rights and other collective goods. Such a reputation, leaders believe, will bring social benefits in the form of legitimacy, esteem, and standing in the international community. At least early on in the norm life cycle, states' policy choices may favor image promotion that acknowledges new norms even as their underlying preferences remain unchanged. Interviews, government documents, and NGO strategies point to the importance of reputation as a social incentive influencing states' commitment to new arms export policies at the international level, despite material incentives pulling them in the opposite direction.

THE CONVENTIONAL WISDOM:
DEFENSE INDUSTRY PREFERENCES

Scholars commonly trace states' weapons procurement and export policies back to powerful defense industry preferences for unregulated trade, linked to the military-industrial complex.[4] From this perspective, governments are in essence held captive by economic, electoral, and security needs to cater to defense industry wishes—even more so when defense companies are state owned. Companies use their close relationship with the state and position of economic power to turn government policy in their favor, seeking to maximize profits and expand export-market shares.[5] Clearly, concern for defense industry well-being has been a major roadblock to cooperative export restraint in the past. However, in this case, deference to defense industry preferences is not a compelling explanation for state policy: governments have adopted new policies and supported the ATT *without* industry consent, leaving industry with the choice to get on board or lose its voice on the issue entirely.

This recent turn of events is surprising. The defense industry's close and supportive relationship with the state as its primary investor, customer, salesman, and licensing authority is to be expected (Stanley and Pearton 1972:85). Governments are intimately involved in the arms trade from the initial financing, research, and design of weapons to the purchasing and export promotion of those weapons. In the process, a complex web of institutions takes root in which government, military, and industry actors reinforce one another's interests. This relationship is ostensibly sustained by states' security need to maintain a viable defense industrial base and is a relatively constant feature across social systems, regardless of domestic political structure, type of government, or degree of industry nationalization.[6] In democracies, it also receives external reinforcement by creating electoral bases in centers of defense production. Politicians support local production lines as an important source of employment and avoid policies that could potentially result in job loss—and therefore vote loss—in their home districts (Keller 1995; Markusen et al. 1991).

The ICBL campaign, although resulting in the landmark Ottawa Mine Ban Treaty and helping to put humanitarian arms control on the agenda, did not break with MIC expectations. Indeed, NGOs worked within the constraints posed by military and industrial interests. Their ability to demonstrate the lack of economic and military utility for APL contributed significantly to the campaign's success. Military officials acknowledged that they considered APL unreliable and of limited strategic value.[7] In addition, the global arms trade had been saturated by an overabundance of cheap APL, which were an insignificant portion of the defense industry's exports (International Committee of the Red

Cross 1996; O'Dwyer 2006). Instead, the business of *removing* landmines—for which the treaty pledges financial support from its signatories—is a far more technology-intensive, expensive, and profitable endeavor for companies (Beier and Crosby 1998; O'Dwyer 2006). It was therefore with the blessing of key military and industrial players that the treaty was able to garner such sweeping governmental support.

The same cannot be said for conventional arms more broadly. Conventional arms are the cornerstone of military strategy and an industrial base important to political, security, and economic interests. Andrew Moravcsik (1993), for example, points to the dominance of domestic industrial preferences in determining governments' defense procurement and production policies. Similarly, Asif Efrat (2010) cites these entrenched domestic economic and political interests in top arms-exporting states as the reason behind the weak results of the UN small arms process. These interests remain strong and face a potentially rough and uncertain road ahead as many states cope with defense cutbacks and budget-austerity measures. Yet "responsible" arms export policies have gotten support *in spite* of defense industry preferences, not because of them. Indeed, the cases I describe next point to reluctant industry support only in cases of prior government support.

FRANCE: STATE AND INDUSTRY, TIGHTLY BOUND

The MIC has long been an important force in the politics of French arms exports, where pressures to sell abroad have been driven by economic considerations and met with consensus on the right and the left.[8] France also traditionally has a strong statist system of market governance. In the defense industry, the state is often the client, the banker, the insurance provider, the shareholder, and even at times the owner (Boyer 1996). Edward Kolodziej describes the French MIC as "a government within a government," with the "formidable resources and influence to elicit the political and economic support for what it wants as the price for its cooperation" (1987:213; see also Freedman and Navias 1997; Labbé 1994). Industry recruitment from the ranks of former military personnel is common, and the educational system early on creates tight networks among bureaucrats, military, and industry officials. Moreover, the lines of communication between government and industry are regular, especially during export promotion and decision making ("French Move" 1998; interview 59108220; Kolodziej 1987).

Exports are an important tool of the French state to bolster an ailing defense industrial base (Freedman and Navias 1997; Graves 2000; Sarkozy 2008). Indeed, even as France has come to support new multilateral export restrictions, it has considered the arms trade essential for weapons procurement, economic power, foreign relations, and national sovereignty.[9] Between its support for former colonies, its desire to establish itself as a "third pole" during the Cold War, and the economic imperative, politicians and their constituents have fiercely supported the arms trade. Despite the state's best efforts, however, French defense exports fell by almost half between 1990 and 1995, strengthening the economic calculus to export promotion (Hébert 1998:140). By the end of the decade, the largest land armaments firm—the state-owned Groupement industriel des armaments terrestres (commonly known as GIAT)—still "relied on exports for over 50% of its total turnover" (Graves 2000:90). Even more significantly, by 2005 more than 80 percent of aviation production was being exported (interview 63308220). In a country with persistently high unemployment rates, moreover, France has been one of the slowest to cut its military spending and has resisted privatization trends, which lawmakers have feared will close factories and risk job losses in their constituencies (Graves 2000; Guay 1998; Lewis 2004; Sarkozy 2008).

As a result, France's support for the ATT is unexpected, especially given the fact that it was made without the consent of the defense industry. As one industry representative commented, although the ATT now seems like a good development to "level the playing field," that was not industry's initial reaction (interview 63308220). In the past, the industry was "very hostile to any control that results in a drop in exports" and fought to introduce less restrictive controls (Labbé 1994:213; see also interview 59108220). It believed that additional restraints would force it to follow economically harmful rules or risk the consequences of disobeying them (interview 63308220). Given the government's firm public commitment to UN processes, however, the defense industry has faced a new choice: support new regulations and have its voice heard in the codification process ("telling the diplomats the reality of the business") or get left out of the process entirely. It has opted for the former as the "only viable position" because it is better to have a say in rules it will have to follow regardless than to leave rule making to those without the expertise to understand their effect on the industry (interview 63308220).

THE UNITED KINGDOM: CROSS-PARTISAN GOVERNMENTAL SUPPORT

Although UK defense companies were privatized in the 1980s, their influence and importance have also been common features in British politics.[10] The British defense industry has been a source of employment, technological innovation, national security and defense, and foreign-policy clout.[11] Exports have long been seen as a matter of "commercial pragmatism," crucial to defense industry survival and actively promoted by Labour and Conservative governments alike (Stanley and Pearton 1972:91). The Defence Export Services Organization in the UK Ministry of Defence is in charge of export promotion, supported by the Export Credits Guarantee Department, an interdepartmental committee chaired by the Treasury.[12] Both parties believe that without exports the defense industrial base would be significantly weakened and jobs threatened, especially in the post–Cold War defense downturn.[13] On average, defense companies currently export about 40 percent of their product (Cook, Foss, and Scott 2004:21; interview 39307200), up from 20 percent in the 1980s (Kapstein 1997:83).

In short, industry "has influence where it matters in Whitehall," regardless of the party in power (interview 39307200). Prime Minister Margaret Thatcher presided over an "arms export revival," including the most profitable deals in British history, the Al Yamamah deals, in 1986 and 1988 (Phythian 2000b:20–21). At the time, the press and policy makers lauded the program to export aircraft and training to Saudi Arabia, which enabled the United Kingdom to continue an important production line and support thirty thousand jobs (Spear 1990; Phythian 2000b).[14] Labour was also strong on defense during its return to office. Although elected in 1997 with a commitment to ethical arms transfers and leading multilateral initiatives, it simultaneously promised to maintain the strength of the defense industry (Gummett 2000:269). As a result, some scholars and critics argue that the British government has remained distinctly pro-export and has framed its export reform agenda to allow a permissive interpretation of new criteria (Cooper 2000; Stavrianakis 2008).

Traditionally, industry could be counted on "to mount a vigorous defence of the status quo—or continue to stress the need for further deregulation" of arms transfer controls—and governments in turn did not push for more regulation (Davis 2002:119; Pearson 1983). Nevertheless, the United Kingdom announced its intention to promote a global ATT in September 2004 and expanded the initiative to include major conventional weapons in March 2005. Industry, however, did not become a supporter of the initiative until June 2006, long after the government took on its ATT leadership role (Fidler 2006; interview 33207200). Interviews reveal two reasons for its eventual support: first and foremost, a leveling of the global playing field[15] and, second, the anticipated benefit to the defense industry's national reputation.[16] Following Labour's strong commitment to an ATT in its election manifesto, the British defense industry—like the French—decided that it was better to have a say in the process and that multilateral controls are the "only way to do it" (interview 39307200). It began to actively promote the ATT abroad, along with the government and NGOs. However, this did not occur until the government's own commitment to legalizing responsible arms export standards worldwide was made public and had demonstrated its staying power.

GERMANY: ARMS INDUSTRY
AT ARM'S LENGTH (IN PUBLIC)

For historical reasons, the German state has maintained a public distance from the arms industry. During World War II, the military and the defense industry were drawn under Nazi control, leading to a distinct postwar distaste for any signs of preferences for policies associated with German militarism. Even as the German defense industry rebuilt in the 1950s and beyond,[17] its relationship with the state has maintained at least some public distance. Small arms producers today, for example, note the government's more passive approach to their problems, stemming, in their view, from their negative historic image (interview 46307255). The German government therefore may not face the same potential industrial barriers to support new arms restraints as many other top exporters.

Even so, by the 1970s, Germany had reestablished a highly concentrated MIC, albeit less visible to the public eye (Homze 1981; Brzoska 1986). Contact between bureaucrats and industry lobbyists is regular, especially through the defense committee of the Federation of German Industry (Bundesverband Deutscher Industrie) (interview 44307255). Industry often recruits retired military officers "to make use of their inside experience and contacts with former colleagues" (Cowen 1986:234). Governments have also supported exports and state offsets for exports, a role that has grown since the late 1990s, even as "responsible" arms export criteria hit the international agenda.[18] Although there is no official agency to promote German defense goods abroad, military and foreign attachés in German embassies are tasked with such activities and often trained by the Federation of German Industry to be informed about German products (interview 44307255). Exports have grown in importance as defense spending drops and the government wishes to "[keep] the German defence industry German" (Mulholland 2005:23; see also Mulholland 2003 and interview 44307255). As a corporatist state, Germany also maintains a close relationship with labor and seeks to prevent job losses. Ian Davis observes, for example, that "the employment argument" has "enabled the arms companies to elicit some support for a relaxation of the arms export rules among trade union representatives" (2002:161; see also Brzoska 1989; Graves 2000; Pearson 1986).

Because the German domestic arms market is comparatively small, arms exports are used to "extend production runs, spread research and development costs and decrease other per-unit fixed costs" (Graves 2000:78). The export market was initially established through overseas military aid in the 1960s and helped to rebuild the postwar defense industry (Haftendorn 1971). Moreover, it fits with the country's "deeply rooted" export orientation (Wulf 1996:31). Since the 1970s, Germany has consistently been a top MCW exporter and relied on exports for a majority of its defense products. Experts estimate that about 70 percent of German defense product was exported in 2007 (interview 44307255). As such, both right and left governments have tried to balance the "necessary evil" of arms exports with a culture of arms export restraint (Pearson 1986; see also Brzoska 1989; interview 46307255; Wulf 1996).

Despite Germany's domestic arms export restraints,[19] its defense industry has refrained from publicly backing similar restraints at the international level. Germany announced support for an ATT in July 2005, but industry has maintained a low profile on the matter. Although it gives its opinions to the government when asked, it consciously avoids looking too aggressive or taking its concerns public (interviews 44307255, 46307255). From some industry representatives' perspective, legal sales are not the real problem, and government attention is focused on the wrong issue (interview 46307255). Nevertheless, faced with higher domestic restrictions, the defense industry does want to level the export-market playing field (interviews 15107255, 44307255, 46307255). It also says that it cannot afford the long-term loss of reputation that might result from being seen as unsupportive of global export restrictions, even if restrictions might be costly to it in the short-term (interview 46307255). Thus, although the German defense industry has fought for a less restrictive interpretation of domestic laws and policies in the past, it has been neither a block nor a catalyst for German support of multilateral initiatives.

BELGIUM: A REGIONAL DIVIDE

Belgium relies heavily on exports to keeps its defense industry afloat, especially in light of limited domestic demand and the end of the Cold War (Weidacher 2005). Between 1983 and 1993, defense industrial employment fell by half, sales declined by 45 percent, and major companies were forced into bankruptcy or foreign ownership (Hassink 2000:83). Exports continue to form the industry's backbone. By the end of the 1990s, exports accounted for about 80 percent of total defense sales, more than half of which are small arms (Castryck, Depauw, and Duquet 2007:28). Even before the post–Cold War decline, however, Belgian small arms firm FN Herstal's "order sheets [read] like an atlas index" as a matter of survival (Stanley and Pearton 1972:70).

Arms sales and their relationship with the state are complicated by Belgium's delicate system of federalism. Since 2003, regional governments have been in charge of arms transfers licensing in line with rules that are at least as restrictive as those set by federal law and policy.[20] Nevertheless, exports have been less transparent and arguably more permissive in Wallonia, where the state–industry connection is much more explicit and potential recipients may be less controversial than in Flanders.[21] In Flanders, exports outside of Europe and North America, which typically account for more than 75 percent of licenses, are limited (Duquet, Castryck, and Depauw 2007).[22] As a result, Geert Castryck, Sara Depauw, and Nils Duquet state, "the decision whether to grant or deny an export or transit licence is generally not a difficult one for the Flemish Government," and license denials are rare (2007:91). Even so, Flemish licenses in 2006 at the time of the initial ATT vote had dropped considerably from figures for 1999–2004 (Castryck, Depauw, and Duquet 2007; Duquet 2008; Duquet, Castryck, and Depauw 2007; Flemish Peace Institute 2007a).

Wallonia's defense exporters are much larger, in terms of both value and amount, and feature more traditional military goods, including small arms. In 2006, Wallonia exported €760 million worth of military goods to sixty-four countries. Most of these goods go to North America, the Middle East, and western Europe (Parlement Wallon 2007). FN Herstal, the dominant firm, derives its sales almost completely from outside Belgium (Weidacher 2005). Without a buyer when FN Herstal was sold off by its French parent company in 1997, the Walloon government took on ownership to preserve the industry and employment (interview 31307211). Economic downturn and high unemployment have meant an even closer relationship between the industry and the Walloon state as well as stronger public support for that relationship. As a result, more restrictive export legislation entails higher, more direct costs for Wallonia (Vranckx 2005), which accounts for two-thirds of Belgian defense industry employment (Hassink 2000).

Despite this regional variation in state–industry relations, however, the regional governments are not responsible for Belgian export control law, which is set by the federal government. Moreover, policy decisions in multilateral fora are supposed to reflect federal and regional interests, but in practice the federal government's foreign-policy choices lead the way (interviews 24107211, 25107211). Although industry is now thought to be in favor of international export restraints for the level-playing-field benefits they might provide, it has not pushed for support in Belgium or elsewhere.[23] With the divorce of policy making and policy implementation, the federal government is freer to support shared export standards. Industry influence appears greater at the regional level—where both Flanders and Wallonia have supported the well-being of their defense companies (Hassink 2000)—and may instead translate into variation in strictness of policy implementation rather than in variation in policy itself, as I explore in chapter 5. Like Germany, then, the Belgian arms industry appears to have been neither a constraint nor a motivation for Belgium to support more restrictive export standards.

UNITED STATES: THE MODEL
MILITARY-INDUSTRIAL COMPLEX

The United States, of course, is the original model for the MIC. Its government depends on defense manufacturers to serve "as guardians of 'national security' " (G. Adams 1981:21). Manufacturers, in turn, expect that the Department of Defense will ensure that their costs are reimbursed and their profit margins maintained. The government also actively promotes U.S. defense products abroad through demonstrations and tax subsidies.[24] U.S. firms traditionally produced solely for the Pentagon, which often gave preference to American companies (Guay 1998). In the post–Cold War era, rapid restructuring, a larger domestic market, and a wider foreign customer base has meant that the U.S. industry has not suffered the same degree of downturn as its European counterparts.[25] As a result, only the U.S. defense industry has a market at home to support itself "without incurring prohibitive costs or a drastic decline of quality" or relying on exports to survive (Moravcsik 1992:40; see also Guay 1998).

Weapons programs receive support from the Department of Defense, all branches of the military, and Congress. Defense companies often hire retired public servants to supplement their political connections and influence. During the 1990s, the defense industry was also given an institutional presence to voice its opinions in the DOS's Defense Trade Advisory Group. In addition, contract money linked to weapons programs makes specific areas of the country dependent on those companies and contracts for jobs, which can win votes for incumbent politicians.[26] Thus, the mutual dependence of the three points of the MIC "iron triangle"—industry, bureaucracy, and congressional appropriations—was born, giving industry a strong voice in government decision making.

The United States was the only country to fully oppose all UN multilateral initiatives before 2009. Even so, this opposition was not the result of industry influence or economic need. The level-playing-field argument has so far not motivated U.S. companies to lobby for an ATT. Despite being faced with "one of the most complex and far-reaching policy apparatuses for reviewing and regulating arms sales" (Nolan 1997:131), U.S. defense companies export at higher rates than their European counterparts and are far less dependent on those exports for survival. U.S. industry has not come out in opposition to the treaty, however, and tends to stay distant from the issue, focusing instead on loosening bilateral controls with close allies.[27] As such, the U.S. defense industry cannot be credited with either past U.S. opposition or present U.S. support. Instead, U.S. opposition—driven by a vocal pro-gun lobby and a distaste for binding international agreements—has led industry to focus its attention elsewhere, while support has similarly come without its involvement.

INTERNATIONAL REPUTATION: SOCIAL INCENTIVES IN INTERNATIONAL INSTITUTIONS

Major democratic arms exporters now support "responsible" arms transfer control policies despite their past preferences and the costs to their defense industries and foreign-policy autonomy. They have gone ahead with new national and multilateral trade regulations *in spite* of weapons producers' wishes. Defense companies in most countries rely heavily on exports to maintain production lines and must seek out new markets in times of economic downturn. Even if defense industry preferences have become arguably less important to states as companies have downsized since the early 1990s, this declining importance provides merely an opening—and not an explanation—for governments' active support for new arms transfer standards. As I show in chapter 5, domestic public pressure also largely pushed policy adoption.

Rather than domestic motivations, I argue that major exporters have strategically chosen to support new arms export controls out of concern for their international reputations—that is, their desire to be seen by other states (and the diplomats representing them) as "good international citizens." As norms surrounding small and major conventional arms evolved over the course of the 1990s to encompass human rights and human security, so too have the expectations by which states make arms trade policy—even those states that have not internalized new norms.[28] These dynamics are strongest in the context of international institutions, which, as social environments, "[create] sensitivity to particular kinds of status markers" (Johnston 2008:151). For the conventional arms community in the post–Cold War era, intense discussions have regularly taken place at the UN and Wassenaar Arrangement as well as in numerous regional organizations such as the Organization for Security and Cooperation in Europe and the EU.[29] These institutions define common policy expectations, publicize states' policy choices to other states and NGOs, and provide fora for the diplomatic interaction necessary to motivate states' concern for reputation. The payoff, in turn, can be social and psychological, even if material gains are absent (Johnston 2008).

In this case, reputation serves as a social incentive, with consequences for states' legitimacy, esteem, and standing in the international community.[30] For those states whose identities are strongly tied to their cooperative membership in international institutions, support for "responsible" arms transfer policies stems in large part from a perceived need to maintain (or better) their reputations as "good international citizens." Democracies especially want to be seen as dedicated to human, social, and economic rights as well as to other collective goods. The analysis here therefore focuses primarily on states' perceived *concern* for reputation rather than on their actual reputations as perceived by other international actors. It looks first at the institutional setting in which norms for "responsible" arms transfer policy have evolved since the late 1990s and the agreements that these institutions have produced. Second, it uses in-depth interviews, government documents, and other evidence to assess states' motives for supporting "responsible" arms export controls in each of the five case studies—France, the United Kingdom, Germany, Belgium, and the United States. In doing so, it highlights major exporters' social reputational concerns in international politics as the source of their policy commitments.

CREATING POLICY EXPECTATIONS: THE INSTITUTIONAL SETTING

International institutions provide a setting in which diplomats interact and develop states' reputations over time. Johnston maintains that social incentives vary with an institution's size and decision-making rules. Where groups are large and decisions are made by majoritarian rules that place members' policies on record, he argues, these incentives will be stronger (2008:31–32). In the case of "responsible" arms transfers, decision-making rules have clearly played an important role: early on, consensus requirements at the EU and UN led to politically rather than legally binding agreements.[31] Yet Johnston's argument also suggests that states can hide behind consensus to avoid paying the social costs of dissent. In reality, however, states cannot assume that their opposition will go unnoticed. Especially where NGOs are allowed a place at the table, dissenting states are often publicly "named and shamed."[32] Even in closed-door meetings, the relevant in-group of participant states knows precisely who opposes a popular proposal and can judge accordingly. In each of the institutional settings I outline here—the EU, the UN small arms process, and the UN General Assembly—dissenting states are identified and criticized, regardless of decision rules. States' concern for reputation, in turn, becomes an important motivation for policy support in each setting.

THE EUROPEAN UNION: CODE OF CONDUCT ON ARMS EXPORTS

The politically binding EU Code of Conduct and its eight criteria to guide conventional arms export decision making passed by a unanimous decision of the fifteen members of the European Council of Ministers in June 1998. The code's legally binding successor agreement, the Common Position on Arms Exports, similarly passed in the council (with twenty-seven member states at the time) under consensus rules in December 2008.[33] In general, the EU Council of Ministers—in which heads of state or their relevant ministers represent member-state interests—prefers unanimity. On sensitive issues such as foreign and security policy, policies are typically negotiated before a vote to facilitate consensus.[34] The council also serves as a regularized setting in which leaders meet to discuss and debate issues. From 1970 to 1993, the number of council meetings almost doubled, with foreign policy one of the topics most often discussed (Fligstein and McNichol 1998:70, 71). The council also established the Working Group on Conventional Arms Exports in 1991, intended to compare national practice and discuss potential harmonization. In doing so, it helped to usher in agreement on common criteria, and it has continued to meet regularly to discuss the interpretation and implementation of the Code of Conduct and the follow-on Common Position.

The council is widely seen as a highly secretive institution, whose deliberations and decisions are conducted "far from the public gaze" (Hayes-Renshaw 2002:65). Yet neither its public unanimity nor its lack of transparency could hide French opposition to the legally binding Code of Conduct—an opposition that other members and NGOs openly criticized.[35] Prior to 2008, France supported legalizing the code only if the EU lifted its arms embargo to China—itself a very public debate, in which consensus could not be reached.[36] However, as I discuss later in the chapter, it reversed its position and led the transformation of the code into the Common Position during its 2008 EU presidency. In doing so, France has conformed to its European peers' expectations, seeking recognition for the restrictive and responsible nature of its arms transfer policies (interviews 59108220, 60108220). Consensus therefore neither prevented France from weakening the initial EU Code nor protected it from criticism for doing so. And as social reputational pressures have built up in both the EU and UN over time, France has felt compelled to conform.

Research into EU member states' arms export practices casts doubt on the strength of their policy implementation and the depth of their socialization into new export norms (Erickson 2013b). Most recently, the Arab Spring has shone the spotlight on EU arms exports to dictatorships despite members' commitments to EU and UN policies (M. Bromley 2012; Dempsey 2012). Nevertheless, when it comes to policy support, the Council of Ministers and the Working Group on Conventional Arms Exports have provided a setting in which "responsible" export controls have become attached to perceptions of the quality of states' EU membership.[37] As Alyson Bailes observes, "There are signs that [the code] has created something like a virtuous circle of pressure for improvements of policy formulation and enforcement, both within the EU and among states preparing themselves for accession" (2004:v). Institutional pressures have thus made EU members early responders to new policy expectations. They have also cleared the path for EU exporters' support of the UNPOA and the ATT. In fact, the decision to legalize the code in 2008 was a product of members' concern for their own reputations as well as for the EU's reputation, which they feared would be undermined by the code's nonbinding status as they sought to promote a legally binding ATT.[38]

THE UN SMALL ARMS PROCESS: PROGRAMME OF ACTION

Like the EU, consensus rules at the UN small arms conferences have been more significant for the content and form of the agreement than for dampening reputational effects. Consensus rules are common in the UN when controversial issues are on the table and are standard practice in the arms control community (interview 5406225; Marín-Bosch 1998; Peterson 2006). Although many supported a legally binding agreement addressing illicit *and* licit small arms transfers already in 2001, consensus was elusive. The United States, to the surprise of many, announced on the opening day its intention to oppose what it considered a fundamentally flawed document and its negotiation "red lines" (Karp 2002; SAS 2002:219). It was adamantly against entertaining any proposals that were legally binding or that included provisions that could restrict licit transfers or civilian possession. The final UNPOA was therefore only politically binding and dealt only with the illicit small arms trade.[39]

Consensus meant that the conference had to bend to U.S. wishes. But it did not mean that supportive states would not advertise or criticize U.S. opposition. U.S. allies, other states, and NGOs roundly rebuked the United States in public for blocking otherwise popular efforts. However, U.S. opposition also allowed other "less influential" opponents to maintain a low profile (SAS 2002:220; Wyatt 2002). One expert noted that active U.S. opposition actually managed to make Russia and China, who were less vocal, "look good" despite their own lack of support for more restrictive measures (interview 5406225). In fact, it is difficult to identify with certainty which states joined the U.S. opposition, suggesting that consensus rules might shield smaller opposing states from reputational damage if a larger state's opposition becomes the magnet of international attention.[40]

This first small arms conference resulted from numerous UN reports and sessions in the 1990s on the problem of SALW proliferation.[41] The idea for a global agreement on small arms took off after the success of the landmine treaty in 1997. Attendance included 169 member states as well as forty-two NGOs invited to address the conference.[42] Some NGOs, however, argue that one of the downfalls of the conference was the decision to hold it in New York rather than in Geneva (interviews 4206225, 5406225, 9206225), where NGOs had explicitly sought to develop a small arms constituency in the 1990s (interview 7206225). Geneva is the home of the Conference on Disarmament, the UN Institute for Disarmament Research, and a plethora of arms control NGOs. Geneva-based diplomats were therefore more likely to be knowledgeable about small arms issues (interview 4206225, 5406225). In contrast, New York–based diplomats had rarely worked on small arms issues and lacked basic expertise (interview 4206225). Thus, although both cities had an established group of regularly interacting diplomats, Geneva's diplomatic population in 2001 more readily linked small arms policy with "good" international citizenship.

In the final hours of the conference, states agreed to a watered-down UN-POA "strictly in the interest of reaching a compromise" that could enable future global action (UN Department of Disarmament Affairs 2002:80; see also Greene 2002). In the face of "prolonged and difficult negotiations" on an issue barely on the international agenda a few years prior, it was a major accomplishment (UN Department of Disarmament Affairs 2002:89). The 2001 conference recognized and defined the "problem of small arms," raised small arms awareness, established a humanitarian dimension to the issue, identified like-minded states, and forced states to voice their positions (SAS 2002; Greene 2002; Krause 2002; Wyatt 2002). It also led to the International Tracing Instrument (2005) and to Groups of Governmental Experts on arms brokering (2007–2008) and ammunition (2008). Nevertheless, the 2003 and 2006 review conferences could not garner consensus to legalize the UNPOA or expand it to include humanitarian export criteria. Despite active NGO campaigning and broadening state support, the United States in particular remained a stalwart opponent and stalled the process from going beyond the existing document. Yet the failure of the 2006 conference did not doom global arms export controls. Rather, its failure spurred lead states to take their case to the UN General Assembly, where the supportive majority could rule, not the opposition voices of a few.

THE UN GENERAL ASSEMBLY: ARMS TRADE TREATY

When the small arms conference process deadlocked in July 2006, leaders sought a new institutional setting to tackle arms export controls. Moving to the UN General Assembly with its majoritarian voting rules prevented any one state from blocking an otherwise-popular initiative. In December 2006, the General Assembly voted 153 to 1 to initiate a process to create a legally binding ATT regulating all legal conventional arms transfers. The United States was the lone "no" vote; twenty-four others abstained, including China, Israel, and Russia. Measures so widely popular in the General Assembly signal that a new norm has become "widely shared" and is a standard of conduct often cited and defended (interview 5406225; Peterson 2006:101). Majoritarian voting intensified reputational concerns carried over from the small arms conferences. Many states did not want to be on record as opposing the initiative alongside the United States—whose poor reputation on the issue was well established.[43]

Reputational pressures in the General Assembly cannot be isolated from the earlier small arms conferences. States that had agreed to language and initiatives in the context of the conferences found it difficult, if not impossible, to oppose them when it came to the ATT (interview 5406225). By the end of the July 2006 small arms conference—and before the General Assembly vote was even scheduled—Cuba, Iran, and Pakistan had withdrawn their opposition to global arms transfer principles, leaving the United States alone in its resistance (SIPRI 2007:432–33). In fact, leaders used the July conference as a sounding board to decide whether to move forward in another forum (SIPRI 2007:433). The result was a decision to pursue a separate ATT in the First Committee meeting in October 2006 and the General Assembly in December 2006.

Although the UNPOA deals with a wide range of complex issues related to illicit small arms transfers—which some identify as its strength and others as its downfall[44]—the ATT focuses solely on legal arms transfers. This was an area where agreement had evolved over the course of several years and regular diplomatic meetings, moving from "much more resistance" in 2001 (Greene 2002:197) to near-consensus by 2006. These expectations for arms transfer policy carried over to the General Assembly. Nor did states' reputations—good or bad—get left behind in the transition. Concern for "good international citizenship" connected to arms transfer policy has played out across institutional venues, regardless of their voting rules. With the United States clear that it would not budge, leaders moved to the General Assembly simply because it offered the ability to move forward and subsequently reaffirm the ATT by majoritarian vote.

Other ATT discussions were nevertheless subject to consensus. The 2008 Group of Governmental Experts was unable to reach consensus on specific treaty contents, largely again because of U.S. opposition but with some states also questioning the human security agenda.[45] Meetings of the Open-Ended Working Group in 2008 and 2009 kept the process in a holding pattern until the United States announced its support in late 2009—on the condition that negotiations proceed by consensus—and thus enabled the process to move ahead. With only Zimbabwe opposed, the UN voted in December 2009 to set ATT negotiations for 2012 with a series of preparatory meetings in 2010–2012. Although the 2012 negotiations "showed that there appeared to be broad acceptance by states of the need to agree to a treaty to regulate the conventional arms trade," they also laid bare two key contentious issues: the scope of items covered and the inclusion of human rights and human security in arms export criteria (Bromley, Cooper, and Holtom 2012:1041–42). In the end, after some debate about the precise language, human security criteria were included in the final text, but ammunition and transfers to nonstate actors were not included in order to keep the United States on board.[46] The ATT passed the General Assembly with a vote of 154 to 3 on April 2, 2013, and opened for signature on June 3 with sixty-seven states signing on the first day. It enters into force ninety days after the fiftieth state deposits its ratification instrument on December 24, 2014.[47]

REPUTATIONAL CONCERNS: MAJOR SUPPLIER STATE SUPPORT

Within these institutions, diplomats have met frequently to interact and develop expectations about arms transfer controls. As one German official stated, "Over the work, you get to know each other" (interview 15107255). These meetings in turn provide fora in which states establish their reputations on "responsible" arms transfers and humanitarian issues more broadly. In a dramatic reversal of past trends, support for such policies has become widespread. An important source of this support across cases, as indicated in the case studies, stems from the reputational concerns of states deeply embedded in and reliant on these international institutions.

I use in-depth interviews with key players in arms export policy making—government, NGO, and defense industry representatives—to illustrate the effect of governments' reputational concerns on their policy commitments (see appendix B for information about interview data and coding).[48] First, many participants directly connect states' policy commitment to their image promotion abroad. Second, participants reveal an acute awareness of how the stringency of their policies stacks up in relation to their peers' policies, making comparisons about whose are the "best" and "most responsible." Finally, ministries of foreign affairs typically spearhead state policies, not their economic ministries, which, some participants contend, turns the focus away from states' economic interests and toward their international reputations. Although the U.S. case demonstrates that some states—especially superpowers—may choose to distance themselves from international institutions,[49] such cases remain the exception, and even the

United States has since reversed its public opposition to multilateral arms export controls in response to reputational concerns.

These references to state identity, image, reputation, and "looking good" help to confirm the social reputation argument and were often given in response to questions asking participants to describe their government's policies and explain its support for "responsible" arms export initiatives. I was careful never to ask questions that would direct participants to discuss reputation, image, or comparisons with other countries' policies. If participants or other evidence had instead highlighted prospective material gains (military or economic) from new policies or lead states' coercive efforts to collect cross-national support, a realist or neoliberal explanation would be more persuasive. As it is, although respondents expressed some concern over economic and foreign-policy costs, they focused instead on social reputational concerns as a strong motivating force behind their support for "responsible" arms transfer policies and related international initiatives.

In general, after the Ottawa Treaty in 1997, governments "didn't want to be seen as being on the wrong side of history" with new humanitarian arms control initiatives (interviews 7206225, 34207200, 35207200, 58107255).[50] They believed that support for "responsible" arms transfer policies—such as the landmine ban—would be "good for their international profile," a point that lead states and NGOs have emphasized in lobbying potential supporters (interviews 37207200, 34207200, 35207200). Although conventional arms present different regulatory challenges than landmines, the Ottawa experience changed international expectations: it altered how states' define appropriate arms control behavior as well as what social gains they believe can be made from their own support of related humanitarian arms control policies. One NGO representative, for example, observed that humanitarian arms control has become "fashionable." He stated, "The landmine ban established this high moral ground. . . . [I]t looks pretty bad if you don't support it. This has led to the habit of thinking you can look morally good by supporting weapons-related initiatives" (interview 34207200).

As small arms garnered international attention following the landmine treaty, policy support became, according to one government official, "really a beauty contest among diplomats who don't want to be looked at uneasily by their peers" (interview 58107255). Opposition also meant being seen as "in bed with the [United States]," whose own reputation had suffered because of its policies (interview 34207200). States saw the potential for reputational damage if they opposed new policies, but also for a certain "kudos that come with being seen as in the forefront" (interview 39307200) of humanitarian arms control issues if they were to come out in support of them.[51] In the words of one NGO advocate, "They want to look good; that's pretty much it" (interview 34207200).

Support for the UNPOA, the ATT, and similar international policies could "give an image that they are doing something" (interview 38207200) and taking "some responsibility" for "moral concerns of the impact [of the arms trade] on the developing world" (interviews 40107200, 34207200, 41107200). Thus, although officials may express doubt over the utility and feasibility of new policies in private, it is "almost unthinkable that [states] would say this is a bad thing" (interviews 41107200, 43107200).

THE UNITED KINGDOM: SETTING THE REPUTATIONAL BASELINE

The United Kingdom was an early mover on humanitarian arms export policies. Unlike other major exporters, it first embraced new arms transfer policies in response to scandal in domestic politics (see chapter 5) and took on a leadership role to promote those policies at the EU and UN.[52] In doing so, it has played a significant role in shifting the standard of good policy among major democratic exporters, providing a reference by which they can compare their policies and assess whether they measure up. Early support and leadership from a major exporter once resistant to common export controls made the United Kingdom a critical state in setting off the reputational beauty contest among democratic exporters. As the other case studies make clear, British support, along with the momentum provided by the success of the landmine treaty, created a reputational baseline for "responsible" export controls and set off a norm cascade, making support for new initiatives not only possible but also expected.

The United Kingdom has taken on a leadership role for two key multilateral "responsible" arms export initiatives, both with an eye to its international reputation. First, the Labour government led the creation of the 1998 EU Code of Conduct. In addition to pleasing domestic audiences and diffusing the costs of unilateral export controls, its leadership was intended to express—and confirm—the United Kingdom's responsible, humanitarian reputation (Blair 1997; Dunne and Wheeler 2001; Robbins 1997). Labour sought to use its "responsible" policies to signal the United Kingdom's new image not just to constituents at home but also to peers abroad, cementing "good international citizenship" as the foundation of postcolonial British foreign policy.[53] Leadership on arms transfer controls, it believed, would "look pretty good if [it could] pull it off" (interview 37207200). Although some note that British policy implementation has been poor (Cooper 2000; Dunne and Wheeler 2001; Mayhew 2005), this poor performance does not seem to have undermined its reputation abroad. Rather, the UK government saw its ability to rally multilateral support for the EU Code and later for the ATT as a reputation-building success (interviews 41107200, 32107200).

Second, since 2004 the British government has spearheaded multilateral transfer controls at the UN in an effort to repair its international reputation, which took a hit following the 2003 Iraq invasion (interviews 4206225, 35207200, 37207200). According to reports, "Britain's human rights policy had been weakened by the Iraq war, military action in Afghanistan and terrorist attacks against the U.S." (C. Adams 2004). Interviewees suggest that joining the ranks of ATT leadership was a strategic move on the part of the then foreign secretary Jack Straw at the helm of the Foreign and Commonwealth Office, hoping to recapture the United Kingdom's popular "ethical foreign policy" image of the late 1990s and show that it could "be a force for good on the world scene again."[54] It was also a chance for Straw to "leave his mark on the issue" and rescue his own domestic and international standing after Iraq.[55] Indeed, although Prime Minister Tony Blair had approved Straw's initial support for a small arms–only ATT, some argue that the same could not be said for Straw's 2005 announcement that broadened the initiative to include all conventional arms (Straw 2005). The move was unexpected even among other ATT supporters and cemented not only British ATT leadership but also Straw's legacy as the architect of the expanded scope of the ATT, which would pass by wide margins eight years later.[56]

Yet it seems likely that in the hands of another ministry less invested in international reputation, the United Kingdom would have eschewed its leadership role. The Department of Trade and Industry, the Department for International Development, and the Ministry of Defence are also deeply involved in UK arms trade policy and practice. The Department of Trade Industry works closely with industry and is concerned about the economic costs of transfer controls. The Department for International Development has often been frustrated that policies do not go far enough to address its concerns for sustainable development, and the Ministry of Defence takes a more technical role. The Foreign and Commonwealth Office, in contrast, has been more concerned about international image and public diplomacy (Martin and Garnett 1997). It has chosen and promoted policies as a way to cultivate UK reputation and the image necessary to attract followers to its initiatives (interviews 32107200, 40107200, 41107200). Less invested in either ethical or economic interests, it has also been able to take the lead inside the government to ensure that policy is unified across ministries when promoting initiatives abroad, despite differences in bureaucratic preferences.

Even so, the government has wanted to make its policies appear more than "just a British idea" (interview 32107200). Although UK support convinced many major exporters (interview 41107200), its colonial history has made its leadership more sensitive for some importing states. It has therefore worked with affected states and NGOs to make the ideas "[pick] up resonance within an organization" to encourage agreement (interview 321072c0). British NGOs have also been closely involved with the government's policy promotion, even as both sides seek to maintain at least the appearance of mutual independence. Indeed, although the government's support and promotion of "responsible" arms export standards helped new initiatives spread, NGOs claim the ideas behind them. NGOs had sought an international code of conduct since the early 1990s and worked closely with Labour to shape its foreign-policy agenda prior to its 1997 electoral victory (interviews 33207200, 35207200, 37207200).

Whether in spite of or because of its commitment to promoting defense exports alongside ethical arms transfers, the United Kingdom has created a strong international reputation for leadership on arms export controls and set the policy standard for other top democratic exporters. Its success with the EU Code of Conduct encouraged it to take the lead on the ATT, and the Blair government believed its international status was enhanced as a result. UK leadership on the issue has continued under subsequent governments, with support from the Conservative-led coalition government especially showing how changes in expectations since the mid-1990s can alter past political opposition. Most importantly for the purposes of this chapter, UK government leadership—at times in partnership with NGOs[57] and the defense industry—has helped to set policy expectations, trigger social reputational concerns, and accelerate support worldwide.

GERMANY: MULTILATERALISM AND CIVILIAN POWER

Germany's arms transfer policy and its foreign policy more broadly have been profoundly shaped by World War II. As a rule, postwar Germany sees itself as a strong supporter of multilateral initiatives and wishes to cultivate a reputation for good international citizenship. According to one official, Germany supports new arms transfer policies, "basically because [they] sounded good and that's what Germany does" (interviews 16107255, 44307255). In general, it is very important for the government to be seen as international, multilateral, and "the best European" (interviews 16107255, 44307255). Germany stands behind UN principles in rhetoric, if not also in action, with multilateralism as "the central reference point [of German foreign policy]" (Grossmann and Hummel 1997:21–22). In fact, because the United Kingdom had declared its strong support, officials believe that "Germany couldn't *not* do it" without risking the appearance of being "irresponsible" and uncooperative (interview 45207255, 19407255).

Germany's public support for common export controls has come despite private skepticism about the merits and feasibility of multilateral "responsible" arms transfer criteria. Many in Germany and elsewhere "did not anticipate the [ATT] initiative to pass through and formalize so quickly at the United Nations."[58] Officials have worried that multilateral principles were neither practical nor efficient and risked taking attention away from other initiatives with the potential for more concrete results (interviews 15107255, 19407255, 45207255). This distinction between public support and private skepticism illustrates that even in Germany—where support for multilateral initiatives is assumed to be an intrinsic element of national identity—reputational concerns can be an important policy consideration.

Cognizant of the growing public-relations element of the small arms issue, the Federal Foreign Office (Auswärtiges Amt, AA) has gone from thinking that post-UNPOA initiatives were "nothing serious" to championing an ATT and shared export standards (interview 19407255). Officials want Germany to be recognized as a leader on small arms and related issues. They believe that as a major arms exporter and a larger EU country, Germany has a responsibility to lead, especially on arms control and disarmament (interviews 14107255, 15107255, 16107255). With Canada and other countries already championing small arms control, Germany went "looking for something else" and saw the ATT process as a public-relations opportunity after failing to press hard enough to achieve a binding treaty on ammunition controls (interview 19407255).[59] In its 2007 EU presidency, Germany kept the issue on the EU agenda. Even so, experts note that although Germany reliably supports policies, it often stops short of overcoming major-power opposition (interview 19407255). As a result, it has not been recognized as a lead state on par with the United Kingdom, presumably because the AA has chosen a backseat in non-European fora.

Germany takes pride in its history of arms control and disarmament (interview 14107255) and sees itself as well qualified to promote "best practice guides for different areas of small arms" (interview 14107255). Officials consistently emphasize the restrictiveness of German policies, especially in comparison to EU requirements and other members.[60] Annual arms export reports describe German policies in multilateral fora and contain a section titled "German Arms Exports in International Comparison," in which the government emphasizes its outreach activities and international cooperation, while downplaying the size of its arms exports in comparison to other major exporters. Officials also compare Germany's leadership efforts in the EU to those of the United Kingdom, Netherlands, and France and note that Germany is one of the most active states on the small arms issue at the UN (interview 15107255). Germany thus expresses a keen awareness of its standing among European leaders and how its policies stack up in comparison.

It is worth noting that, like the United Kingdom, Germany's strong support of "responsible" arms control would have been less certain had the AA not been the key agency deciding German policy. Ultimately, it is the AA leadership's decision to push an issue on the foreign-policy agenda (interview 19407255). And, as one official notes, "there is a difference between the principles the AA will follow and what the [Ministry for Economics and Technology (Bundesministerium für Wirtschaft und Technologie)] will follow" with important consequences for German foreign policy (interview 14107255). As the foreign office, the AA is more concerned with international principles and multilateralism and more critical of arms exports, especially as they relate to public diplomacy and support for human rights. AA diplomats represent Germany in the EU and UN and seek to build its reputation for civilian power. In contrast, the Ministry for Economics and Technology is more supportive and tolerant of arms exports and is not the public face of German foreign policy. It is less invested in multilateral fora and seeks instead to defend the status quo of national arms export controls.[61]

Given the AA's existing interest in multilateralism and arms control, NGOs did not see a need to push it to adopt "responsible" arms transfer policy (interview 17207255). Rather, they see themselves as "work[ing] in the same direction" though consultation, research, and regular government–NGO working group meetings (interviews 17207255, 10407255, 45207255). In some respects, these relationships are improvised as initiatives emerge and develop. As one official noted, "Germany has never had a strong opinion on how to [relate to] NGOs" and engages them to some extent as a matter of public diplomacy (interview 58107255). For their part, NGOs focus on ensuring policy implementation, stating that if the government signs on, "we know what's been promised, and [it also knows] we'll follow up" on its export decision-making practices (interview 17207255).[62] By appealing to the policies to which the government has publicly committed, NGOs seek to enhance "responsible" arms transfers in practice as well as on paper, in line with Germany's own self-image as a cooperative civilian power,[63] a compliance dynamic I explore further in chapter 5.

As a civilian power, Germany promotes a foreign policy focused less on hard power than on building norms of global governance (interviews 10407255, 16107255, 44307255). It has a "fairly strong belief in the logic of transparency and in multilateral regimes" (interview 14107255) and "aims to foster working together with other countries and developing rules" (interview 16107255). It wants its arms transfer policies to reflect this point of view (interview 10407255). According to one official, "If there is a code of conduct, we apply it," regardless of practicality (interview 15107255). Moreover, Germany would not want to be "the one left behind," accused of *not* supporting multilateral policies (interview 58107255). Indeed, as Germany seeks to play a peaceful, constructive role in the international community, adopting policies that uphold its public image as conforming with multilateral policy standards is a key factor behind its support for "responsible" arms transfer initiatives.

FRANCE: CHANGING POLICY
TO BUILD REPUTATION

Following in the United Kingdom's steps, France announced its backing of a global ATT in 2005 (Chirac 2005) and has since become a strong supporter of multilateral "responsible" arms export controls (interviews 59108220, 60108220). Until that time, however, France had opposed shared legally binding criteria that "could 'force' it to give up some of its, by European standards, liberal arms export policies" (SIPRI 1999:439). Even its support for the 1998 EU Code of Conduct was prefaced on the condition that the code refrain from issuing legally binding criteria—a condition that it dropped a decade later, clearing the way to legalization. Absent—at least initially—a supportive defense industry, an interested domestic public, and an active NGO community, France's policy shift has been largely a matter of promoting a "good" reputation in the international community. In general, France's global interests are "intimately linked to [its] *rang* [rank] and *grandeur* [greatness] and to the notion, with deep historical roots, that global interests enhance French power and influence in Europe" (Gregory 2000:10; see also Utley 2000). As one official noted, "the role of image" is an important consideration for French foreign policy[64] and has carried over into its policies on multilateral export controls (interview 59108220).

Like Germany, France seeks recognition as a leader on the EU Code of Conduct, UNPOA, and ATT, but in private it is somewhat skeptical of policy initiatives. Officials note that France places a high priority on promoting multilateral arms export initiatives and is one of the most involved states in promoting small arms control on the international agenda (interviews 59108220, 60108220).[65] At the same time, they are concerned about the sovereignty and security implications of imposing shared standards on "the last place of freedom," conventional arms sales, and are unsure of the value of UN processes (interviews 59108220, 60108220). Indeed, France has sympathized with past U.S. opposition, suggesting it, too, might prefer a narrower document focused on regional implementation were it not for its concerns about reputation in EU and international politics (interview 60108220). Indeed, other than the United Kingdom and other major European exporters, France's main point of comparison on arms trade policy is the United States. France compares itself to the United States as a fellow major power with exceptional global responsibilities, as a major arms exporter with an admired system of national export controls, and as a world leader in human rights promotion (interviews 59108220, 60108220; Tardy 2007).

Shaun Gregory argues that France uses its UN activity to promote "a positive humanitarian image for France and the support of French norms and values in the international system" (2000:169). As support for "responsible" arms export policies has become expected in international politics, France has thus shifted its own policies to align with these expectations. In particular, it has used its newfound, visible policy support to overcome its past reputation for arms export liberalism at home and policy obstructionism abroad. Since 2001, the government has identified two tracks in the UN and wants to be a part of the "good group," which includes EU small arms leaders, such as the UK and the Netherlands (interview 60108220). This is also a way for France to distinguish itself as more responsible than the (initially) obstructionist United States, although the results of this strategy for France's reputation have perhaps not been as successful as the government had hoped. Officials argue that French arms export policies have been unfairly criticized as too liberal simply because France is "more responsible" than others in reporting its sales figures, and they take pride in what they see as the restrictive and "responsible" nature of French policies (interviews 59108220, 60108220). Stated one official, "The French image is perhaps not that positive outside, but if you see the work of each person in the process, then it is difficult to see how you could do it better" (interview 59108220). Moreover, officials cite France's experience in arms control, its large export market, and the complexity of its domestic export mechanisms as attributes that enable it to provide quality leadership on this issue (e.g., interview 59108220).

France's policy shift also seeks to strengthen the EU's reputation as a global actor. France promotes multilateralism as a way to enhance and exercise its international influence, linked to its membership and leadership in the EU (Tardy 2007; Wood 1997).[66] The EU's inability to legalize the Code of Conduct due to French opposition had hindered the EU's ability to advocate for a legally binding ATT and be a credible global actor more broadly. Stalling legalization therefore became contrary to French foreign-policy interests beyond the arms trade. In addition, France also believed that not only supporting but *leading* the legalization of the EU Code after coming out in support of an ATT would signal its membership in the "good group" of states and draw a sharp contrast between its cooperative approach and U.S. hostility.

The decisions to support an ATT and the legalization of the EU Code came from Presidents Jacques Chirac and Nicolas Sarkozy, leaving the Ministry of Foreign Affairs (Ministère des affaires étrangères) and Ministry of Economics and Finance (Ministère de l'économie et des finances) to follow (interview 60108220).[67] NGOs have also been on the sidelines of French policy making.[68] The government takes the view that "states lead, not NGOs," on the issue of "responsible" arms transfer policy (interview 59108220). In fact, French NGOs did not develop the background to become actively involved in arms export policy until the ATT vote in 2006, long after the government had announced its support. Both sides now say they are satisfied with French policies and the government's receptiveness to NGO input, although NGOs have not been invited to take part in French UN delegations (interviews 59108220, 64208220). Government officials and NGOs say that this hands-off approach to French policy may be in part explained by the fact that France "already [has] a quite restrictive regime" (interviews 59108220, 62208220, 64208220). As I show in chapter 5, NGOs are beginning to turn instead to monitoring policy implementation (interviews 61208220, 64208220). Moreover, France's concession to legalizing the EU Code was a point of satisfaction for states and NGOs pushing an ATT at the international level. However, to get the government to this point, changes in what would promote its reputation connected to the arms trade in the international community were necessary, with the standard set by the United Kingdom and opportunities for France to showcase its responsible policy positions.

BELGIUM: MISSED OPPORTUNITY FOR LEADERSHIP

Observers argue that Belgian support of multilateral arms trade standards stems largely from the government's "looking over its shoulder at others" (interview 26207211). They suggest that the government did not want to "hang [its] neck out on this one" and supported new initiatives mainly because of British leadership and the policy standards set by the United Kingdom (interviews 26207211, 30207211). In fact, some Belgian NGOs—which were otherwise satisfied with the federal government's leadership on humanitarian arms control—regret that an opportunity was missed to position Belgium as a leader on small arms as it was on the landmine treaty (interviews 29207211, 30207211).

The federal government, which had been an early promoter of linking small arms to sustainable development (Rossel-Cambier 1997) and an APL treaty leader, had been preoccupied by its regionalization of national arms export licensing after 2002 (see chapter 5).[69] Moreover, in the process of regionalizing policy implementation—but not policy making—some observers have worried that Belgium's international reputation would suffer (interviews 52207211, 53207211). In their view, divorcing arms trade policy from arms trade practice would threaten the perception of Belgium's sincerity and its ability to impact other countries' positions on the issue (interview 52207211). Nevertheless, there is no evidence that this has occurred,[70] suggesting that states' arms trade policy implementation—unlike their policies—receives little attention outside their borders.

Despite the regionalization of export licensing, Belgian arms trade policy is still coordinated by the federal Ministry of Foreign Affairs in line with European and international expectations.[71] Although the ministry takes input from the regions "on practical measures," it "will not accept [input from] regions that will hinder pursuing an [ATT] as a Belgian policy goal" (interview 56107211).[72] Officials view cooperation as a matter of "[supporting] our principles on the multilateral level," but they also acknowledge that it has been driven by "pressures to support . . . lead nations" in international fora (interview 56107211). And because economic interests are more closely represented at the regional level (interview 27207211), the Ministry of Foreign Affairs is freer to pursue concerns about Belgium's reputation abroad, alongside its goals to protect human rights and democracy (Houben 2005). This focus also allows Belgium to have influence, as officials see it, because its policy decisions can be seen as part of a more neutral image rather than swayed by global economic or foreign-policy interests (interview 55107211).

Arms control is "considered a central issue in Belgian policy," and shared standards of "responsible" arms transfers have not been controversial (interviews 56107211, 57207211). According to one NGO representative, "Like all human rights topics . . . everyone is proud to support [the ATT]" (interview 57207211). The defense industry, too, has learned that Belgium "will do it if the UN wants it" (interview 31307211). Moreover, Belgium takes pride in its "progressive" laws and avoids projecting an "arms salesman" image.[73] Officials and NGOs are quick to point out that only Belgium has adopted the EU Code into its national legislation. Belgium sees its arms trade policies as "best of class" and "quite ethical" compared to other states' policies (interview 57207211). NGOs note that government policy often outpaces their lobbying and that the public has been largely absent from relevant policy discussions (interviews 52207211, 29207211). So they instead focus more on implementation at the regional level, noting that the regional and federal governments "don't need civil society voices" on policy formation (interviews 26207211, 57207211).[74]

With its successful collaboration on the Ottawa Treaty, Belgium has sought to build on its reputation as a humanitarian leader. Officials state that Belgium seeks to be seen as a "problem solver" in international politics: "We've solved quite a number of problems, have objectivity, and define a well-balanced decision, [even] punishing our own industry on mine production" (interview 55107211). To maintain its reputation, Belgium therefore sees a need to support policies consistent with the image it projects to the international community. It has also had to overcome perceptions as a historic center of illicit arms trafficking.[75] Ultimately, although missing a leadership opportunity on arms exports was a lost chance for Belgium to advance its social reputation, it did not inflict reputational damage. What does cause such damage—at least based on the

U.S. experience—is opposition to popular multilateral initiatives, even where national policies might be classified as "responsible."

THE UNITED STATES: FROM OPPOSITION TO SUPPORT

Until late 2009, the United States was the only state to vote against the ATT process and the primary voice of opposition on UN small arms initiatives. It is certainly active in regional and international institutions, but its opposition suggests that it may see itself as less beholden to the reputational concerns faced by others by virtue of its perception of its "exceptional" position and power in the international system. This does not mean that U.S. leaders are uniformly unconcerned about U.S. image abroad. The United States has engaged in "public diplomacy" across administrations (Goldsmith and Horiuchi 2009). Rather, U.S. policy suggests that U.S. leaders may be more flexible in their concern for international reputation, dependent on domestic politics, party ideology, and foreign-policy agendas.[76] Thus, even as the George W. Bush administration's opposition to "responsible" export initiatives showed a disregard for reputational concerns, the Obama administration's October 2009 announcement of support for the ATT process (Clinton 2009) seems an effort to engage in reputation repair and signal renewed multilateralism to the international community.

For many, the strident opposition coming from the United States was puzzling. U.S. arms export policies are considered among the best in the world. Thus, from a practical standpoint, new global standards would not likely require substantive changes in U.S. policies. Sensitive issues such as civilian firearm possession and transfers to nonstate actors were kept explicitly off the table to keep the United States at the table. During the Cold War and after, the United States had even led initiatives to globalize its best practices and establish shared arms transfer controls (U.S. DOS 2001). President Carter initiated talks with the Soviet Union in 1979, and President George H. W. Bush supported the P5 talks in 1991 (see chapter 3). In 1999, the Republican-majority Congress passed legislation requiring the president to start working on an international arms sales code of conduct. The United States also claimed a leadership role in the preparations for the 2001 UN conference and in global small arms control more broadly (SAS 2002; U.S. DOS 2001; U.S. General Accounting Office 2000). According to a 2000 U.S. General Accounting Office report, U.S. leadership had helped to develop international standards to prevent illicit small arms transfers; strengthen small arms export controls; create and strengthen multilateral initiatives on small arms; and provide assistance to other states to destroy excess weapons stocks (5).

Starting in July 2001, however, U.S. policy shifted abruptly. The move damaged its international reputation, quickly earning it an "obstructionist" image (SAS 2002; SIPRI 2007). According to pro-control NGOs, the United States was "seen as the bad guy by a lot of states," with an "arrogant" attitude, "no interest in abiding by the rules," and an inability to "play well with others" (interviews 48207002, 51207002).[77] Even states skeptical about arms trade control sought to distance themselves from what was seen as the extreme U.S. position to spare themselves the hit to their own international reputation.[78] Yet the U.S. position in this case was not an isolated incidence of U.S. opposition to multilateralism, nor was this the first time the U.S. had derailed multilateral arms export initiatives, including initiatives it nominally supported (see chapter 3). Its opposition should therefore not simply be written off as concern for domestic electoral concerns but can be seen as a larger pattern of skepticism toward binding international instruments in general.

Some observers of the UN small arms meetings argue that U.S. opposition can be traced back to the influence of the National Rifle Association (NRA) on the George W. Bush administration (interview 48207002; Karp 2002). The United States explicitly cited concern for domestic civilian gun possession as justification for its opposition (Greene 2002), and the NRA presence was clear: according to Rachel Stohl, "This influence ranges from the presence of NRA board members on the US delegations at the UN and other multilateral meetings to . . . NRA positions in policy statements and speeches" (2006:10).[79] In addition, the NRA has sought to use the issue to rouse its membership base, making it the only significant segment of the U.S. public attentive to—and angry about— UN initiatives (see chapter 5). NRA executive vice president Wayne LaPierre refers to the small arms conferences as a concerted effort by the UN "to strip the Second Amendment from our Constitution" and "take guns away from every law-abiding citizen in the world" (2006:ix, 22).[80] This argument seems to resonate with some constituents, whose idea of U.S identity is rooted in a national self-image tied to the western frontiersman, explorer, and farmer (Squires 2000; Uviller and Merkel 2002). The NRA also fears that UN small arms measures might restrict civilian possession outside U.S. borders and so has advocated against gun control in other countries (Bob 2012).[81]

Of course, the United States already regulates its foreign sales of small and major conventional arms, with standards that are not vastly different from what ATT supporters proposed. Nevertheless, the NRA set off a small but vocal domestic constituency strongly opposed to multilateral arms trade initiatives and has mobilized sustained opposition to the ATT by U.S. senators.[82] Because of the Republican Party's close relationship with the NRA, the Bush administration's considerations of this constituency's reactions could have been significant to its political calculus. Certainly, these considerations affected the strategies of pro-control NGOs, which saw the costs of getting involved under the Bush presidency as far outweighing the benefits (interview 48207002). A Democratic administration, they believed, would be less beholden to NRA interests. Indeed, it seems unlikely that the Obama administration will win support from the core NRA constituency under any circumstances, making it perhaps freer to follow other policies at the UN.[83] Even so, the U.S. request to delay the final ATT approval to after the July 2012 negotiations seems likely to have been motivated by electoral concerns, with the Obama administration not wanting an American "yes" vote to hurt the chances of more conservative Democrats facing tight races at the polls in November.

However, throughout the ATT process, the UN and ATT leader states have catered to U.S. interests and explicitly kept civilian possession of firearms off the table, thus making it difficult to attribute sustained U.S. opposition to Second Amendment concerns.[84] Proposed documents have dealt only with the international trade in conventional arms. The Obama administration has publicly supported the ATT, while also reminding UN delegates that the ATT negotiations are "not an attempt to intrude, either in principle or process, into states' internal activities, laws, or practices concerning the domestic possession, use, or movement of arms" (Mahley 2012). Prior to the final negotiation in March 2013, the American Bar Association (2013) confirmed that the proposed ATT is consistent with the Second Amendment and federal court rulings to date. The final ATT formally acknowledges the "sovereign right of any State to regulate and control conventional arms exclusively within its territory, pursuant to its own legal or constitutional system."[85] Despite formally excluding civilian possession from the scope of the treaty, U.S. ratification—requiring two-thirds Senate majority—is highly unlikely in the near future, in large part because of NRA lobbying and electoral influence.

Yet the bigger picture shows U.S. opposition to multilateral transfer controls prior to 2009 as part of a larger pattern of U.S. aversion to multilateralism. Although expressions of U.S. exceptionalism under the Bush administration may have been less nuanced and less attentive to its international reputation, perceptions of exceptionalism are not unique in American politics.[86] Exceptionalism is embedded both in the U.S. self-image as "an agent . . . for good in the world and for righting geopolitical wrongs" (Sperling 2007:171) and in how other members of the international community view its "lack of consideration for the majority" (Smouts 2000:48). Certainly, the United States had "downgraded multilateralism as a substantive goal of American foreign policy" after September 11, 2001 (Sperling 2007:182). The Bush administration's opposition to multilateral initiatives extended beyond small arms to include the Anti–Ballistic Missile Treaty, the updated Biological Weapons Convention, the Kyoto Protocol, the International Criminal Court, and the Convention on Cluster Munitions. Pro-control NGOs in particular have noted this "anti-international agreement atti-tude" that seeks to avoid obligations enabling ncn-U.S. rules "to govern US foreign policy" and tie its hands in the war on terror (interview 51207002). Yet it should not be forgotten that it was the Clinton administration that first refused to sign the Ottawa Treaty. Citing exceptional U.S power and responsibility, it argued a need at times to put aside international norms and rules.

For the arms trade, this aversion to multilateralism has meant—independent of the NRA or partisan preferences—a rejection of external restraints on the ability to use arms transfers as a political tool (R. Stohl 2006). Such rejection, of course, is not new to U.S. policy or practice and has prevented U.S. cooperation in the past (see chapter 3; Erickson forthcoming). Arms trade experts point out that the United States has consistently resisted subjecting its arms exports to human rights criteria in favor of other foreign-policy objectives, regardless of the party in power (Hartung 2001b). Even in U.S national policy, presidents have preserved the ability to make exceptions for exports "in the national inter-est."[87] U.S. support for the UN small arms processes during their planning phase under Bill Clinton was not a given, despite what some organizers might have believed at the time. In fact, the origins of U.S. opposition to the processes may actually have come under the Clinton administration (interview 50207002), which took a simultaneously supportive and "cautious" approach to the issue (Karp 2002:189).

The Obama administration, too, has emphasized arms transfers as a means to promote U.S. national security and foreign-policy interests (Shapiro 2012). Nevertheless, in late 2009 it publicly announced its (qualified) support for the ATT process. Its concerns about consensus and behind-the-scenes negotiations over acceptable language have suggested ongoing reservations about strong, binding export controls, but ATT support has offered the United States easy reputational gains abroad. Studies report that U.S. reputation had suffered as a result of its unilateralist actions and apparent disregard for international norms and rules during the Bush administration (American Political Science Associa-tion 2009; Chicago Council on Global Affairs and WorldPublicOpinion.org 2008). Once in office, the Obama administration made a concerted effort to ad-dress this problem by publicly adopting policies and positions on popular interna-tional initiatives.[88] Its public ATT support—whatever its private reservations—is a product of its reputation-building efforts, signaling a break with the past and a new tone of U.S. foreign policy for international audiences.[89]

Reputational concerns have been more consistent across European export-ers, which are more deeply embedded in international institutions with peer states to which they constantly compare themselves. In contrast, because of U.S. national origins and confidence in domestic institutions, the U.S. self-image may not consistently rely on its status in international institutions.[90] Yet disregard for international norms and institutions under the Bush administration in particular has discredited U.S. policies and damaged U.S. reputation that "no amount of 'public diplomacy'" can fix (Walt 2005:231; see also Goldsmith and Horiuchi 2009). The consequences may be—like the widespread support of the ATT despite U.S. opposition—a distancing of other states from the U.S. foreign-policy agenda (Walt 2005). Its perception of superior power may be why the United States can value its international reputation less but also why it may need to improve that reputation. In particular, the social benefits attached to a good reputation may help it to cultivate its soft power, assuage the international community's fears, and promote a stable and rule-bound international order (see Ikenberry 2001; Koh 2003).

Major exporters' support for "responsible" arms transfer policies has spread dramatically since 1998. Yet military security, economic incentives, and domestic political gain seem largely absent from states' decision-making calculus. Indeed, for states with large defense industries dependent on exports to survive, signing on to "responsible" arms export controls may be perceived as costly at least to their economic well-being, if not also to their national security. In the next chapter, I show that public opinion also has little interest in governments' arms export policies. As a result, material preference-based explanations provide little insight into states' policy choices. Instead, states adopt "responsible" arms transfer policies out of concern for their international reputation, despite their private reservations about the value of new norms, and in response to social pressures from other states and the social benefits reputation can provide. In the context of international institutions, diplomats and leaders observe their peers' policies, discuss new initiatives, and adopt new expectations for "good" arms transfer policies and for their "good international citizenship" more broadly. By supporting these policies, states hope in turn to build, repair, and maintain their reputations as cooperative, peaceful, and human rights–oriented members of the international community.

Reputational pressures have been potent among major European exporters despite their past policies of arms export promotion. This is not simply a European phenomenon. As I show in the concluding chapter, reputation has important effects on the arms transfer policies of states outside the EU as well. Moreover, the U.S. case demonstrates that states may indeed have cause for concern about reputational damage, especially when opposition to one policy joins a long list of similar behavior on other issues associated with "responsible" membership in the international community. Yet reputational pressures at the international level may not extend to policy compliance. States may have been socialized into expectations for new arms export policies, but, as chapter 3 shows, these norms have mostly not been internalized in practice—at least so far. In particular, without international monitoring mechanisms or other forms of peer review, states' "irresponsible" practices can escape criticism even as these same states seek reputational kudos for their "responsible" policies. To that end, the next chapter examines governments' concern for *domestic* reputation in the context of arms trade scandals as a major factor behind those changes in practice that they do exhibit.

5. Explaining Compliance

DOMESTIC REPUTATION AND ARMS
TRADE SCANDAL

As states began to ramp up support for humanitarian arms control policy in the late 1990s, arms trade practice was emerging from its historic secrecy. In some cases, revelations of past export behavior had damaging domestic consequences. In Argentina, for example, scandal broke in 1995 with reports of a series of secret deals sending thousands of tons of arms and ammunition shipments to Croatia and Ecuador between 1991 and 1995 (Deutsche Presse-Agentur 1995).[1] It took six years to formally charge former president Carlos Menem in 2001 with authorizing the sales in violation of a UN embargo and a regional peace agreement. Despite his claims of innocence, most Argentines believed him guilty, but few believed he would be convicted. After being released a few months after his arrest due to lack of evidence, it took another ten years before an Argentine court would acquit Menem and seventeen other defendants, calling the arms deals a "foreign policy decision and a non-punishable political act" (Tarbuck 2013). But in 2013 the tide turned: an appeals court convicted Menem and a bevy of top officials of illegal arms smuggling and levied prison sentences ranging from four to seven years.[2]

The dealings reached deep into the Argentine administration, implicating fifty cabinet officials, military commanders, and personal advisers. A Buenos Aires news agency labeled the affair "an international blunder of unforeseeable

magnitude for the country" ("News Agency Says" 1996). According to one official, it "complicated [Argentina's] image abroad" ("Argentine Foreign Minister"
1996). Argentina has sought to compensate for these deals with a strong commitment to "responsible" arms transfers, becoming an ATT leader.[3] Yet the
costs of bad practice publicly revealed were even more tangible in domestic
politics. The scandal ended political careers, further deteriorated trust in government, and embarrassed the government at home and abroad.

This is merely one arms trade scandal among many in the post–Cold War
era, but it illustrates the difficulty of arms trade accountability, the far-reaching
implications of scandal, and the importance of reputation to states and their
leaders. "Irresponsible" or noncompliant arms export behavior often goes unnoticed, but when it is noticed, the consequences can be severe. Other states
with reports of arms export scandals since the early 1990s include Belgium, Bulgaria, Colombia, France, Germany, India, Poland, Slovakia, Slovenia, South
Africa, Sweden, Switzerland, Ukraine, the United Kingdom, and the former
Yugoslavia.[4] EU members have been shamed for past arms sales to dictatorships
in the Middle East and North Africa, spotlighted by the Arab Spring (M. Bromley 2012; Dempsey 2012). With growing transparency and shifting export norms,
arms trade scandals have become more widespread. Because governments prefer to avoid the domestic reputational damage and political fallout scandals can
cause, scandal—and threat of scandal—may in some cases help promote arms
export restraint among democracies.

This chapter explores the effects of domestic political pressures on states'
compliance with their commitments to "responsible" arms export controls. For
the most part, policy implementation has been weak, and changes in practice
slow to appear. Decision makers rarely perceive material or normative incentives to pursue new arms transfer policies for a domestic audience. The defense
industry, as I have shown, is a reluctant late supporter of multilateral controls
and favors export promotion. The broader public, as this chapter demonstrates,
is typically unaware of arms export policy and practice, with one important exception. Public attention to the arms trade is piqued by scandal brought on by
media attention to violations of a state's fundamental values and self-image
through "irresponsible" arms exports.

I argue that it is the prospect of arms trade scandals and the cost to reputation—
and with it, the cost to power and legitimacy—at home that affect how well
governments implement new arms trade policies. Government sensitivity to
arms trade scandal may not be able to provoke sweeping changes in export practice, but, lacking international enforcement, other options are limited. Governments' perceived scandal sensitivity increases in tandem with improvements in
transparency, allowing NGOs to spotlight "irresponsible" exports in the media
and inflict reputational costs. The case studies reveal that *both* transparency and

pro-control NGOs are necessary to improve accountability among democratic exporters, separate from—but perhaps aided by—international commitments to new export standards. For that small subset of scandal-prone cases where violations of rules and values are the most clear-cut and likely to come under public scrutiny, the policy–practice gap can begin to narrow. These findings suggest that transparency measures, although developed before new arms trade initiatives, can be harnessed to promote relatively "better" (though so far not "good") arms transfer practices. It also has important implications for ATT implementation, which I discuss in the concluding chapter.

PUBLIC OPINION AND DOMESTIC STRUCTURE

At first glance, it might seem far-fetched to expect states' arms trade policy and practice to reflect public opinion. The close relationship between governments and defense industries indicates that the preferences that count will not be those of the broader public but rather those of the defense industry. Industry has the political importance and the inside connections to make its voice heard. Although, as I have already argued, states have committed to new humanitarian arms trade controls in spite of defense industry preferences, the noncompliant export practices described in chapter 3 hint that industry wishes have not been forgotten. Indeed, the statist nature of arms transfer decision making suggests that any other societal influence would be hard pressed to make a substantive impact on state behavior. Across the board, arms transfers must be approved for export by government agencies through complex internal processes that are often understood by a handful of experts and not subject to advance public scrutiny.[5] Moreover, if the public does care, it may do so to preserve industry to safeguard national security and employment.

When it comes to foreign-policy making in general, scholars are divided about the role of public opinion. Many question the public's interest in foreign policy. Even at the height of the Cold War, only a few defense issues, such as nuclear weapons, stimulated cross-national public attention (Capitanchik and Eichenberg 1983). In the 1990s, policy makers perceived a decline of U.S. public interest in foreign policy in favor of domestic issues.[6] Apart from a small "attentive" segment of constituents, the mass public is often described as detached from, uninterested in, and poorly informed about foreign-policy decisions, except possibly with respect to international crises.[7] Moreover, it is less likely to focus on "complicated and more remote foreign policy issues," such as arms transfers, leaving such affairs in the hands of the experts (Small 1996:69).

Literature on the "NGO-ization" of politics, however, suggests that security issues can be popularized with the right strategies (Petrova 2007; Price 1998;

Rutherford 2000). For example, NGOs were able to engage public interest in a landmine ban by promoting a clear, simple campaign goal backed up by personal stories with humanitarian angles.[8] The resulting groundswell of public support helped pressure governments into accepting new norms of APL nonuse (Petrova 2007; Rutherford 2000). In the case of small arms control and the ATT, pro-control NGOs hoped that the success of the landmine treaty could be replicated. However, similar tactics have been difficult to apply to conventional weapons more broadly. Guns and other military equipment are discriminant by nature. They are also basic tools for police and military and in some states legally owned by private civilians, making a ban unwelcome. As a consequence, the issue and message alike with respect to conventional arms are more complex and divisive in some countries: to restrain arms transfers under specific conditions— not simply to ban them. Yet this also means that a campaign to promote "responsible" arms transfers has difficulty resonating with the public with the same ease as one about landmines (Brem and Rutherford 2001; O'Dwyer 2006).[9]

Interviews confirm the more cynical view of public opinion when it comes to arms export controls.[10] Government officials, NGO organizers, and industry representatives in all five cases believe that the public is uninterested and uninformed about arms transfers. Even in Germany, where public criticism of the arms trade is long established, the public does not have a sustained interest in arms transfer policies or activities. A bad image of the arms trade simply "does not express itself strongly."[11] People are often unaware of arms production, and the media typically finds the issue "too complex" to report on with regularity (interviews 11407255, 45207255).[12] Similarly, although peace is a broad rallying point in Flanders and the public attitude toward the arms trade is negative there (Flemish Peace Institute 2007c), actual interest in relevant policies is low, just as it is in Wallonia, where the public tends to see arms exports more positively.[13]

This trend is even more pronounced in the other cases. The UK public and media—despite a well-developed NGO culture—are typically uninterested in the arms trade.[14] In the United States, pro-control NGOs see the arms trade issue as "really a hard sell in general" (interviews 48207002, 50207002, 51207002).[15] Although polls find that 57 to 60 percent of Americans support international arms trade regulations,[16] it is a hot issue only among the NRA membership, opposed to such controls. Public opinion may therefore contribute to U.S. opposition, but it cannot explain U.S. support (see chapter 4). France, too, has signed on to new standards without any clear domestic incentives to do so. Government, NGO, and industry representatives report that the media and public remain uninterested in and unaware of the issue.[17] Moreover, NGOs have acquired the expertise and professionalization necessary to influence arms export policy making only since 2006 as a *result* of the ATT process at the UN, after France had announced its support (interviews 59108220, 60108220).

Indeed, in all of the cases, interviewees observed that public pressure is not responsible for recent policy developments; the public simply is not interested. As a result, domestic structure[18] is also less important for explaining states' policy choices. Scholars often point to domestic structure as the mediator between public preferences, the groups that represent and shape them, and government decision making (Checkel 1999; Risse-Kappen 1991, 1995a). Yet where public preferences are ambiguous, weak, or absent, characterizing the structure through which they would travel loses value. Thus, liberal structures such as the United Kingdom, where governments should be more constrained by society, are as little constrained on arms export policy as more statist structures, such as France, where the state can typically dictate the direction of policy more freely.

Democracies are never fully immune from domestic constraints, of course. Although governments have faced little domestic pressure on their arms export policies, they have become relatively more sensitive to the effect that the implementation of such policies can have on their domestic image. As I show next, transparency and pro-control NGO activity can lead governments to perceive a greater likelihood of scandal stemming from (certain) arms export deals. When arms exports that deeply violate domestic and international values are discovered and publicized, they can create public attention where none previously existed. In the face of scandal, governments attempt to preserve their domestic reputation and political position. They may therefore approach clearly objectionable arms deals with more caution in order to avoid scandal and its reputational costs.

TRANSPARENCY AND SCANDAL: DOMESTIC COSTS FOR NONCOMPLIANCE

As much as the public officials and civil society leaders interviewed agree that domestic publics lack the interest, coherence, and force to influence states' arms export policy choices, they also point without hesitation to one instance in which the public does pay attention. The unveiling of seemingly "irresponsible" or unscrupulous arms transfer deals sanctioned by the government against strongly held national values and international norms can spark scandal.[19] Scandals generate public attention and outrage. Their consequences can include a loss of government legitimacy and electoral retribution. When faced with heightened threat of scandal, governments are more likely to avoid those arms transfers likely to raise public ire, but they are sheltered from condemnation as long as their behavior can fly under the public radar.

Until the 1990s, arms trade scandals were almost nonexistent, and governments could regularly transfer arms without fear of public backlash. Informa- ·

tion about the arms trade was mostly hidden from public view, and civil society was largely unorganized to raise concerns. The point is not that scandal was impossible—after all, the United States had the Iran–Contra Affair—but that low-level transparency made these events incredibly rare and their threat minimal.[20] As transparency initiatives have increased available information, however, the arms trade has become more susceptible to public criticism. When criticism is widespread, organized, and linked to clearly stated national values and international commitments, it can damage a government's reputation. An active pro-control NGO community[21] can serve as a watchdog, expose "irresponsible" deals in the press, and frame certain transfers as violating human rights and other national values. Such groups have claimed a growing presence in politics in recent years as NGOs have found a place in UN policy making and prominent scandals have prompted domestic groups to organize around the issue. This combination of active pro-control NGOs and arms trade transparency creates structural conditions that make arms trade scandal more likely in domestic politics.

Figure 5.1 illustrates the importance of high levels of both arms trade transparency *and* domestic pro-control NGO activity for increasing governments' scandal sensitivity. Under these conditions, governments may perceive a greater likelihood of arms trade scandal and become relatively more cautious in their

Pro-control NGO community

		High activity	Low activity
Arms trade transparency	**High**	*High* scandal sensitivity (Belgium-Flanders, Germany, UK)	*Low* scandal sensitivity (France, U.S.)
	Low	*Low* scandal sensitivity (Brazil, South Africa)	*Low* scandal sensitivity (Belgium-Wallonia, Israel)

FIGURE 5.1. SCANDAL SENSITIVITY IN DOMESTIC POLITICS.

choice of arms export partners. Where arms trade scandals have already tarnished governments' reputation, this dynamic can be particularly potent. Scandals can prompt governments to improve transparency or NGOs to mobilize
around arms trade issues, in turn easing scrutiny of future export decisions.
Yet even where these conditions are present, only a small segment of cases
might actually be prone to scandal and prompt better government compliance. Arms deals to the most egregious human rights violators and severe
conflict zones may be best able to attract high-profile media attention and
public backlash if revealed. In this way, the public may have a limited but
powerful indirect effect on arms trade practice. However, in less clear-cut
cases or where these conditions are absent, public interest may remain dor-
mant, allowing government to pursue less "responsible" practices without
fearing reputational damage.

TRADITIONS OF SECRECY AND SILENCE IN THE ARMS TRADE

Before the 1990s, only the United States and Sweden regularly issued arms export reports, and other states feared losing customers if deals went public. With
the 1991 Gulf War, however, supplier states experienced firsthand the consequences of unchecked regional arms buildups and instituted the UN Register
of Conventional Arms. Some states passed additional transparency measures at
home in response to domestic fallout over secret arms sales to Iraq. The EU also
included an information-sharing component in its 1998 Code of Conduct in
response to NGO and EU Parliament lobbying to make such information public (M. Bromley 2012). Although unevenly executed overall,[22] reporting became
increasingly widespread among democracies especially and coincided with the
growth of transparency norms in world affairs.[23] Arms trade transparency has
since enhanced scandal sensitivity by providing information about government
practice, without which public accountability would be far more difficult.

Secrecy was long the rule in the United Kingdom, and not just for arms exports,[24] making scandal outbreak difficult. Information about the arms trade
was "hard to come by," and the trade was thus "undebated" (Phythian 2000b:80).
Before 1987, the United Kingdom did not maintain export-licensing statistics
even for its own internal usage (UK House of Commons 1991, debate on April
26). Moreover, there was "a time-honoured lack of specificity about the details
of individual defence export contracts, justified at least as much by reference to
commercial as to state secrecy" (Gummett 1999:115; see also Phythian 2000a).
This culture of secrecy dates back to the late 1800s but began to lose public
credibility in the 1980s (Ponting 1990; Vincent 1998). By 1992, with the exposure

of British defense exports to Iraq, it became a rallying cry for Labour's success-ful bid for power against Conservative secrecy and the wider "culture of sleaze" in the 1997 general elections. Annual public reports began in 2000 after the new government led the adoption of the 1998 EU Code of Conduct.

Belgium also maintained a tradition of arms trade secrecy. However, revela-tions about exports to Iran and Iraq in the 1980s led the Parliament to institute an annual arms export report in 1991 (Carlman 1998; Flemish Peace Institute 2006). Nevertheless, public information remained 'extremely succinct and con-fidential" (Mampaey 2003), and reports did not identify recipients until re-quired by the EU Code. Regional governments have been in charge of annual reports since 2003, when they took over arms export licensing. Flanders has of-fered more frequent and detailed information about its arms trade than man-dated by federal law (interviews 21407211, 24107211, 53207211). One expert stated that Flemish measures had progressed so that "the public knows more now than parliamentarians knew before" (interview 21407211). Wallonia adheres to federal transparency requirements, but reports can be more difficult to obtain (interviews 21407211, 2720721). A primary goal for Walloon groups is improved reporting to enable campaigning on specific cases or issues (interview 27207211). Increased transparency overall makes it possible for NGOs to react quickly to mobilize public opinion through the media on cases of problematic export deals in a way that was impossible before (interview 29207211).

Although France and Germany have contributed regularly to the UN Regis-ter since the 1990s, neither issued annual public reports until required by the EU. Their first reports appeared in 2000, covering transfers for 1998. Previously, Germany had "a very limited reporting process" and provided only aggregate arms export totals each year in accordance with its 1961 Weapons of War Con-trol and the Foreign Trade and Payments Acts (Chrobok 2004:47; see also Carl-man 1998).[25] The French state had also "discourag[ed] a sustained flow of pub-lic information" (Kolodziej 1987:280). Starting in 1983, the French government gathered information relating to arms sales but kept it classified and released only aggregate information to the Senate and National Assembly on a postex-port biannual basis. These reports also did not identify any specific recipient countries (Carlman 1998:14). French media and civil society did not attempt to fill the information gap on their own. Edward Kolodziej attributes their lack of activity in part to France's lack of a "well-established tradition of investigative reporting . . . and a well-developed network of independent security and arms control research centers" (1987:281). Moreover, unlike Germany, France has not been shy about its aggressive export policies, which have largely avoided domes-tic criticism and are linked to a broad foreign-policy consensus and a desire for an independent military policy (Boyer 1996; Kolodziej 1987). Relevant NGOs have emerged along with transparency measures only in recent years. In response, officials have become more concerned about the public image of the arms trade, as I show later in this chapter.

Of the cases at hand, only the United States has a history of arms trade transparency predating the 1990s, making it "the most notable exception to the prevailing pattern of secrecy" in the arms trade (Lumpe 1999b; see also Kemp and Miller 1979; Schroeder 2005). Transparency in major conventional arms transfers was already a point of public concern by the late 1970s, connected to the perceived unchecked use of arms sales as a tool of foreign policy (Kemp and Miller 1979; U.S. Senate 1979).[26] By the early 1990s, "the vast majority" of U.S. major conventional arms transfers were public (Goose and Smyth 1994:96). In 1996, the United States also began reporting disaggregated data about small arms transfers (Lumpe 1999b), making its policies in this regard an early model of openness (Schroeder 2005).

Yet even as national arms export reporting has spread since the 1990s, more information does not automatically lead to more accountability, as the U.S. case shows. The presence of an NGO community willing and able to call governments to task on their "irresponsible" exports is also necessary. NGOs seek out and comb through reports to spotlight questionable deals in the media and public. As the cases show, without *both* arms trade transparency and active pro-control NGOs to spotlight apparent government hypocrisy, scandal is possible but not feared. Together, they can increase governments' scandal sensitivity and drive them—in some cases—to be more selective about their export partners. A major scandal can also enhance a government's scandal sensitivity directly by teaching it firsthand the potential costs of scandal and indirectly by prompting legislative reform and NGO activity. The key point, as I demonstrate in the following sections, is that the anticipation of criticism and scandal can push governments to scrutinize and better justify arms export decisions that they anticipate might trigger public outcry if made known.

THE UNITED KINGDOM: SCANDAL AS INCENTIVE FOR LEADERSHIP

The British Arms to Iraq scandal broke in the wake of the 1991 Gulf War and helped the Labour government get elected in 1997, prompting policy changes and international policy leadership. New transparency measures, a commitment to "ethical" arms transfers, and a newfound role for NGOs in the policy-making process, have had consequences for British scandal sensitivity and arms export practice. These changes place the contemporary British case in the high-transparency-active NGO category, giving existing NGOs clear standards by which to judge government export behavior and more information by which to do so. The government, in turn, has become more concerned about its domestic reputation and arms exporter image, although for some critics at the expense of more substantive, far-reaching reform (Cooper 2006; Stavrianakis 2008, 2010).

ANATOMY OF A SCANDAL

The Arms to Iraq scandal tarnished the ruling Conservative Party's reputation and helped usher in a "totally different world" of arms export decision making (interview 32107200). In the late 1980s, British media did not widely consider clandestine arms sales to Iraq an issue worth pressing (Negrine 1997). Yet by 1996 the *Financial Times* had denounced the British arms trade as "a culture corrupted by the absence of checks and balances against the power of the executive and by an obsession with secrecy" (Stephens 1996). It was the Iraqi use of British weapons against British troops in the Gulf War that raised public ire and party politics that kept it going. The resulting scandal changed the terms of the arms trade debate and public expectations for government practice and contributed to the 1997 Labour victory and its commitments to government transparency and "ethical" arms transfers. These policy changes have left the government more sensitive to the threat of arms trade scandal, even as it seeks to support exports abroad and defense industry employment at home.

The illegal sale of British arms to Iraq during the 1980s initially appeared to be the sole responsibility of private firms. Published policy from 1985 clearly prohibited the transfer of any lethal equipment to Iraq (Cooper 1997; Leyland 2007). Throughout 1990 and 1991, officials claimed the policy had not been changed and denied the legal sale of arms to Iraq by British firms (UK House of Commons 1990, debate on December 3, and 1991, debates on January 31 and July 1). The blame instead fell—at first—on three executives from defense manufacturer Matrix Churchill, who went on trial in 1992. The trial collapsed, however, when former minister of trade Alan Clark testified that the government had known of the sales all along (Pilkington 1998; Tomkins 1998). He also admitted to counseling companies to "stress the civil applications of their equipment [in their license applications] even though they knew that it would be put to a military use" (B. Thompson 1997:2). From Clark's admission, it became clear both that the government had supplied arms to Iraq that were used against British troops and that it had made a "secret change of policy" on arms sales, which it kept from the Parliament and the public (House of Commons 1992, debate on November 10).

One day after Clark's testimony, Prime Minister John Major called for an independent investigation, to be run by Lord Justice Sir Richard Scott. According to Colin Pilkington, the investigation was "[t]he most severe test of government secrecy and ministerial accountability for many years" (1998:198–99), illuminating in excruciating detail hidden governmental practices. The government had reportedly not intended the investigation to take on such a broad scope (Norton-Taylor, Lloyd, and Cook 1996:31). Nevertheless, Scott's inquiry took three years, interviewed 276 witnesses, including Major and Thatcher, and reviewed two hundred thousand pages of official documents. Its findings, released in the 1996 Scott Report, stated that the government had purposefully and repeatedly "misled parliament in breach of ministerial accountability," prevented "crucial evidence about arms sales being revealed," and "collectively conceal[ed] government policy from parliament" (Pilkington 1998:201; see also Cooper 1997; B. Thompson 1997; Tomkins 1998).

The issue captured public attention and was followed closely by the news media. Why did the Scott inquiry resonate when the arms trade otherwise did not? Two reasons, unrelated to the exports themselves, are key. First, the inquiry simply made for "good entertainment" (B. Thompson 1997:1; Tomkins 1998). As Matthew Baum argues, scandals and trials can be "easily framed as compelling human dramas" and attract soft news media and consumers not ordinarily interested in politics or foreign policy (2002:91). The Scott inquiry contained "the ingredients of a good popular drama, spies, criminal trials and internecine squabbling amongst ministers and officials" (B. Thompson 1997:1). *Guardian* reporter Richard Norton-Taylor even cowrote a play based on the inquiry, which ran in London (Norton-Taylor and McGrath 1995).

Second, the "sleaze factor" came into its own with the Scott inquiry (Lee 1999; Phythian 2000b). For secrecy and hypocrisy to trounce accountability in a democracy was itself scandalous. Multiple sex scandals and minor arms trade scandals had plagued the Tory government, and Arms to Iraq was the biggest, spreading the blame to the party as a whole.[27] What was most clear to the electorate was "the hypocrisy and hint of double standards" (Pilkington 1998:184). Indeed, it was the issue of accountability on which most press reports focused.[28] Opinion polls showed that 87 percent of the public "thought ministers had misled Parliament, and 54% had done so deliberately," and more than 60 percent were in favor of ministerial resignations ("The Scott Report" 1996). It was felt that such illegal and secret trades were simply unacceptable behavior for a good democracy, a sentiment echoed in debates in the House of Commons and House of Lords (UK House of Commons 1996, debates on February 15, 19, 26).

The immediate political aftermath was surprisingly minimal given the uproar the scandal had caused. Analysts argue that the length of the report, combined with Scott's vague language, made it subject to spin on both sides (Negrine 1997; Pilkington 1998). The government gave itself eight days' advance access to read the 1,800-page report before the parliamentary debate on publication day, compared to three hours given to Parliament member Robin Cook as the Labour representative (Pilkington 1998:201; Norton-Taylor, Lloyd, and Cook 1996). The government survived a vote of confidence by one vote, and the Scott Report faded from public attention (Tomkins 1998:13). By the 1997 election, however, it returned. The public had begun to condemn "all government ministers as shifty" (Pilkington 1998:202; Vincent 1998). Labour itself "made much use of the Scott Report" (Lawler 2000:293), stressing themes of ethics and transparency as a part of its election strategy (Worcester and Mortimore 1999:71). In this sense, the scandal was the catalyst for policy change that, as I describe next, has made the government more sensitive to future scandal.

CONSEQUENCES FOR ARMS EXPORT DECISION MAKING

In the words of one official, "the Arms to Iraq scandal had a dramatic effect" on the new Labour government, even if the changes were not immediate or automatic (interview 41107200). Not only did Labour have "to contend with the same pressure against sleaze in the changed climate" after the Scott inquiry (Lee 1999:301), but it had also provided a baseline of commitments against which its own progress could be measured. Its promised reforms—to engage in an ethical arms trade, overhaul arms export legislation, and make transparent the processes of policy making in the arms trade and otherwise[29]—provided civil society with both the standards by which to judge its progress and the means to do so. Although these commitments were coupled with others to support defense exports and employment, they were a departure for British defense export policy, which earlier had not existed apart from "the longstanding objective of increasing the volume of sales of conventional weapons," with export decisions "made on an *ad hoc* and pragmatic assessment of changing, and often conflicted, British interests" (D. Miller 1996:360).

Labour had in essence "paint[ed] itself into a corner," requiring that it take action when it came to power (interview 37207200). Appointing longtime arms trade critic Robin Cook as foreign minister helped signal its commitment to the cause. It also took a highly visible leadership role on arms exports in multilateral fora and opened up export decision making to scrutiny by NGOs. These policy changes not only helped build the government's domestic and international reputation but also greatly increased its scandal sensitivity. Once shut out of policy making, NGOs—including Amnesty International, Oxfam, Saferworld, and others—were invited in.[30] Arms trade transparency also went from a limited practice at best to an extensive practice with an "unprecedented" level of detail and frequency (Gummett 1999:115), enabling new scrutiny of export practices.

The Labour government introduced a role for NGOs in policy making that the previous government had resisted. Several years before the 1997 elections, Labour had begun to work with pro-control NGOs on its foreign-policy agenda (interview 35207200). NGOs also provided some of the expertise needed to make criticisms of Conservative arms trade policy and practice during the Arms to Iraq affair (interview 37207200). The consequences of "cozying up" to NGOs while in opposition, however, meant that the postelection period became "payback time for NGOs" (interview 32107200). Groups continued to work with Labour, which opened up bureaucracies to their input as a matter of good public relations.[31] As one official stated, "It makes sense to take their opinions seriously" when NGO media access could mean potential embarrassment through reports and articles in the press (interviews 40107200, 41107200, 43107200; see also Grant 2000).[32]

Also as a result of the Scott inquiry and its findings, the Labour government began to lift "the veil of secrecy" hiding arms export decision making (Phythian 2000b:81; see also Gummett 1999; interviews 32107200 and 41107200). Publishing an annual report has made UK arms trade practice "subject to scrutiny," whatever the ruling party (interviews 41107200, 32107200). In the past, the "sweeping categories" used to fulfill UN reporting requirements effectively hid the substance of British practice from view and made criticism by Parliament or NGOs difficult (Gummett 1999; Tomkins 1998). In contrast, newer, more detailed reports show Parliament, the media, NGOs, and the public "the types of arms-related equipment provided by British companies to particular countries" and reveal where the problems lay (Gummett 1999:115).

Foreign Minister Cook presented the first annual report to the Select Committee on Foreign Affairs, stating, "We can all take satisfaction that Britain is now the most transparent of all the European countries in how we handle arms licences." He added that the reports should "enable Parliament, public, NGOs, to invigilate whether we are standing by [the new] criteria, making sure that we are not breaking those criteria" (Cook 1999, testimony on November 3). Parliamentarians and activists took him up on it. Questions on arms transfers to Indonesia, Pakistan, China, Zimbabwe, and other locations arose immediately (Lawler 2000).[33] In its first report, moreover, the administration listed some "questionable shipments" to Sierra Leone during its first eight months in office (Lawler 2000:292). Cook and the administration were tainted by the subsequent Arms to Africa affair, which taught them early on that NGO involvement and transparency may not only serve their domestic reputation but also harm it. More recently, in 2012, a report from the All-Party Parliamentary Group on International Corporate Responsibility critiqued government export credits, including arms deals to Saudi Arabia and Zimbabwe.[34]

Party image and reelection are major concerns for politicians, and the British are no exception. What changed in the United Kingdom was not these concerns, but the ease with which a party's reputation could be damaged. Labour also sought to promote arms exports, but with the growth of transparency and NGO activity, officials "seem genuinely worried" about the potential consequences (interview 35207200). Amnesty and Oxfam in particular "can mobilize significant constituencies," and Labour might easily lose support from voters important to it (interview 35207200). NGOs have adapted their strategies by seeking to get the media interested and asking questions to build public attention to certain cases (interviews 32107200, 33207200). The arms trade "doesn't become an issue until you get headlines," and scandals "raise [its] profile."[35] Simply stated, "Ministers care about what gets on the front page" (interview 35207200). With NGOs watching and waiting, the government became more keenly aware of the public-relations problems that "irresponsible" arms exports can create and claimed a more restrictive approach to its arms trade practices. The Tory-led Cameron government has continued the United Kingdom's public commitment to "responsible" arms exports. Moreover, its rapid decision to revoke licenses to North Africa and the Middle East in light of the Arab Spring suggests concern for how arms exports to a repressive region in the public spotlight will be received (Saferworld 2011).

GERMANY: HIGH SENSITIVITY AND ACTIVE CIVIL SOCIETY

The German case highlights a longtime public commitment to restrictive arms export practices that has been called to account more reliably in recent years as NGOs have gained access to government arms export reports. Since World War II, Germany has been extremely sensitive to arms trade scandals and has experienced public backlash in response to some of its export decisions. As transparency measures have grown to accompany an established and active NGO community, the German government continues to be a relatively more scandal-sensitive case. Yet in recent years it has also occasionally sought—in "a wide break from the German foreign policy consensus" with widely unpopular results—to use weapons supplies to counteract growing demands for German troops abroad, demands that sit uncomfortably with its civilian power identity (von Hammerstein et al. 2012:21).

THE HISTORICAL CONTEXT

Germany's arms transfers have been powerfully shaped by World War II (Davis 2002; Pearson 1986; Wulf 1996). As the federal minister for economics stated, "The uncontrolled proliferation of weapons, as well as industrial goods and knowledge with the weapons can be produced, leads to a grave danger to the peaceful co-existence of people. In this knowledge, and also on the basis of Germany's historical experience, the Federal Government feels a special responsibility for a restrictive Arms Export Policy" (German Minister for Economics 1993:1).

The arms industry was closely affiliated with Hitler and the Third Reich, becoming a symbol of militarism from which postwar Germany sought to distance itself. Over the years, domestic opposition to arms transfers has been strong (Brzoska 1989; Davis 2002; Pearson 1986).[36] Governments have responded to this political unease by prohibiting arms deliveries to "areas of tension" in 1965 and abandoning all major military aid programs by the end of the 1960s (Davis 2002:156; see also Cowen 1986). Officials have also avoided the appearance of using arms transfers as a foreign-policy tool and, unlike most other major arms producers, have declined to promote arms sales abroad (Davis 2002; Pearson 1986). Laws have been designed to "achieve the benefits [of arms transfers] without the stigma" and to avoid the embarrassment of approving problematic export requests (Pearson 1986:532, 533). Politically sensitive arms export requests are adjudicated not by bureaucrats in the Federal Office for Economics and Export Controls (Bundesamt für Wirtschaft und Ausfuhrkontrolle) but instead handed up to an interagency commission.

In 1980, pending arms deals to Saudi Arabia and Chile initiated a public debate over specific decision-making criteria. As Regina Cowen observes, "Governmental disengagement and the consequential divorce of arms exports from foreign policy [had] greatly encouraged the commercialization of arms transfers," leading to serious concerns about a "credibility gap" between arms export law and practice (1986:269). Yet the debate was not about loosening restrictions; indeed, there was broad consensus to maintain a restrictive stance. Rather, it focused on how to better define existing political rules and organize the decision-making structure (Cowen 1986:269).[37] Following the adoption of export guidelines in 1982, the proposed deals to Saudi Arabia and Chile were denied (Cowen 1986:270). The public has also made clear over time its disapproval of specific arms deals, including to Indonesia, Saudi Arabia, Turkey, and Israel.

Public attention has both generated and been sustained by an NGO community that pushes arms export restraint, which "has been an important issue of morality and political culture for a wide variety of groups and institutions" (Davis 2002:160; see also Brzoska 1989). Amnesty Deutschland, Oxfam, peace research institutes, religious groups coordinated through the Joint Conference Church and Development (Gemeinsame Konferenz Kirche und Entwicklung), labor organizations, and the Berlin Information-Center for Transatlantic Security have all taken an active interest in the arms trade. In recent years, small arms NGOs have gathered monthly with relevant government bureaucracies to discuss developments in small arms and other conventional arms control policy (interview 14107255). New transparency measures since 2000 have made government decision making more public. Thus, although the German public—like the public elsewhere—is typically focused on internal issues,[38] it has also demonstrated a continued discomfort with arms exports in the context of international peace and its own postwar identity.[39] Controversy across the political spectrum over Chancellor Angela Merkel's more liberal arms export practices in recent years further illustrates the broad public consensus over arms export restraint. Merkel knows that arms exports are unpopular among voters, especially "if authoritarian regimes like Saudi Arabia secure their power with German weapons" (von Hammerstein et al. 2012:25). With Afghanistan still fresh in everyone's mind, she has nevertheless risked paying the social costs, hoping to avoid even more unpopular decisions down the road to send troops into conflicts overseas.

CONSEQUENCES FOR ARMS EXPORT DECISION MAKING

German press and civil society groups had begun to pay careful attention to arms export practices even before official reporting began in 2000.[40] Otfried Nassauer and Christopher Steinmetz observe, "Heated discussions regularly ensue on the political and moral acceptability of shipping tanks, rockets, submarines, or personnel carriers abroad" (2005:1). Such discussions, however, have not meant that the government has exported only to controversy-free destinations. Rather, it has simply sought to avoid the public *appearance* of irresponsible arms transfers to avoid reputational costs at home. First, it has used coproduction arrangements to bypass more stringent domestic restrictions, suppress arms export tallies, and avert public condemnation for certain deals (Brzoska 1989; interview 11407255). For example, coproduction arrangements allowed German antitank missile exports to Syria from France in the 1970s and the export of German missiles to Taiwan from the United States in the early 1990s (Peel 1993).[41] Second, decision makers have a "declared preference [for] sales to NATO [North Atlantic Treaty Organization] countries," which face lower restrictions in German law and generally do not present strong human rights concerns (Davis 2002:157). However, with the exception of Turkey, as I explain shortly, NATO exports are also not controversial among the public, which values alliance cooperation.

NGOs—especially with improvements in arms trade transparency—keep a watchful eye on the government's export decisions. Officials are keenly aware of the potential for scandal as they adjudicate export requests (interviews 14107255, 58107255). Governments have gotten into the most trouble over export decisions where the legalistic approach has insufficiently reflected national values.[42] For example, although human rights was not a criterion for refusing arms transfers until 2000, already in 1993 the Kohl government came under fire for exporting used East German ships to Indonesia because of violations in East Timor (Peel 1993).[43] By 2003, Germany no longer permitted arms transfers to Indonesia, and weapons once supplied by German companies came instead from Turkey and Pakistan through licensed production (Kleine-Brockhoff and Kurniawati 2003).

Arms transfers to Turkey have been a particularly sensitive subject, pitting support for human rights against support for NATO.[44] Yet although German export law and practice privilege NATO allies, Parliament embargoed Turkey in November 1991 in response to human rights violations against the Kurds (Davis 2002; Kinzer 1992). The Christian Democratic Union (CDU, Christlich Demokratische Union Deutschlands) government—apparently without top officials' knowledge—attempted to reconcile its problem by covertly supplying fifteen tanks to the Turkish government. The strategy backfired. In March 1992, Turkish forces attacked Kurdish areas with what witnesses reported to be German-made tanks. The Panzeraffäre spread, Defense Minister Gerhard Stoltenberg claiming that his officials had supplied the tanks without his knowledge. With state elections scheduled for early April, the Social Democratic Party (SPD, Sozialdemokratische Partei Deutschlands) highlighted the scandal in its campaign, even naming as an arms trafficker rival CDU candidate who was a former Defense Ministry aide (Kinzer 1992).[45]

Fearful that damage to the government's image would worsen despite its postreunification popularity, Stoltenberg dismissed senior aide Wolfgang Ruppelt in hopes of ending the affair (M. Fisher 1992; Kinzer 1992; "Unter dem Druck" 1992). This tactic also failed. Calls for a sign of responsibility at the top grew, and Stoltenberg finally gave in to public pressure and resigned.[46] The Süddeutsche Zeitung, the major newspaper in the CDU stronghold of Bavaria, declared that "the illegal tank delivery to Turkey has now conclusively ended the political career of the minister"—a man once considered a possible future chancellor ("Kritik an Stoltenberg" 1992). Chancellor Helmut Kohl and the press alike declared Stoltenberg's duty to resign, whether he had known the illicit transfers had taken place or not (Casdorff 1992). In turn, the affair left that generation of CDU leaders acutely aware—by firsthand experience—of the high costs to be paid for politically unpopular arms transfers.

Arms exports to Turkey have since been treated with a greater degree of caution for fear of political backlash (interview 45207255). The CDU government installed another embargo against Turkey in April 1994 just prior to elections (Davis 2002; Sariibrahimoglu 1992) and denied transfers in 1999 in response to civil society pressure (interviews 18207255, 19407255, 45207255). In 2003, the SPD government declined a tank order to prevent its coalition with the Greens from collapsing. Tank exports specifically became much more difficult because of the use of tanks in Turkey's human rights violations, despite the importance of the land armament vehicle sector for the German defense industry. Other defense goods, such as ships and submarines, pass through the export decision-making process with greater ease and less political concern (Mulholland 2003).

NGO and media criticism of numerous arms transfers since the mid-1990s have stopped some noncompliant sales from going forward to prevent further public backlash—but, as the 2011 Saudi Arabian tank deal showed, certainly not all. The public becomes more attentive when a deal explodes in the press and becomes a scandal with political liability.[47] It was difficult to cultivate sustained improvements in government practice in the 1990s without transparency (interview 11407255), but, according to one NGO representative, new transparency measures since 2000 have enabled a central mobilizing strategy targeting the government's policy–practice gap: "The biggest difficulty is being heard. With scandals, [public] interest picks up; you need examples to awaken interest. The easiest way to act is to look at the export report and use what's already public. We criticize in relation to political guidelines, the law the government sets out for itself, and its obligations" (interview 17207255).

High-profile conflicts and severe human rights abuses serve as potential scandal material for organizations scrutinizing export reports. Industry analysts note, for example, that the government would be unlikely to grant export licenses to China even if the EU arms embargo were lifted, "as human rights issues there would raise too much opposition" (Mulholland 2005:22). In 2002, after pressure from NGOs in the press, the government denied small arms exports to Nepal. Prior to the decision, Amnesty and other groups noted that Nepal was embroiled in internal conflict and engaged in massive human rights violations. Approving the license would therefore be a clear violation of German export law and policy (Deutsche Gewehre 2002). The government listened, and NGOs counted it a victory (interview 17207255)—but not one easily repeated elsewhere, as the Belgian case demonstrates.

More recently, however, the Merkel government has pushed the boundaries of acceptable arms export practice in Germany, facing widespread public backlash for secret deals exposed and denied. In 2011, officials publicly denied making a deal to sell 270 Leopard tanks to Saudi Arabia after press reports of a similar deal leaked earlier in the year drew protests and outcries of scandal ("Saudi-Arabien" 2011). Similar deals were delayed in response but in some cases have since been approved. In 2014, reports surfaced that divisions within the government over sending battle tanks to Saudi Arabia may have stalled or ended the deal altogether (Agence France Presse 2014). Despite multilateral commitments and domestic anger, Merkel has sought to implement dramatic changes not just in German arms export practice but also in national arms export policy. For Merkel, the perceived failures of Afghanistan loom larger than arms trade scandal, prompting weapons sales to regions of potential conflict so that those countries can use them instead of German soldiers to maintain peace and stability down the road (von Hammerstein et al. 2012:25). She has conceded to providing the Bundestag more information sooner on new deals but has rejected calls for a new arms trade supervisory body.

Concern for national and international norms is expected for Germany with its civilian-power-based foreign policy.[48] Clearly, however, government restraint in arms export behavior is not simply self-motivated, rooted in identity and deeply embedded normative commitments. CDU and SPD governments alike have pursued arms transfers contrary to stated national values, only sometimes pulling the plug due to public backlash. The pressure of public accountability and the fear of the high costs of scandal have thus motivated some compliance. But it also shows that perceived political expediency may come at the expense of arms export restraint, especially when the various demands of civilian power clash with each other and political power is not credibly threatened.

FRANCE: LOW SENSITIVITY WITHOUT NGOS

France has taken a place in the high-transparency-active NGO community category only since 2006. French NGOs began to organize around the arms trade issue in 1998 in response to revelations about French arms deals to Rwanda in the early 1990s. Scandal was a catalyst not for government policy reform but for emerging NGO activity. However, NGOs were unable to mount sustained lobbying and mobilization efforts until after the ATT process got under way at the UN. Transparency, too, was poor until new measures were adopted in 2000 in response to the EU Code of Conduct. The threat of scandal therefore remained low in the eyes of the government, while new NGOs struggled to engage on the issue, and transparency was lacking.

THE RWANDA AFFAIR

France has long pursued aggressive arms transfer practices with little public criticism. Without NGOs to push the issue, the media have maintained a largely apolitical stance. Even in cases of would-be scandals, they have refrained from probing too deeply to gather information or expose evidence. This is not for lack of potential material. France has often received criticism from outside its borders for its arms export deals. It has an active arms trade with Francophone Africa, has transferred large volumes of defense materials to Iran and

Iraq during the 1980s, and has liberally interpreted the EU arms embargo to China. As a result, the case demonstrates not only the difficulty of inciting arms trade accountability but also, with the Rwanda Affair, the transformative role scandal can play in mobilizing NGO interest in the arms trade.

During the Cold War, even severe violations of national law had difficulty creating any traction for arms trade scandal. For example, in November 1987 reports surfaced that despite an arms embargo France sent $120 million of arms to Iran from 1983 to 1986 (Gaetner 1987; Greenhouse 1987; Pontaut 1987). A secret Ministry of Defense (Ministère de la Défense) follow-up to the 1985 l'Affaire Luchaire (named after the arms manufacturer responsible for the sales and initially believed to have acted without government knowledge) suggested that the deals had taken place with the tacit approval of top officials in the Socialist government.[49] By some accounts, moreover, kickbacks of 3 to 5 percent had landed in Socialist Party coffers. The news was leaked to pro-right magazines by the then prime minister Jacques Chirac, who was lagging badly behind François Mitterrand in the polls in the lead-up to the 1988 presidential elections (Greenhouse 1987; Webster 1987a).

Yet despite the ingredients for a good scandal—seemingly corrupt high-ranking politicians, secret embargo-busting shipments to a country affiliated with terrorist attacks and hostage holders, an official denial, and an upcoming election— the affair soon died without causing political damage or affecting the public arms trade discourse. The reasons highlight both the lack of sustained public interest and the lack of nonstate actors capable of instigating sustained public interest. It was unclear the degree to which Mitterrand himself could be touched by the accusations, and the corruption charges were a relatively nonprovocative issue among voters (Hoagland 1987; Jacobson 1987b; "That Damned Elusive Mitterrand" 1987). The public was overwhelmed by a plethora of scandals amid the preelection "scandal wars" (Webster 1987b), which lessened the impact of the news and reinforced the cynicism with which voters had begun to view all politicians (Jacobson 1987a; Markham 1987a). The public also did not appear shocked by the developments. Arms exports were not often publicly questioned. For many, defense policy was simply "sacred ground and out of bounds" (Webster 1987a). And without the presence of NGOs, the apparent indifference of the media and public—a silence both pervasive and deliberate, according to Jean-Paul Gouteux (1998:230)—could go uncontested.

Most importantly, the ministry report emerged in the middle of a recession, when economics issues trumped all others among the electorate and was already a key driving force behind the French arms trade ("That Damned Elusive Mitterrand" 1987). The report clearly "establishe[d] that the Socialists' decision to overlook these exports grew out of official concern that nearly 1,000 jobs would have been otherwise lost in the factories run by the Luchaire company"

(Hoagland 1987; see also Markham 1987b). Instead of violating French values, the deals were seen as *confirming* them—medicine for an ailing industry important to employment and economic well-being (Webster 1988). The issue was for many not a matter of morality and irresponsible exports but rather effective policy making by whoever was responsible within the government (Echikson 1987).

After the Cold War, the possibility for critical media attention seemed to have emerged in reports of French arms transfers to Rwanda. Yet the absence of an active NGO culture[50] initially left calls of foul play to sources outside France. France was a major supplier of arms to Rwanda after the start of the 1990 war and the 1993 Arusha Accords.[51] Arms flows and training were (and still are) key parts of French military cooperation in Africa, and French military relations with Rwanda dated back to 1975. This was no secret—France treated Rwanda like its former African colonies. The key questions were whether France shared in responsibility for the 1994 genocide and whether it had violated the May 1994 UN arms embargo.

France only acknowledged deliveries from 1990 to April 1994, when the massacres started. In 1994 and 1995, however, foreign NGOs released evidence in the international media accusing France of sending arms to Rwanda after it knew of the genocide and after the UN arms embargo was imposed (Austin 1995; HRW 1994). The big media splash came from a 1995 BBC report including testimony that France "had delivered munitions to the FAR [Forces armées rwandaises (Armed Forces of Rwanda)] when the genocide had already been underway two days" (McNulty 2000:115). Belgian journalist Colette Braeckman found further evidence of a May 1994 arms deal (1994:116). An HRW report (Austin 1995) claimed that French arms shipments after May 1994 were simply diverted through Zaire.

The weapons were said to have "expanded the conflict," "facilitated violations of international law[,] . . . and increased human rights abuses" (Goose and Smyth 1994:90). Although machetes were the weapons of choice, small arms were also instrumental in rounding people up for easier and more efficient mass killings (Goose and Smyth 1994; Verwimp 2006). Although the French media briefly reported the government's alleged "complicity in the genocide" (Callamard 1999:157), both the media and government were largely unresponsive to external pressures. Without NGOs inside France to sustain domestic criticism, what might have had devastating political consequences elsewhere died down with little significance in French politics.

It took another four years to initiate an official inquiry into the events. In 1998, *Le Figaro* broke with tradition and accused the government of supplying the missiles used to shoot down Rwandan president Juvénal Habyarimana's airplane, alleging that it had continued arms shipments into the summer of 1994 (Burns 1998; "France Denies" 1998).[52] The government claimed that all shipments were halted on April 8, more than a month before the embargo. Yet in a rare turn of events media criticism was heavy enough and public sensitivity to genocide strong enough (La Balme 2000:274) that the government appointed its first-ever parliamentary commission to look into French overseas military activity. With global humanitarianism and the birthplace for human rights central to French identity (McNulty 2000:105; Tinsley 2004), complicity in the genocide seemed a fundamental violation of French national values.

The Quilès Commission was groundbreaking. African policy "was traditionally an area shrouded in mystery and run from the president's office" (Melvern 2000:233). However, the commission's report was not similarly novel.[53] It declined to make any conclusions related to arms trade practices and absolved France of any responsibility for the killings, despite some errors in judgment (Whitney 1998). The source of the weapons also went unaddressed (McNulty 2000). In fact, the report eschewed the arms issue altogether. Rather than being an exercise in transparency and accountability, it simply "repeated rumour, speculation and intrigue and to date the most basic facts have still to be established" (Melvern 2000:234).

Once again French policy traditions and the dearth of organized civil society combined to prevent a scandal from imposing damaging consequences on politicians.[54] First, because the investigation did not offer conclusions on the arms trade, the issue remained shrouded in secrecy and essentially dropped away with no one to revive it. Relevant NGOs were new and weak—formed in response to the affair (McNulty 2000:106)—and had not been integrated into domestic discourse. The press remained reluctant to push the government too far. And although public attitudes toward humanitarianism had become more pronounced in the midst of the 1997 landmine campaign, l'Affaire du Rwanda resulted in no direct repercussions for the government.

Second, France's Africa policy gave considerable discretion to the executive and shielded it from domestic criticism (Kroslak 2007). France treated Rwanda as if it were a French colony and maintained close relations with its government (Callamard 1999; Klinghoffer 1998; Melvern 2000). The support seemed natural: the Hutu had "had a social revolution, constituted the majority, and Habyarimana, like one of the leaders of the French revolution, would eventually emerge as the strong man of the democratization process" (Callamard 1999:173).[55] France also wanted to ensure that Rwanda stayed within "the Francophone fold," a key policy concern since 1990 (Klinghoffer 1998:86; see also Callamard 1999; Kroslak 2007). The institutionalized relations and dependence of Francophonie was perceived as a cornerstone of France's continued global *grandeur* and advancement of global interests (Gregory 2000; Kroslak 2007). Thus, although misjudgments may have been perceived, France's overall policy did not diverge from accepted practices.[56]

CONSEQUENCES FOR ARMS EXPORT DECISION MAKING

The Rwanda Affair did not have any direct consequences for French arms trade practices, nor did it inspire legislative reform. Significantly, it did spark civil society organization on the arms trade.[57] However, NGOs remained weak until 2006, stopping policy makers short of developing a heightened sense of scandal sensitivity and leaving media a passive actor. Although a new discourse of "responsibility" arrived in French politics as a result of events in the 1990s (Roussel 2002), it remains to be seen how fully it will translate to arms exports. The nascent NGO community born of the Rwanda Affair has become more professionalized since the 2006 ATT process, opening up new avenues for accountability to regional and international norms and agreements. Greater transparency, too, has come about due to international commitments.

Minor scandals since 2000 have so far lacked the teeth to encourage serious reform. "Angolagate"—in which government officials were charged with trafficking Soviet-made weapons to Angola during the 1990s—resulted in the arrest of Mitterrand's son and former Africa adviser Jean-Christophe Mitterrand in 2000 (Gee 2000; Henley 2001). In 2004, he was found guilty, fined, and given a suspended jail sentence. In 2009, Interior Minister Charles Pasqua was also convicted of corruption charges, responding with, as one report put it, a call "for an end to the official secrecy act on documents concerning arms sales" (Hollinger 2009). The arrests and initial trials appeared to mark a change in French responses to arms trade scandal and a somewhat more aggressive media with a lower public toleration for corruption (Bell 2001; interview 60108220). However, an appeals court acquitted Pasqua on all charges in 2011 and cleared other defendants of arms-trafficking charges, leaving the impression that perhaps the French justice system was not so concerned with arms sales after all (Thréard 2011).

Although one official claims that "in a democracy, regardless of whether there are strong NGOs, everyone is afraid of what can be said" (interview 59108220), France's reputational concerns began to appear only with the professionalization of the NGO community since 2006. Officials now express image concerns connected to France's arms trade and increasingly fear the negative public attention arms trade scandals generate (interview 59108220). Arms export decision makers are careful to keep detailed records, showing exactly what has been transferred and that each transfer is within the law: "You have to leave things crystal clear for years down the road when they could be questioned" (interview 59108220). Officials also take care to note what they see as the highly restrictive nature of French arms export law. They add that France has largely ceased to export small arms to Africa because of the political risk (interviews 59108220, 60108220). These developments suggest a growing sense of responsibility and an interest in relatively more restrictive sales in response to reputational concerns.

In addition, the government has begun to engage with NGOs, noting that the NGO culture has transformed radically in recent years (interviews 59108220, 60108220). Indeed, the government's receptiveness to parliamentary, public, and civil society input "is brand new, and not just an issue for weapons" (interview 64208220). NGOs agree that their relations with the government have improved in recent years and that they too are more competent in their arms export control advocacy (interviews 61208220, 62208220, 64208220). Nevertheless, they are still finding their way in relatively new territory. Government reports are frequently released too late to impact policy substantively (interview 61208220). Moreover, arms export control advocacy has often been an issue tacked on to existing organizations whose resources and main concerns are devoted elsewhere (interviews 62208220, 64208220). It is perhaps too early to tell, therefore, how well NGOs will really be able to affect French arms export practice.

Even so, existing levels of transparency have aided civil society's transformation by giving NGOs information with which to criticize the government (interview 61208220). Yet accountability in France lags behind that in the other European cases. NGOs are still transforming from reactive to proactive, and although some past deals have been questioned, the government has yet to be critiqued on contemporary decisions. With claims that France had helped to arm Chad at the beginning of its February 2008 civil war (interview 61208220) and questions about arms exports in the context of the Arab Spring, opportunities have emerged for arms control advocates to assert their political perspective. If they do, it could have far-reaching consequences for French arms trade practices.

THE UNITED STATES: LOW SCANDAL SENSITIVITY

Despite high arms trade transparency since the late 1970s and a large-scale, global arms trade, the United States has suffered little domestic criticism of its arms transfer practices. As Susan Waltz observes, there is a distinct gap between its "principled policy" calling for restraint in arms transfers and its actions that "do not easily fit within the bounds of the policy that is publicly promoted and lauded" (2007:3, 4). Yet successive governments have remained relatively impervious to scandal. The cause, I argue, has to do primarily with the absence of a pro-control NGO community with an active voice in American politics.

GOOD LAWS, BAD PEOPLE?

The United States has a record of steady arms exports—small arms especially—to human rights violators and conflict zones in the Middle East, Africa, the former Soviet Union, and Asia. Reports of transfers to Indonesia, Sierra Leone, Nepal, Iraq, and others have had dire political consequences for governments elsewhere but have raised little commotion in the United States. As in France, this lack of notice is largely due to the absence of an active pro-control NGO community, which reinforces—and is reinforced by—the lack of public interest in the issue. As a result, arms exports maintain a low profile in the United States, and government scandal sensitivity remains minimal.

The Iran–Contra Affair of the 1980s might appear to be the one exception. It started as two separate scandals about covert U.S. arms transfers to Iran and Nicaragua. The first broke in October 1986, when Nicaraguan Sandinistas shot down a U.S. cargo plane and broadcast the existence of a U.S. military resupply chain for the Contras, which was seen as a clear violation of U.S. law and detrimental to the image of the U.S. government. With the Boland Amendments in 1982 and 1984, the Reagan administration had been legally prohibited from assisting the Contras through military aid.[58] The second scandal broke a month later with reports in a Lebanese magazine, picked up by the U.S. press, of U.S. arms sales to Iran. Despite the U.S. arms embargo and Reagan's policy of not negotiating with terrorists, it appeared as though the White House had traded arms for hostages. The president claimed that the sales had been intended primarily to normalize relations with Iran, not to release hostages (Walsh 1997:10). However, the shock the public felt at "the revelation that the administration had been saying one thing publicly and doing the opposite clandestinely" dragged the news into the media spotlight and formed the heart of the scandal (Draper 1991:470; Trager 1988).

But in late November 1986, the administration's admission that the two scandals were in fact intimately related immediately overshadowed both (Cohen and Mitchell 1988; Walsh 1997).[59] The larger scandal involved the diversion of funds from the arms sales to the Contras. Although the affair damaged Reagan's domestic reputation, it did not lead to public backlash against U.S. arms sales. In fact, it had little if any perceptible effect on U.S. arms transfer policy or practice. Instead, it became preoccupied with questions of who knew about the diversion of funds and whether, as in Watergate, the corruption reached all the way up to the president (Draper 1991:497; Wroe 1991). Indeed, Iran–Contra coverage was so strongly shaped by Watergate and its focus on what the president knew and when that it left the arms sales issue on the sidelines (R. Busby 1999; Kornbluh and Byrne 1993; Trager 1988).

Although Americans conceded that laws had been broken and policies ignored, many supported the anti-Communist goals behind the arms sales. Oliver North—the scapegoat and hero of the affair—won over the public with his appearance of patriotic virtue during congressional hearings (Walsh 1997; Wroe 1991). He invoked reminders of "America's own struggle in the War of Independence," blamed Congress for not supporting the Nicaraguan "freedom fighters," and painted the arms supplies as a necessary and just policy (qtd. in Wroe 1991:68; see also Walsh 1997). Like the French Luchaire Affair in a sense, defendants of the Reagan administration saw its policies and practices as broadly in line with and justified by U.S. interests and U.S. values.

In the end, Iran–Contra "was left as a scandal whose natural constitutional denouement—the fall of the man at the top—had never happened, and whose true nature would possibly never be known" (Wroe 1991:iv). Its focus on Reagan's culpability, which it was unable to establish with any certainty, severely limited its consequences for arms trade policy—or for the national security apparatus in general (Koh 1990; Kornbluh and Byrne 1993). This was not a foregone conclusion: Reagan's approval ratings crashed with revelations of his administration's illicit activities, and many—including White House advisers and the media—thought the affair could topple his presidency (Thelen 1996; Walsh 1997). At the time, Iran–Contra was seen as damaging the president's reputation, revealing his vulnerabilities, undermining his ability to lead, and possibly exposing him to impeachment.[60]

But answers to the question "What did the President know and when?" were elusive (Wroe 1991:iv; see also Cohen and Mitchell 1988; Kornbluh and Byrne 1993). Extensive document shredding and questions about Reagan's memory prevented a resolution. Many doubted his ignorance: the issues were centerpieces of his policy agenda on which he received daily briefings, and "the diversion was no fringe detail" to keeping them alive (Walsh 1997:24; see also Kornbluh and Byrne 1993). However, as Harold Koh states, "The Iran–Contra committees' inability to find a smoking gun damning the president effectively mooted the impeachment question, leading several members to act as if their inquiry were exhausted" (1990:19). The public, too, seemed to want the issue to drop. In the long run, Reagan remained personally popular, and no one wanted to deal with the aftermath of another Watergate (R. Busby 1999; Cohen and Mitchell 1988; Walsh 1997). It was only in 2011 that the 1991 reports by prosecutor Christian Mixter were made public, revealing that although Mixter had found that Reagan had been briefed on the weapons shipments, neither Reagan nor Vice President George H. W. Bush was criminally liable (Associated Press 2011).[61]

Iran–Contra was instead generally blamed on "bad people" not "bad laws" (Koh 1990:2). Admiral John Poindexter, deputy national-security adviser, and North, his aid, were fired and prosecuted (and then pardoned in 1992), but reforms were not forthcoming. Unlike other cases, scandal did not ignite fear of public reaction to other "deceitful" arms transfers.[62] Indeed, Iran–Contra demonstrates that scandal does not guarantee governments' sensitivity to future scandal, especially when its effects are dependent on assigning blame to a single leader. Scandal sensitivity is heightened when scandal encourages institutionalized policy reforms and the emergence of NGOs seeking to hold governments more accountable to its policy commitments. The pairing of transparency and organized civil society is at the core of enhancing the domestic threat of scandal. Lacking an active pro-control NGO community and evidence linking "irresponsible" exports to the top, U.S. administrations have been able to proceed largely without regard to public retribution when it comes to their arms transfer practices.

ANOTHER CASE OF U.S. EXCEPTIONALISM?

Aside from illustrating the lack of credible threat for scandal resulting from "irresponsible" export deals, the U.S. case also makes clear the need to distinguish between pro-control and pro-gun NGOs. The United States does in fact have a well-resourced, high-profile NGO community involved in the arms issue. However, these groups, in contrast to groups concerned about the issue elsewhere, are strongly opposed to multilateral export controls (see chapter 4). The NRA, "by far the largest and most influential of groups opposing gun-control legislation" (Finch 1983:26), represents the "active" contingent of the U.S. public on this issue. Its focus on civilian ownership rights makes it largely uninterested in export accountability. Instead, its work on the arms trade has focused on U.S. foreign policy and on rousing its constituents to stave off international standards it believes might undermine the Second Amendment, not raising public ire about U.S. export practices.[63]

It is not unusual for a country to lack active arms trade NGOs. What makes the U.S. case exceptional is its strong pro-gun NGO community with its active constituency, which has the ear of policy makers and has overwhelmed smaller pro-control groups[64] from mobilizing a broader (and less interested) public. In contrast, European gun organizations consider themselves observers of and not participants in the political process. Although U.S. pro-control groups have lobbied Congress and the administration on some laws and export cases (interviews 48207002, 50207002, 51207002), they have insufficient means or will to generate the public interest needed to press for export accountability (interviews 48207002, 50207002). Congress, moreover, is "relatively uninformed about the impact of small arms proliferation and . . . tend[s] to be overly cautious and deferential to pro-gun perspectives and views" (Stohl and Hogendoorn 2010:38).

During the George W. Bush administration especially, pro-control groups felt that the arms trade was an issue that was "not going to have a lot of successes" and placed it lower on their agendas as a result (interviews 48207002, 50207002, 51207002). Yet even under the Obama administration, pro-control NGOs have been slow to engage in advocacy at home, focusing their limited resources on shaping the U.S. role in UN processes. Moreover the NRA has been active in communicating to Congress its opposition to those processes, pushing to prevent ATT ratification.

Iran–Contra has not been followed by other arms trade scandals, and decision makers have not been pushed to change arms export practice, which is seen as vital to support allies in the Middle East and Central Asia. In 2012, the Obama administration resumed deliveries to Bahrain after Congress briefly suspended a deal over Bahrain's crackdown on protesters and American NGOs. Arms sales to Persian Gulf states have increased dramatically in recent years with otherwise little reaction from Congress or the public. As in the Cold War, the public has accepted arms exports justified by national-security arguments. In the long term, the consequences of low NGO activity may therefore reach further than case-by-case accountability. NGO campaigns can help shift public values and interest. As Rachel Stohl and E. J. Hogendoorn observe, "The connection between small arms and human suffering . . . has not been made successfully by the U.S. government or advocacy groups" (2010:38). The United States now supports "responsible" export controls. It remains to be seen if pro-control NGOs will hold it accountable to those commitments or if the hurdles set by the NRA and public disinterest are simply too high to overcome.

BELGIUM: TWO REGIONS, TWO TRADITIONS

Until 2003, Belgian arms export policy and practice were decided by the federal government. Early export reports, initiated amid emerging scandal in 1991, did not name individual recipients, making it difficult for NGOs to raise specific concerns. Transparency and export controls grew after the EU Code of Conduct was developed, activating NGO criticism of certain export deals. With export decision making regionalized in Belgium in 2003, scandal sensitivity now varies across the two major regions. Although both regions have some level of pro-control NGO activity, only Flanders has maintained a level of transparency with which those NGOs can wield information to spotlight government hypocrisy. In contrast, lower transparency in Wallonia leads to lower scandal sensitivity and the perception that government practice is less restricted.

REGIONAL DIVIDES

Like many of its allies, Belgium was implicated in an Arms to Iraq scandal in the early 1990s. The 1990 murder of Canadian-born weapons engineer Gerald Bull in Brussels—his base for the Iraq "supergun" project[65]—brought Belgium firmly into the Arms to Iraq intrigue. In the process of investigating propellant manufacturer Poudrières réunies de Belgique's (PRB) role in illegal sales to Iraq, former deputy prime minister André Cools uncovered connections between PRB, the Iraqi supergun project, and Bull.[66] Cools was murdered in 1991, soon after receiving documents implicating Belgian civil servants in the affair. According to reports, civil servants had been bribed "to secure the use of Belgian air force freighters to ship cargoes of 'supergun' propellant to Iraq" and allowed defense goods destined for Iraq to pass through customs without proper authorization (Foster, Cleemput, and Lambert 1991).

Unlike in the British affair, only low-level career bureaucrats appeared to be at fault in this scandal. Nevertheless, arms export reform—which had been simmering since accusations of lax controls in the late 1980s—was quick to follow the murder of Cools, preventing the scandal from developing further.[67] In August 1991, Parliament passed legislation to institute some reporting and stricter controls based on conflict and human rights, making Belgium an early mover on humanitarian export controls at the domestic level.[68] The law also gave final decision-making power to an interministerial committee (in practice, the minister of the license-requesting company's region) to allow decisions to reflect the exporting region's economic and normative concerns. The reform was a distinct change for Belgium, which had been "notorious as [a world center for the arms trade] since the Middle Ages" and where international arms trafficking from ports and airports had flourished (Lowther 1991:5).[69]

Arms export decision making became a contentious topic within the government almost immediately, with splits in the coalition over transfers to Saudi Arabia causing Parliament to dissolve in late 1991 (Flemish Peace Institute 2007a).[70] Yet although the new law introduced national reports, public transparency remained low, with the first report in 1994 limited to geographic zones and not including individual recipients (Mampaey 2003). The report did provide think tanks, peace groups, and other organizations—active on the arms trade since the 1970s and 1980s—with some new information, but debates were still mostly intergovernmental. In particular, Flemish peace parties, which are opposed to arms exports as a rule, made decision making contentious and at times exposed it to the public eye, especially for non-NATO transfers to the Middle East and developing world.

Controversies spread as transparency improved and NGOs became increasingly involved in generating public accountability.[71] The issue exploded in 2002 with the authorization for Walloon producer FN Herstal to export machine guns to Nepal despite strong public opposition (Vranckx 2005; Weidacher 2005). A few months earlier Germany had denied weapons to Nepal, which was embroiled in civil war. As a result, Belgium's approval not only seemed to circumvent Belgian law but also introduced complex issues under the EU Code of Conduct about knowingly approving a deal previously denied by another EU member (Donnay 2002; 2007a; Vranckx 2005).[72] The government made its initial decision by consensus behind closed doors in July 2002 and justified it by declaring that the situation in Nepal had changed and that the sale would support a young, fragile democracy (Dombey 2002; Flemish Peace Institute 2007a; interview 52207211).

Nevertheless, once the deal was made public a month later, it prompted the resignation of one minister in the ruling party coalition[73] and revived regional tensions. Flemish leaders cried foul and called for the suspension of the licenses (Belgian Chamber of Representatives 2002). The government nearly collapsed, saving itself only by agreeing to incorporate the EU Code into federal export law (Vranckx 2005). Yet the sharp regional division over public expectations for arms export accountability remained unresolved, and the Nepali licenses continued to attract criticism from Flanders. The longer-term resolution in 2003 left federal arms export laws in place (incorporating the EU Code) but transferred their execution to the regional governments just before the Nepali licenses required a divisive renewal decision (Crutzen 2003).

Flemish party leader Hugo Coveliers summed up the source of the consensus for the decision: "With this law we will avoid a great deal of tension in our federal state" (qtd. in Otte 2003). The decision freed Flemish politicians from public backlash against "irresponsible" Walloon licenses and Walloon politicians from Flemish reluctance to approve Walloon export deals (interviews 21407211, 24107211, 57207211). Both sides appeared satisfied. Flemish commentator Jorn De Cock noted that "Flemish politicians will soon need to have no more twinges of conscience over controversial arms supplies by FN Herstal" and can focus on an "ethically inspired foreign policy" (2003). Walloons in turn, felt that regionalization would allow them to export weapons "as they see fit" (Otte 2003). Ultimately, the decision was "mainly a question of accountability to [the] public" because the values of the electorate to which decision makers in Belgium are accountable are regional, not national (interviews 20307211, 21407211).

THE "REGIONALIZATION OF CONSCIENCE"

The regionalization of arms export decision making highlights fundamental divisions within Belgium.[74] In the past, Flemish politicians and activists had mainly criticized Walloon practice, painting a picture of "the good Flemish pacifist versus the cynical Walloon merchant of death" (Mampaey 2002:13).[75] The fact that most Flemish defense exports were dual-use technologies not clearly identifiable as weapons also helped its image seem "innocent" and "cleaner, even if it [wasn't]."[76] Flemish politicians could therefore more easily avoid public perceptions of "irresponsible" arms exports.

Since 2003, however, each region has had to take responsibility for its own decisions. Flanders faces a clear chain of public accountability brought on by a culture of NGO activism and strong arms trade transparency, which has markedly increased scandal sensitivity. Even as the Flemish government has ratcheted up transparency standards, it often feels compelled to avoid critiques from civil society (Flemish Peace Institute 2006; interviews 21407211, 24107211, 53207211).[77] NGOs have criticized and lobbied the government, "really focusing on [policy] implementation" (interviews 57207211, 24107211). The government faced criticism early on for dual-use transfers to Algeria, Colombia, Liberia, India, Israel, and Pakistan. It countered by arguing that it did not approve the export of guns but rather the export of displays, lighting, and airport equipment (Brinckman 2005; Verschelden 2006a, 2006b).[78]

As one official remarked, "[Export decision making is] not that easy when you have the responsibility" (interview 55107211). Indeed, some in Flanders have since regretted regionalization as a result (Otte and Verschelden 2006). Even so, regionalization was seen as "an opportunity for the Flemish region to demonstrate [that] we can do it better, more ethically" (interview 21407211). The Flemish government is therefore increasingly cautious and reluctant to approve export deals, resulting in longer processing times and higher refusal rates (interviews 20307211, 24107211). Arms trade experts state the vast majority of favorable export decisions in Flanders "go to trustworthy destinations" in industrialized countries. Approximately half of denials are made for administrative reasons such as missing documents. The other half are for political reasons, such as human rights and security (interview 21407211).

The Walloon government, in contrast, lacks high scandal sensitivity. In 2003, Minister-President Jean-Claude van Cauwenberghe declared his intention to conserve the federal regime and its ethics and standards (Crutzen 2003:10). Yet Wallonia has a reputation—whether accurate or not—for a less restrictive, more economic approach to arms export decision making, in part because the Walloon public is more positive toward the defense trade, which is a major employer in the region (interview 20307211). In addition, transparency is lower and government access for NGOs is more difficult in Wallonia than in Flanders (interviews 53207211, 21407211, 26207211).[79] Export reports are slower to be released and contain fewer export details. One NGO representative noted that the public reports simply do not provide useful information with which to criticize the government and mobilize the public (interview 27207211).

The rare instances of pressure on Walloon export decision making have come from the federal government, not from NGOs or the public. The divorce between policy making and implementation created by regionalization has given rise to difficulties in reconciling regional practice with federal foreign policy. Wallonia's 2005 approval of an export license for the New Lachaussee Company to build an ammunition factory in Tanzania is a key example of this unique policy–practice gap. The federal government argued that the decision would undermine its policies to support humanitarian arms control, oppose illicit arms trafficking, and promote a peacemaker role in the region (interviews 21407211, 53207211; Verbruggen et al. 2005). Wallonia had no legal obligation to grant the federal government's request or any direct stake in its foreign policy. Yet its retraction of the license also seems unrelated to the negative public attention the case generated once it hit the news. In fact, one official noted that the issue did not have a "naturalistic appeal" to the public absent the sudden press coverage (interview 55107211). Nevertheless, the regional government agreed to cancel the license "purely because of the power of the political party" (interview 52207211): there is no hierarchy of governments in Belgium, but there is a party hierarchy. Federal parties are above regional parties, which are often starting points for political careers (interview 26207211).

The Tanzania episode suggests an alternative, albeit rare, path for export accountability and demonstrates the difficulties inherent in separating the agents of arms transfer policy from arms transfer practice. Overall, although regionalization bucks the trend of greater international convergence on arms trade issues, it also demonstrates governments' concern for avoiding the costs of domestic backlash against unpopular export decisions. Both active NGOs and transparency are critical for establishing and enhancing this domestic reputational dynamic. Yet, as the contrast between regions in Belgium shows, improved accountability can—but does not necessarily—translate into improved compliance with new export standards.

Domestic politics cannot explain the adoption of "responsible" arms transfer policies in most cases, but it can have limited consequences for policy implementation. Governments ordinarily have little reason to adhere closely to new arms transfer standards, which can be costly to foreign and economic policy. Material interests can therefore help to explain states' broader patterns of noncompliance. However, they have trouble accounting for those rare but important instances in which governments *do* seek to close the policy–practice gap. Although often shielded from public attention and buried in complex bureaucratic procedures, arms exports that violate national values can under the right conditions come to light and cause scandal. Policy makers—especially those with scandal experience—may seek to avoid "irresponsible" exports when the threat of scandal appears high. Scandal can also lead to reform. However, where civil society or transparency or both are weak, the threat posed by scandal declines dramatically. This points to the importance of both information about government activity and the existence of an NGO community able to act on the information that transparency provides. Transparency in the hands of an active civil society can increase scandal sensitivity and cause governments to respond with greater restraint—at least in a limited set of those most high-profile and egregious (i.e., scandal-prone) export deals.

Domestic politics is clearly limited in its ability to produce a sustained and widespread compliance dynamic. But in the absence of international accountability mechanisms, it is domestic politics that may be best able—among democracies at least—to reshape national arms export cultures in light of new arms transfer norms. Arms trade transparency measures provide the means by which civil society can call policy makers to account. Governments' public commitment to the ATT and other multilateral agreements can also facilitate and enhance NGO critiques of arms export practices by clearly articulating their values and norms. The five cases described here show how variation in transparency and civil society involvement affects governments' scandal sensitivity and emerging willingness to impose export restraint in some cases. They also show that scandal sensitivity can be tempered by the historical national relationship with the arms trade, foreign-policy values, and national political priorities. In the final chapter, I consider these conclusions in the context of the book's broader theoretical and empirical questions and offer insights into its lessons for the implementation of the Arms Trade Treaty.

6. Conclusions and Implications

Questions and controversies about the supply of weapons to Syria have been at the heart of debates about the appropriate and prudent international response to its conflict since 2011. Russian arms transfers to the regime have been widely condemned, but arms embargo proponents failed to neutralize Russian and Chinese opposition at the UN. As the conflict dragged on, the debate in the United States and Europe shifted from embargoing arms transfers to supplying rebel groups. In 2013, the United States announced its intention to arm Syrian rebels, and the EU let its embargo to Syria lapse, enabling it to do the same. These decisions have been praised for showing support for the opposition without putting troops on the ground. They have also come under fire for the potential security costs that arms transfers may bring, including their diversion to terrorist groups, role in conflict escalation, and use in human rights violations. The complex interests, conflicting values, and murky ethics in the Syrian case are symptomatic of the tensions inherent in the contemporary arms trade as a whole.

The Arms Trade Treaty attempts to clarify these dilemmas and encourage export restraint in cases such as Syria. It lays out—for the first time—legally binding principles to restrict small and major conventional arms exports to human rights violators, conflict zones, and recipients that risk of diversion to illicit markets or terrorist actors. This is a dramatic policy achievement once thought impossible. Despite widespread support for the ATT, however, putting these principles into practice is often messier in reality than it seems on paper, as Syria shows. The conventional arms trade has long been seen as necessary for states' foreign policy, national security, and economic well-being. Yet the effects of arms export decisions can have long-lasting consequences for the states and populations on the receiving end. Arms supplies may enable or prolong conflict and repression, destabilize societies, and undermine human security. In the post–Cold War era, many of these problems with conventional arms—small arms especially—have become more difficult for states to ignore as bloody internal conflicts hit the front page of newspapers and as affected states and NGOs have begun to voice their concerns. Hundreds of thousands of people die each year as a direct or indirect result of armed conflict and by firearms in nonconflict areas. Moreover, extensive research has explored the causal connections between conventional arms proliferation and conflict, human rights, governance, and development in importing states.[1]

A handful of states export the vast majority of global legal conventional arms, but until recently these states have been subject to little external regulation regarding their export decisions.[2] In the past, states have openly or clandestinely supported many conflicts and abusive regimes with arms supplies. Today, although states continue to face decisions about whether to supply arms to buyers who may use those arms to provoke conflict or harm civilians, new rules and norms have introduced human security to the political calculus of arms export decision making. These new "responsible" arms export norms fight against supplier states' long-held national-security, foreign-policy, and economic interests. Nevertheless, most major democratic exporters in recent years have agreed to restrict their arms transfers to war-torn and repression-prone destinations—at least in theory.

In this book, I have explained why major arms-exporting democracies have committed to multilateral humanitarian export controls, despite their past opposition, and to what effect. First, I have argued that states' social reputational concerns account for their commitment to the ATT and related multilateral initiatives. Second, I have attributed marginal changes in export practice, amid a persistent gap between states' arms export policy and practice, to some governments' concerns for their domestic reputations in the face of arms trade scandal. These findings have consequences for understanding—and possibly improving—conventional arms control and for the broader relationships between commitment and compliance in international affairs. In this concluding chapter, I summarize the main findings of the book, explore their implications for IR theory beyond state reputation, and offer a brief analysis of three additional non-European arms exporters: Israel, South Africa, and Brazil. I end with a series of policy implications for ATT implementation and for how states collectively reconcile their conflicting interests and obligations in world politics more broadly.

SUMMARY OF FINDINGS

The empirical findings suggest reasons for both pessimism and optimism for the prospects of conventional arms control. On the one hand, they demonstrate that past hostility to shared export policies has been replaced with a strong endorsement of them—at least on paper. The states once most resistant to "responsible" arms transfer standards are now among their biggest proponents. Major European exporters that once firmly opposed similar policies on economic grounds today vocally endorse new standards of export control, despite ongoing concerns for the viability of their defense industries. The United States is an exception in that it unilaterally (and temporarily) supported similar policies during the Cold War but was the leading opponent of recent initiatives until late 2009. On the other hand, the findings also reveal a glaring disconnect between states' "responsible" policies and their often "irresponsible" practices. Accountability can be rare and may require the confluence of pro-control NGOs and arms trade transparency. Commitment can come without compliance: state behavior is hard to change.

The first part of the book assesses broad historical trends in conventional arms trade policy and practice and seeks to account for contemporary changes in international arms trade norms. It highlights the persistent failure during much of the twentieth century to achieve multilateral arms export controls, which were doomed by entrenched norms of sovereignty and the material stakes that major powers attach to their arms trade. Poor human rights records, I show, did not significantly deter arms exports in practice. It was the confluence of four key events in the 1990s, I argue, that created new expectations for interstate cooperation on policies intended to curb the detrimental effects of conventional arms proliferation: Arms to Iraq scandals following the 1991 Gulf War, high-profile civil and ethnic conflicts, the success of the 1997 Ottawa Mine Ban Treaty, and the growing role of NGO advocacy in international affairs. These events resulted in a new and dramatically different normative environment for the arms trade, drawing attention to human security and putting in place the conditions to generate widespread support for new humanitarian initiatives.

Nevertheless, these new initiatives are costly for major exporters, limiting their foreign-policy autonomy and the available markets for their defense products. Standard explanations for states' commitment to multilateral agreements rest on such costs being outweighed by anticipated material benefits or a sense of normative obligation. States may also support low-cost agreements that simply codify existing practice. These explanations therefore expect states' practice to mirror their policy commitments. Yet statistical analyses examining the SALW and MCW export practices of top supplier states from 1981 to 2010 suggest otherwise. The results indicate that states for the most part have not significantly reduced arms exports in response to recipients' poor human rights performance, either before or after the advent of their support for "responsible" arms export initiatives. And even as states' policies have been closely scrutinized in international politics, they have largely escaped international condemnation for noncompliance. States have chosen to adopt and promote new policies despite the fact that these policies require far-reaching changes in their export practice. Yet it does not appear that states perceive a need to implement these policies in anticipation of material gains or to fulfill normative obligations. Explanations that can account for commitment without compliance are therefore needed.

The second part of the book delves more deeply into states' motives for commitment and compliance using case studies of five major arms-exporting democracies: Belgium, France, Germany, the United Kingdom, and the United States. I show that these states have supported "responsible" arms transfer policies *in spite* of their own material interests, not because of them. Defense industry preferences have followed government support, not led it. Domestic publics have remained largely unaware or disinterested. With high material costs and little to no domestic incentives attached to new policies, what accounts for support from states that once opposed such initiatives? I argue that states' social concerns for their international reputation—made possible by normative changes begun in the 1990s—instead play a prominent part in explaining their commitment to "responsible" arms export initiatives such as the EU Code of Conduct and the ATT.

Interviews with key players in the arms transfer policy-making process, government documents, and secondary literature demonstrate this concern for social reputation in international politics. The United Kingdom was an early mover, setting a new reference point for other now-supportive states, which have carefully chosen their policies as a means to improve their reputation as "good" citizens of the international community. States (and the diplomats who represent them) have sought to conform to social pressures brought on by the new international environment attached to arms trade norms. International institutions serve as sites of norm development as well as venues in which states engage in reputation-building behavior. Those states whose self-images are strongly tied to international institutions are more likely to respond to social pressures in the context of international institutions, seeking praise and social gain from their peers and avoiding censure for their arms export policies. In other words, reputation provides states with a social incentive to act, despite the material costs of doing so. Moreover, although its exceptionalism creates a more complex relationship with its international reputational concerns, the United States too has turned to support the ATT as a low-cost (given its own strong national export controls, unlike other top exporters) part of a strategy of reputation repair since 2009.[3]

Where domestic pressures can play a prominent role is in the policy implementation phase. Democratic governments that face both high arms trade transparency and an active pro-control NGO community may fear backlash from the public unveiling of their most "irresponsible" export deals. Although scandals rarely influence elections, they nevertheless draw attention to governments' arms trade practices and harm their domestic reputations. Past scandals can also induce reforms that enhance transparency and mobilize civil society, increasing the threat of future scandal. Under these conditions—high transparency and pro-control NGO activity—governments can become sensitive to the threat of scandals in cases of deals that showcase the extreme violation of national values or international norms. Even so, this is a relatively small subset of cases in which governments may voluntarily seek to improve policy implementation relative to past behavior. States remain committed to bolstering national defense industries, and overall trends in arms export practice suggest that new norms are not yet broadly influencing state behavior.

A EUROPEAN PHENOMENON? OUTSIDE THE TOP FIVE

This book has focused on cases of top democratic arms exporters in order to examine state support of humanitarian arms control despite strong material incentives to maintain more liberal export policies—precisely what states had done in the past. However, these cases cannot explore whether state support and the reputational pressures I use to explain it are simply a European or Western phenomenon. I argue that although domestic culture and the forces of integration in the EU have made these dynamics stronger, they reach beyond the EU to other exporting democracies as well. A brief look at the politics of arms transfers in Israel, South Africa, and Brazil—democracies that have been late to develop their defense industrial bases but are now medium-size exporters—helps to demonstrate this point.

ISRAEL: CONCERN FOR INTERNATIONAL REPUTATION?

The Middle East and Asia are the only two regions without their own arms transfer control regimes. As a result, Israel—unlike European suppliers—has not been subject to an additional layer of regulatory and socializing pressures to adopt new arms export policies. Indeed, as both an importer and an exporter of conventional arms, Israel has resisted external controls.[4] As an importer, it is intensely concerned about its ability to acquire arms because of its heightened military insecurity (Naaz 2000; Rodman 2007). As an exporter, it takes a market-based approach to arms transfers, often selling arms where other exporters will not (D. Clarke 1995). With hostile neighbors and potentially unreliable suppliers, it perceives an acute need to support the economic viability of its domestic arms industry through exports as a matter of national security (D. Clarke 1995; Naaz 2000). Moreover, a distinct lack of arms trade transparency and NGO activity has prevented any sustained attention to the issue in domestic politics. The government—to an even greater degree than most democracies—is free of reputational concerns attached to the perception of "irresponsible" arms export policy and practice at home.

However, Israel has not been free of reputational concerns in international politics. Despite its resistance to shared export controls and domestic disinterest in the issue, it has wanted to avoid being grouped with the "lowest common denominators" out of concern for its international reputation. In this way, Israel has used the United States as a reference point for its own policies. Its choice has not followed from a perceived need to coordinate and curry favor with the United States. Instead, Israel's instructions to its diplomats for its 2006 ATT vote "were to do one better than the US" (interview 48207002). After 2001, it was clear that the United States would set the low bar for multilateral policy, a position that came with international condemnation and reputational costs. So when the United States voted against initiating the ATT process in 2006, Israel abstained.

In its 2007 ATT statement to the UN secretary-general, the Israeli government asserted that its abstention should be understood "as a call for prudence . . . rather than an objection to the application of a robust and responsible control of the sale and transfer of arms" (UN General Assembly 2007:16). It also stated that Israel "has, for many years, exercised strict control over arms exports through a comprehensive export control mechanism" (15). Like the other cases in the book, the government emphasizes that its policies are in tune with international standards—although many experts would disagree with such a characterization of Israeli arms trade policy and practice. Once the United States changed its vote to a "yes" in late 2009, Israel too joined the ranks of supporter states. It voted in favor of the final ATT in 2013 but has so far not signed it.

In short, Israel has chosen its policy in order to avoid sharing in the international criticism attracted by U.S. opposition. Although Israel is close to the United States and depends on it for substantial advanced weaponry (D. Clarke 1995; Rodman 2007), it nevertheless recognized the broader social costs of aligning with it on the issue. Israel may not have opted for reputation building through policy support, but it was strategic in evading the reputational damage associated with opposing the initiative. As such, the Israeli case highlights two important factors: first, international policy pressures at work in the absence of existing regional norms or policies and in the presence of strong military inse-curities and, second, the extent to which the United States sets the standard of policies to avoid and detracts attention from those "less irresponsible" but still not "responsible" policies followed by nonsupportive states.

SOUTH AFRICA: CONCERN FOR DOMESTIC REPUTATION?

International reputational pressures have also likely helped South Africa trans-form from an early opponent of shared export controls during UNPOA negotia-tions to a firm ATT supporter as it seeks to legitimate its role in world politics.[5] What South Africa contributes to the analysis more significantly, however, are its vivid domestic debates about arms trade practice.[6] In the opening of the book, I described the angry protests that erupted in 2008 in response to the government's decision (later reversed) to allow the transit of Chinese arms through South Africa to Zimbabwe. Despite an active network of NGOs, the incident demonstrated the government's initial lack of sensitivity to arms scan-dals absent arms export transparency. It also showed the public's intolerance of transfers—once revealed—that are perceived as "irresponsible" and contrary to South African values.

On the import side, the government has also faced ongoing scandal over al-legations of widespread bribery connected to its 1999 Strategic Defence Pro-curement—known as "the arms deal"—with numerous European firms. Arms deal corruption charges against Jacob Zuma were dropped just prior to his elec-tion to the presidency in 2009. In 2011, Zuma suspended broader investigations into the matter but reversed his decision later that year after an activist brought suit against the government, "forcing it to revive the investigation on the grounds that it had failed to meet its constitutional obligation to fight corruption" (M. Cohen 2011). Media attention has sparked public interest and outrage regarding government accountability, leading to investigations into fresh revelations of corruption and political meddling in 2012 and 2013

The domestic politics of arms transfers in South Africa complement those of Germany, with historical experience prompting general public and organized civil society concern about the human rights implications of arms exports. Un-like Germany, however, South Africa lacks the transparency to consistently ad-vertise "irresponsible" deals. SAS (2007) counts South Africa among the least transparent small arms exporters. What information has been released in recent years has come too late to affect decision making and has been largely ignored by the media as "only of historical interest" (Lamb 2007).[7] In turn, according to Laurie Nathan, "South Africa's export of conventional armaments has been its foreign activity least consistent with stated policy," which lays out a commitment to human rights on paper but has often turned a blind eye to them in practice (2005:371).[8]

South Africa has numerous organizations dedicated in part or in full to arms trade issues[9] as well as religious and labor groups willing to monitor arms trade activity as they are able and a public willing to mobilize when opportunities arise. But because there are no regular sources of arms trade information, the government can more easily hide less palatable trading partners from critical eyes and reputational damage. Yet its ability to maintain arms trade secrecy may be crumbling as it is forced to address ghosts of arms deals past. And as it seeks a regional leadership role, attempts to cope with gun violence within its own borders and reputational costs of this policy–practice gap and legacy of corruption may grow.

BRAZIL: SEPARATION OF DOMESTIC POLITICS AND INTERNATIONAL POLICY

Brazil developed its defense industrial base in the 1970s and 1980s. Although it is not a large exporter of MCW,[10] it has become a key exporter of SALW in the past decade (SAS 2006). The Brazilian case is particularly instructive as a counterpoint to the United States. It shows that public support for civilian gun possession in domestic politics need not spill over into opposition to arms export controls in international politics. As in the United States, public debates in Brazil over questions of domestic arms control have been intense. Unlike in the United States, however, these debates have not been deployed in foreign-policy debates on conventional arms control. In fact, Brazil has been a strong supporter of "responsible" arms export policies in both regional and international fora.

Gun violence in Brazilian society is notorious (see SAS 2007). In response, Brazil proposed to outlaw commercial arms sales to civilians in 2005. One month prior to the referendum, polls suggested 73 percent favored the proposition, largely because of support from the federal government, the Catholic Church, and a major media conglomerate (Morton 2006). Yet although only a small fraction of the civilian population is thought to own guns, the proposition ultimately failed by a nearly two-to-one margin, primarily because of the intense campaign run by pro-gun groups in the three weeks prior to the election that caught pro-control groups off-guard (interviews 65209140, 66209140; Morton 2006). Clifford Bob (2012) describes a domestic election battle with international participants on both sides and pro-gun groups desperately seeking American resources (albeit without success). In the end, pro-gun groups won by mimicking NRA campaigns, designed to remind voters of their historic fight to overcome dictatorship and to stoke public anxiety about trust in government, human rights, and personal security.

The resounding failure of Brazil's 2005 proposition was lauded as a global triumph by the NRA and used as a global call to arms against UN initiatives (Bob 2012:180). Even so, pro-gun groups in Brazil have not connected the debate about civilian possession to export policies.[11] And although the government has not sought a leadership role on the ATT or on other UN initiatives (interview 66209140), its support for multilateral export controls has not been contested. Brazil sees its foreign policy as grounded in cooperation and compromise, soft power, and international law, connected to its identity as an intermediate power and mediator in regional and international politics (interview 65209140; Lafer 2000; Soares de Lima and Hirst 2006). Brazil may also not have the luxury of shrugging off concern for its international reputation in the way the United States as a superpower can. Conforming to international expectations rather than publicly flouting them, Brazil voted in favor of successive ATT resolutions and signed the day it opened for signature in 2013.

THEORETICAL IMPLICATIONS

The spread of "responsible" arms transfer standards presents IR theory with a difficult task. The gap between states' policy and their practice casts doubt on explanations expecting commitment and compliance to go hand in hand. Ripe with potential costs to economic profits and military power and largely ignored by the public, "responsible" arms export controls are also unlikely to win domestic political gains or future profitable agreements. Weak implementation of new controls suggests that policy changes have not come about because of a deep internalization of new humanitarian standards, either. Even so, states' eagerness to endorse such policies despite the material costs of doing so indicates changing policy expectations in a new normative environment. Explanations must therefore accommodate both states' widespread commitment to popular new policies as well as their relatively consistent noncompliant arms trade practices. By understanding reputation as a social incentive, this book bridges rationalist and constructivist approaches to IR and provides additional theoretical insights for reputation and government accountability, norm diffusion and socialization, and regime formation.

REPUTATION IN INTERNATIONAL
AND DOMESTIC POLITICS

This book's core argument is that states' concern for social reputation in international fora explains their commitment to otherwise costly "responsible" arms transfer policies. In this case, reputation serves as a social incentive for states to choose policies that conform to international norms in public—even norms they have not internalized in private. In particular, where diplomats meet regularly to discuss specific issues, expectations for appropriate policies can be communicated and states' policy choices easily observed..States may therefore choose their policies strategically as a means to preserve, enhance, or repair their reputations in the social context of international institutions. A good reputation can itself be a goal in international politics, bringing positive feedback on a state's identity, or be sought out for other social benefits it can confer, such as legitimacy. Reputation as a social concept can extend beyond the arms trade to other issues, such as states' commitment to climate change initiatives, human rights treaties, development, and humanitarian intervention. In turn, these social incentives can help explain the diffusion of new norms beyond their initial norm entrepreneurs.

In this context, the five case studies examined in this book highlight the importance of political leadership and ministries of foreign affairs in driving states' social reputational concerns in international politics. In many states, arms export policy and its implementation are the responsibility of multiple government ministries (e.g., foreign affairs, commerce, defense, and perhaps others). Although ministries of finance and economics might be more invested in protecting states' material interests with more liberal arms export policies, ministries of foreign affairs or high-level leaders typically take the lead when it comes to shaping and promoting states' policies abroad. These actors interact frequently with diplomats and leaders from other states. Ministries of foreign affairs may also be charged explicitly with shaping the state's image abroad through public diplomacy and related programs. As the state's representatives in multilateral fora, these actors are often more in tune with changing international norms, more subject to international pressures for social conformity, and more deeply invested in maintaining a state's reputation. They may therefore be more sensitive to appeals to "good international citizenship" to commit to such regimes as the ATT and to the reputational costs of opposing them.

The book also argues that domestic reputation can play a role in policy implementation and government accountability. The compliance literature typically looks to international politics to provide states with the incentives—whether material or nonmaterial, formal or informal—to comply with their policy commitments. Yet in some cases domestic politics may also motivate compliance, even when the international community lacks the tools and authority to monitor and enforce state practice. Although hard treaty law can broaden and formalize the domestic mechanisms available to facilitate compliance (Simmons 2009), the prospects of public backlash can also generate some compliance. Scandals impose domestic reputational costs by spotlighting severely "irresponsible" export deals and capturing intensely critical public attention.[12] Scandal sensitivity, I argue, requires both information about a government's arms export activity and an active civil society willing to call attention to "bad" export deals in domestic politics. Where governments perceive a high threat of scandal, they may exercise (comparatively) more restraint in their export practices. Even so, this dynamic may be rare and slow to develop.

Acknowledging reputation as a social concept opens the door to consider states' acceptance of new norms without the internalization of those norms. States can be concerned with the public appearance of social conformity, but the private acceptance and "taken-for-granted" status of norms may take more time to emerge, if they do at all. As a result, when states' policies are highly visible but their practices are not, commitment can more easily come without compliance. In this way, states may strategically respond to changes in the international normative environment out of concern for the social consequences of reputation in the present, despite the potential material costs of doing so in the future. Yet if their compliance remains limited, further questions arise for the processes of socialization and regime formation.

NORM DIFFUSION AND SOCIALIZATION

Although arms trade accountability has been left in the hands of civil society, international institutions have two integral roles in the diffusion of "responsible" arms trade norms. First, they provide formal settings in which states face social pressures to commit to new policies as diplomats interact and behavioral expectations evolve over time. In the case of arms transfers, domestic political pressures in most states cannot do the same. Unlike the landmine campaign, which benefited from popular and interest-group support, "responsible" arms transfers have faced an inattentive public and an initially hostile or reluctant defense industry. Rather, it has been in the context of international institutions that commitment pressures have increased and caused states to rethink their policies. Second, states' support for multilateral initiatives can make rhetorical entrapment[13] a viable means to promote government accountability. Support for agreements makes explicit states' commitment to certain values and norms. In doing so, agreements—whether they are legally binding or not—make incidents of hypocrisy easier for domestic NGOs and the media to spot and spotlight. Both the policy commitment itself and the publicity of that commitment in international institutions enable accountability and concern for reputation to begin to emerge in domestic politics.

So far, however, international institutions have not generated a significant sense of social obligation among states to *comply* with the norms these institutions articulate. State practice has proven difficult to change, suggesting that norm internalization will be a slow and uncertain process. Defense industry interests, a multitude of bureaucratic interests involved in arms export decision making, and a general lack of public attention reduce material and social incentives to institute broad changes in practice. At times, these factors may even work against deeper socialization. Norm diffusion has been rapid and widespread. But although norm emergence has been highly successful in the short term, scholars, policy makers, and activists must all take a long-term view of how "responsible" arms trade norms will evolve and take hold over time. Norm internalization is not inevitable; it will take concerted effort and attention from governments and civil society alike.

Nevertheless, social obligation does win out over material interests as states weigh whether to *commit* to popular policies. Indeed, it lays the foundation for states' reputational concerns linked to their legitimacy and standing in international politics. In contrast, where shared social obligations to commit to policies are absent, reputation fades as a motivation for policy support. This is possible where a state is less dependent on international institutions and "good international citizenship" to define its role in the international community. As the U.S. case illustrates, a hard-power-oriented hegemon may see itself as above or exempt from international social obligations.[14] Yet it may also face greater public scrutiny of its willingness and ability to meet its obligations. The resulting gap between a hegemon's material power and the social foundations of its ability to exercise that power can generate a deep crisis of legitimacy and authority (Reus-Smit 2007). Research finds that U.S. reputation—and with that reputation, its standing, credibility, and legitimacy—took a hit from its widespread opposition to multilateral initiatives throughout much of the 2000s (American Political Science Association 2009; Goldsmith and Horiuchi 2009). In response, the United States attempted to engage in reputation repair and reshape its international leadership role, with potential consequences for the structure and content of global governance for years to come.

REGIME FORMATION

U.S. treatment of international law also has consequences for regime formation and norm diffusion. International regimes may form more readily under the leadership of a hegemon able to coax (or coerce) others to join and continue to cooperate over time (Keohane 1984). When the hegemon is uninterested in or actively opposes cooperation, the prospects for regime formation are uncertain. Some scholars cast grave doubt on regime creation without a willing hegemon acting in its own material interest to facilitate interstate cooperation (Krasner 1983). Others counter that the landmine treaty formed in the hands of middle-power leadership and succeeded without bending to U.S. preferences. In the case of "responsible" arms export controls, U.S. opposition until late 2009 both helped and hindered regime formation and norm diffusion.

Certainly, the absence of one of the most powerful players in the creation of an international regime might cast doubt on that regime's legitimacy (Franck 1990), and opposition from any state will stall cooperation when institutional rules require consensus. Lead states and NGOs have made a particular effort to accommodate U.S. "red lines," hoping to create a treaty that covers a significant portion of the global arms trade by including the United States. In doing so, they simultaneously increase the final product's legitimacy but weaken its contents.[15] Yet despite initial U.S. opposition and in part *because* of U.S. opposition, lead states were able to initiate the process to form a legally binding regime. In fact, when the hegemon's reputation is damaged, its opposition may not be wholly detrimental to regime formation. The opportunity to "look better" than (or not as bad as) the United States has helped garner support for (and lessen opposition to) shared arms transfer controls. The negative perception of a hegemon by a majority of states for eschewing its social obligations may therefore provide an opportunity for others to advance their social standing by behaving "better" than the most prominent objector.

Although the ATT process was pushed forward by U.S. opposition, it nevertheless entered a holding pattern without U.S. support—or at least had to decide how to move forward without U.S. support. This suggests that the conditions under which regime formation may occur and the outcome itself may still be circumscribed in the face of hegemonic opposition. Leaders reduced the scope of the ATT—by excluding regulations on transfers to nonstate actors, ammunition, and civilian possession—simply to keep the U.S. engaged in the process and in hopes of its eventually coming on board. And even as U.S. support in late 2009 catalyzed formal negotiations, behind the scenes the United States sought to maintain the more limited treaty scope and create some wiggle room in the language of treaty obligations.

The strength of changed expectations for "responsible" policy choices may affect lead states' ability to rally a critical mass of supporters in addition to the hegemon's reputation. When consensus over norms becomes more widely diffused through regional initiatives and UN discussions,[16] these conditions can work together to the regime leaders' advantage: the hegemon's reputation will visibly suffer as a result of its opposition, and other states will perceive greater social obligations and reputational consequences linked to their own policy choices. The social pressures to cooperate therefore may be strong even when the hegemon does not contribute to them. If the spread of new norms becomes truncated, however, lead states may have difficulty inspiring cooperation in the absence of hegemonic support.

POLICY IMPLICATIONS

In October 2009, the United States announced its support for the ATT initiative as long as the process remained ruled by inclusion and consensus. This announcement was game changing. Rather than indefinite working groups to keep the process alive as leaders considered how best to move forward without the support of the world's largest arms exporter, formal treaty negotiations were scheduled for 2012. In 2013, with U.S. support, the UN voted by wide margins to approve the final ATT, which will go into effect after the fiftieth state deposits its instrument of ratification on December 24, 2014. As lead states and NGOs now consider how to move from negotiation to implementation, the empirical and theoretical findings of this research carry important implications for legalizing "responsible" arms export controls and similar policy initiatives in the future.

First, how will the ATT achieve substantive behavioral change among major exporters? This question looms large and ultimately affects the treaty's ability to reduce the lives lost and human insecurity generated by "irresponsible" arms proliferation. As I have shown, arms trade practice is slow to change, and the ATT secretariat will have no enforcement authority. Article 14, the treaty's sole formal enforcement provision states, "Each State Party shall take appropriate measures to enforce national laws and regulations that implement the provisions of this Treaty." Much as before, enforcement must therefore fall to domestic politics. Indeed, the ATT's preamble explicitly recognizes "the voluntary and active role that civil society . . . can play in raising awareness of the object and purpose of this Treaty, and in supporting its implementation."[17]

Yet compliance that relies on electoral accountability will be limited even in established democracies. Because the ATT is a legally binding document, domestic courts may formally enforce its provisions and provide additional incentives for compliance (Simmons 2009). This method of enforcement may nevertheless rely on the spread of NGOs as agents of government accountability and arms trade transparency if it is to become an effective path to compliance. It may require financial support from the international community as well as training in ATT provisions, export reporting, and export policy. Lead states and NGOs may also need to nurture domestic NGOs elsewhere so that they are able to engage with government decision makers and national judicial systems on the issue. But even where these conditions are present, consistent and sustained compliance will likely still be difficult and will require both domestic efforts to raise awareness and international efforts to consolidate the interpretation of new standards over time.

Second, initiative leaders must continue to consider how to bring skeptical states on board—especially major arms exporters, such as Russia and China. Understanding the nature of their interests and their perceptions of their roles in the international community may help in doing so. For Russia, reputational pressures may be insufficient. Widespread international criticism over its arms transfers to the Assad regime have been ignored and perhaps may even have strengthened its resolve. Arms exports are seen as vital to its struggling economy. Emphasizing an ability to engage in technology sharing and coproduction—and with them, access to more profitable arms markets—as a benefit of common export controls may be more effective in Russia's case. Conversely, China may respond better to reputational arguments as it seeks social standing, validation, and integration into the international community (Johnston 2008; M. Miller 2013). Indeed, its role in the final ATT negotiations was said to be more constructive than expected, thanks largely to its increasing engagement with supportive African governments.

Finally, continued U.S. participation seems uncertain at best. Its domestic political climate all but ensures that Senate ATT ratification will be impossible for the foreseeable future. Divisive partisan politics and NRA influence in Congress suggest that arguments emphasizing that the ATT will not impose any additional restrictions beyond current U.S. policy will be largely ineffective. Regardless, the eventual inclusion of all top exporters will be necessary to create a regime able to restrict arms flows to problematic areas. If this does not occur through formal treaty signature and ratification, perhaps eventual informal adherence to ATT provisions, as the United States has largely done with the Ottawa Treaty, will lead to changes in the absence of formal legal obligations. For this scenario to be plausible, however, arms trade norms will have to be greatly strengthened. Work by civil society groups can attempt to increase public awareness and interest to enhance accountability, but this work can be difficult and unreliable, especially given other pressing domestic concerns and the complexity of the issue itself. Clarifying international expectations and boosting material and nonmaterial international pressures may also be essential in the long run.

Ambitious policies are an important start, but without the means to expose and punish noncompliance, they do little more than enhance states' reputations without improving human rights and conflict conditions on the ground in recipient states, as ostensibly intended. Adherence to "responsible" arms export norms has so far been weak, even within longer-established regimes such as the EU Code of Conduct. This weak adherence raises serious questions for the ATT and beyond. How can international institutions, state policy makers, and civil society effectively persuade, inspire, coerce, or cajole states to meet their human security obligations in world politics? The evidence here suggests that the ATT faces a hard road ahead and that reliance on domestic accountability may not be sufficient. The norm life cycle does not guarantee that new norms will reach the widespread internalization phase. Keeping compliance in the public eye and ensuring that the social and material costs of noncompliance are clear and certain will require hard work from both the international community and domestic actors.

The "last area of freedom" in arms control is no longer as free as it once was. Rules and norms of small and major conventional arms transfer controls are proliferating. Joining prohibitions on the production and use of "inhumane" and nuclear weapons, conventional arms regulations complete a spectrum of weapons regimes ranging from the protection of individuals' human security to the protection of states' military security. Certainly, compliance on the conventional arms front leaves much to be desired. But the success of new initiatives to set global legally binding standards based on humanitarian principles to govern the conduct of the conventional arms trade is unprecedented in both its reach and its achievements to date.

The role of conventional arms transfers in world politics has clearly shifted in line with changing foreign- and security-policy priorities and practices in the post–Cold War era. This trend may not be irreversible, however. Countermovements associated with the war on terror and new austerity measures indicate that states may be adopting a renewed security and economic mentality with respect to arms transfers. Without further developments to improve government accountability, the policy–practice gap on the arms trade could widen even as major exporters express their support for more "responsible" policies. Reputation can help to explain states' seemingly contradictory behavior, but it can go only so far in reconciling those contradictions in practice.

States' concern for reputation links normative shifts in the international community to strategic policy choices intended to serve state interests—in the case of arms trade, interests that are defined not only by material goals but also by social goals in international politics. Acknowledging reputation as a strategic *and* social concern may also provide insights into states' behavior elsewhere. For example, reputation may help to explain how donor states choose to dedicate and disperse international aid. States may also perceive reputational incentives to support popular multilateral initiatives, such as climate change or human rights, despite potential material costs. Clearly, some states do internalize the rules and norms they publicly endorse. Many others, however, adopt the accepted line in public but not in private, especially where monitoring is poor. Reputation attached to states' international legitimacy and standing helps explain such discrepancies and states' desire to keep up with expectations for "good" or "responsible" policies, even if their private preferences remain otherwise unchanged.

At the intersection of states' material interests and social obligations, conventional arms export controls present policy makers with an especially complex and sensitive task. Small and major conventional arms are the basic building blocks of states' security. At the same time, many see small arms as the "real weapons of mass destruction," killing millions of people each year. On paper, conventional arms transfers have become a tool by which exporters can promote international humanitarian and human rights norms. Yet the gap between states' policy commitments and their less-restrictive practices has gone largely unaddressed in international discussions. Instead, domestic political actors in some cases have sought to constrain states' arms transfers. As ATT signatories prepare for implementation, however, tough questions about monitoring and enforcement remain. Answering these questions will depend on the signatories' ability to strike a balance between states' continued notions of sovereignty and security attached to their arms trade and their evolving ideas of what it means to be "responsible" citizens in the international community. This task will not be easy, but its outcome will have profound consequences for security and human rights around the world.

Appendix A

MULTILATERAL CONVENTIONAL ARMS CONTROL IN THE TWENTIETH AND TWENTY-FIRST CENTURIES

Year	Key talks and agreements	Purpose
1919	St. Germain Convention for the Control of the Trade in Arms and Ammunition	Prevent "problem actors" in areas of colonial influence from acquiring arms
1925	Geneva Arms Traffic Convention	Publicize arms exports
1932–1935	League of Nations Disarmament Conference	Establish production and trade regulations
1949–1994	COCOM for Multilateral Export Controls	Establish conventional and dual-use export controls from west to east
1950	Tripartite Declaration	Regulate arms transfers to the Middle East from the United States, the United Kingdom, and France
1974	Declaration of Ayacucho	Establish Latin American import controls

(continued)

Year	Key talks and agreements	Purpose
1977–1978	US–USSR Conventional Arms Transfer talks	Limit weapons transfers to regions of conflict
1980	Convention on Certain Conventional Weapons (CCW), Protocols I–III	Ban use of conventional weapons that cause "superfluous injury and suffering"
1987	Missile Technology Control Regime	Develop informal, voluntary coordination of national export licensing to prevent the proliferation of unmanned delivery systems of weapons of mass destruction
1990	Treaty on Conventional Armed Forces in Europe	Set troop ceilings and mandated destruction of excess weaponry in eastern and western Europe
1991–1992	P5 Talks on conventional arms control	Attempt to limit arms transfers to the Middle East
1991	UN Register of Conventional Arms	Provide transparency, confidence building
1992	Treaty on Open Skies	Establish openness and transparency in military activities
1993	NGO landmine conference	Consult on possible campaign to ban landmines
1993	Organization for Security and Cooperation in Europe (OSCE) Principles Governing Conventional Arms Transfers	Guide states in conducting arms transfers
1995	UN General Assembly Resolution 50/70B	Create UN Group of Governmental Experts (UNGGE) on Small Arms
1995	CCW, Protocol IV	Ban use of blinding laser weapons
1996	Organization of American States (OAS) Landmine Resolution	Declare goal to eliminate APL in Western Hemisphere, ask states to declare moratoria on the production, use, and transfer of landmines
1996	Amended Protocol II of CCW	Restrict use of APL, antivehicle mines, and booby traps

Year	Key talks and agreements	Purpose
1996	Ottawa Conference Towards a Global Ban on APL	Call for international community to eliminate APL
1996	UN General Assembly landmine resolution	Call for international agreement to ban the use, production, stockpile, and transfer of APL
1996	Wassenaar Arrangement	Establish transparency
1996	UN Disarmament Commission guidelines	Develop voluntary guidelines for conventional arms transfers to conflict zones and unstable areas
1996–1997	UN Panel of Governmental Experts on SALW	Report on the use of SALW in conflicts, their excessive accumulation, illicit production and trade, and means to reduce their destabilizing accumulation
1997	UN General Assembly Resolution 54/54V	Request views of member states and second UNGGE on convening a SALW conference
1997	Ottawa Mine Ban Treaty	Ban the import, export, production of APL
1997	OAS Inter-American Convention Against the Illicit Manufacturing and Trafficking of Firearms	Develop cooperation and information exchange to prevent illicit manufacturing and trafficking of firearms, ammunition, and explosives
1997	EU Programme for Preventing and Combating Illicit Trafficking in Conventional Arms	Establish nonbinding commitments to prevent and combat illicit trafficking from the EU and to assist areas adversely affected by trafficking
1998	EU Code of Conduct on Arms Exports	Provide politically binding common export standards, transparency, and consultation
1998	EU Joint Action on SALW	Combat the destabilizing spread of SALW and help solve problems caused by such accumulation (renewed in 2002)

(continued)

Year	Key talks and agreements	Purpose
1998	ECOWAS Moratorium on Production and Trade of SALW	Ban import and production of SALW (extended in 2001 and 2004)
1998	Small Arms Working Group, Southern African Development Community	Develop policies on SALW
1999	UNGGE on convening a small arms conference	Report on the scope, agenda, dates, objectives, and venue for a SALW conference
1999	OAS Inter-American Convention on Transparency in Conventional Weapons Acquisitions	Establish transparency in reporting of exports and imports and in weapons acquisitions
1999	OSCE Istanbul Summit	Initiate discussions on SALW proliferation
2000	OSCE Document on Small Arms and Light Weapons	Provide details on export control criteria, marking and tracing, and identifying surpluses (politically binding)
2000	Nairobi Declaration on Illicit SALW	Combat problems caused by illicit SALW
2000	Bamako Declaration on Illicit Proliferation, Circulation, and Brokering of SALW (Organization of African Unity)	Recommend national action on SALW issues, create bilateral agreements, and destroy surplus weapons
2000	Brasilia Declaration of Latin American and Caribbean States	Develop common position for 2001 UN SALW Conference
2000–2001	Preparatory Committee meetings on SALW conference	Negotiate procedures and draft programs of action (three total) for 2001 UN conference
2001	Protocol on the Control of Firearms, Ammunition, and Other Related Materials (Southern African Development Community)	Establish regional and international initiatives to combat illicit production and destabilizing accumulation of firearms

Year	Key talks and agreements	Purpose
2001	UN Programme of Action on Small Arms and Light Weapons	Establish politically binding national, regional, and global measures to combat illicit trade of SALW
2002	Wassenaar Arrangement Best Practice Guide for exports of SALW	Establish guidelines for members regarding SALW transfers
2003	CCW, Protocol V on Explosive Remnants of War	Establish responsibility for states to clear weapons left behind and to warn populations of presence of weapons before clearance
2005	UN Firearms Protocol	Adopt crime-control measures, strengthen national licensing procedures, adopt legislation to criminalize the illicit production and trade of firearms, and create firearms marking and tracing
2005	EU Strategy to combat illicit accumulation and trafficking of SALW and ammunition	Provide a common response to problems and threats posed by illicit SALW trafficking; reinforce the need for consistency between security and development policies
2005	UN International Instrument to Enable States to Identify and Trace, in a Timely and Reliable Manner, Illicit Small Arms and Light Weapons	Enable identification and tracing of SALW, promote international cooperation in marking and tracing
2006	ECOWAS Convention	Transform moratorium into a legally binding convention
2006	UNPOA Review Conference	Follow up to the 2001 conference on UNPOA implementation
2006	UN General Assembly Resolution A/61/394 towards an ATT	Establish formal process to begin negotiations on a legally binding ATT

(continued)

Year	Key talks and agreements	Purpose
2006–2007	UNGGE on illicit arms brokering	Establish recommendations for UN steps to control international arms brokering
2007	Oslo Declaration	Commit signatories to concluding cluster munition treaty by 2009
2008	UNGGE on an ATT	Take second formal step to establish scope of treaty in view of future negotiations
2008	UNGGE on ammunition stockpile controls	Make recommendations for UN
2008	Convention on Cluster Munitions	Ban use, stockpiling, production, and transfer of cluster munitions
2008	EU Common Position 2008/944/CFSP	Make Code of Conduct legally binding
2013	UN General Assembly passes the ATT	Provides legally binding humanitarian arms export criteria
2014	UN Arms Trade Treaty	Entry into force

Appendix B

DATA SOURCES AND CODING

This appendix briefly describes the selection and coding of the dependent and independent variables in the Arms Trade Data Set as well as the interview sources and citations. There are two dependent variables: MCW transfers and SALW transfers. The independent variable of interest is importer states' human rights records. The control variables have been chosen to reflect factors that might have a confounding effect on the relationship of interest (arms transfers and human rights) based on the existing theoretical and empirical literature. The Arms Trade Data Set is significantly broader than previous statistical research in terms of the number of supplier states it covers and its consideration of both small and major conventional arms. It therefore seeks to be as comprehensive as possible despite data problems inherent in this field, which has long had to deal with difficulties of measurement and state secrecy that has only recently begun to fade.

COUNTRIES

The data set contains exporter–importer dyad-years from 1981 to 2010 for 22 top SALW- and MCW-exporting countries and 189 potential importing countries. The exporters include Austria, Australia, Belgium, Bulgaria, Canada, China, the Czech Republic (Czechoslovakia), France, Germany (West Germany), the Netherlands, Norway, Israel, Italy, Russia (Soviet Union), South Africa, South Korea, Spain, Sweden, Switzerland, Turkey, the United Kingdom, and the United States.

The subset of ATT supporter states includes all exporter states that voted in favor of the ATT when it passed the UN General Assembly on April 2, 2013. It excludes Russia and China, which formally abstained from voting.[1]

DEPENDENT VARIABLES

Because the political attention to, use of, and data for SALW and MCW transfers are dissimilar, the data set contains separate dependent variables for each. Most analyses cover only trade in MCW—where more historical data are available, transparency is more established, and the weapons themselves are easier to track. However, the most work to build multilateral standards and controls in the past decade has taken place with SALW. The ATT process has expanded international discussions on SALW export controls to include MCW. As I describe later in this appendix, differences between data sources also necessitate coding separate variables for methodological reasons.[2]

Major Conventional Weapons

MCW data are significantly better developed than SALW data. In particular, SIPRI compiles and updates worldwide annual data based on publicly available sources going back to 1950. SIPRI defines MCW as large weapons with a military purpose, covering the following nine categories: aircraft, armored vehicles, artillery, sensors, air defense systems, missiles, ships, engines, or an "other" fulfilling certain qualifications (SIPRI 2007:428–29). Although limited to MCW, SIPRI "provides the most painstakingly researched database" available (Brzoska and Pearson 1994:20) and is an established source in the arms trade literature.[3] Since the 1990s, SIPRI data collection has benefited from voluntary state-created transparency initiatives such as the UN Register and the Wassenaar Arrangement.

The dependent variable for MCW transfers (*mctransfer*) uses SIPRI trend-indicator values (TIV),[4] which are aggregate dollar figures measuring the core price and value as military resources of actual weapons deliveries within an exporter–importer dyad in a given year (SIPRI 2007:429).[5] TIVs are based on an assessment of "the technical parameters of weapons" transferred in a dyad-year. The value represents quantity and quality assigned from "an index that reflects its value as a military resource in relation to other weapons." (SIPRI 2007:429). Although TIVs consider core weapon prices where that information is available,[6] they are not a record of payments made.[7] Because transfers can include gifts or aid, in addition to sales, by way of a multitude of financing methods— including barter, discounts, credit, and cash—the standardized TIV measure is substantially more useful in comparing transfers from year to year and country to country (Brzoska 2004; SIPRI 2007). Moreover, it can better factor in transfers of secondhand equipment, to which it is otherwise difficult to assign a monetary value (Durch 2000:8). Finally, TIVs are a uniform measures across countries over time and are updated as new information becomes available, including as past reports are declassified. Thus, although TIV data cannot be combined with other sources, they are an extremely useful tool for research.

SIPRI consults a wide range of public sources in collecting its data: newspapers, books and reference works, official national and international documents, and periodicals and journals. Some records may require an informed estimate by the researcher and tend to err on the side of being conservative (SIPRI 2007:430). It is important to acknowledge that with respect to public sources, an absence of a recorded transfer in a dyad-year can indicate either "no transfer" or a "so far undetected transfer." However, SIPRI provides the most thorough information available for the global MCW trade.

Small Arms and Light Weapons

The variable for small arms transfers (*satransfer*) is based on raw records compiled by the Norwegian Initiative on Small Arms Transfers (NISAT; see NISAT 2006).[8] NISAT uses the UN definition of SALW, labeling as small arms "those weapons designed for personal use" and as light weapons "those designed for use by several persons serving as a crew" (UN 1997:11). These categories include, for example, revolvers, machine guns, rifles, and ammunition and explosives (UN 1997:11–12). NISAT collects UN Comtrade data[9] as well as available national and regional reports and press research but suffers from the lack of a universal system of reporting and methodology (Marsh 2005:2). As a result, data are not streamlined into uniform definitions and measures of quantity or quality. Moreover, multiple reports of a single transfer may exist but cannot be identified as repeat submissions with any certainty, as I explain later in more detail.

Despite the coding difficulties that arise when states *do* report small arms data, simply tracking the small arms trade is inherently more problematic without their support. As Ian Anthony states, "The rapid and unbroken increase in the movement of standard-size closed containers through ports in countries with a domestic small-arms industry underlines that monitoring of the legal trade can only be done with the consent and cooperation of governments and industry" (1994:34), which have recently become more common (Holtom 2008).

In its first yearbook, SAS called small arms transfers "a unique kind of terra incognita" that "remain statistically primitive and underdeveloped" (2001:61). Since then, however, numerous national, regional, and international sources have appeared, helping generate a broad sketch of the small arms trade.

Because of the rough nature of SALW data, *satransfer* is dichotomous: the number 1 indicates the presence of a transfer in a dyad-year, and zero indicates no record of a transfer in a dyad-year. Three significant data problems necessitate a dichotomous SALW variable. First, the absence of a transfer record does not mean with certainty that no transfer took place—only that one was not listed in the numerous sources used to compile the database. Without completely open government records for all years, it is simply impossible to distinguish a missing variable from a "no transfer" record. This is especially problematic with regard to data from the Cold War, which Nicholas Marsh refers to as the "heyday of gray market arms transfers" (2002:221). The superpowers delivered arms to conflicts worldwide in an attempt "to subvert the global influence of the other by clandestinely arming the enemies of their enemies" (221). Rather, it can only be assumed that the figures are generally underestimates, especially during the Cold War.

Second, one record in a dyad-year may list price and not volume, but another may list volume and not price. The specific number of weapons is also often missing. This disparity makes it difficult to create a variable based on either price or quantity because only partial information is usually available. As SAS points out, "Many governments report only the value or tonnage given in their customs receipts, leaving the actual number of weapons to guesswork" (2003:99). At the same time, the values of transfers—if given—are not necessarily accurate or useful because states may acquire arms through bartering, credit, or gifts as well as cash, which a raw price report does not capture (Brzoska 2004:113; Levine et al. 1997).

Finally, a single dyad-year may list more than one record of a single transfer. As a rule, NISAT utilizes multiple sources ("mirror statistics") in compiling its database and lists every record found for a dyad-year. For example, there may be at least two sources of data on a transfer, one taken from exporting-country reports and the other from importing-country reports (Marsh 2005). This approach helps to broaden the picture of the SALW trade, particularly for exporters or importers who do not regularly submit reports. However, it is impossible to determine whether the records reflect multiple sources on a single transfer or are indeed multiple transfers. Exporters and importers may provide either different types of information (e.g., price or quantity) or even slightly (or grossly) different values for the same type of information about the same transfer. Data aggregation is therefore unwise, and NISAT explicitly advises against it because of the nonstandardized nature of the raw data.

As a consequence, although it is possible to identify whether a small arms transfer has taken place, it is impossible to provide accurate information about the price paid or the amount transferred. Without improved records, *satransfer* is therefore most responsibly coded dichotomously. At the same time, it remains a crucial component of this analysis. Given the dearth of political and scholarly attention to small arms until recently, there is limited knowledge of states' patterns of exports in this area. This gap widens when it comes to quantitative analyses and suggests that using available data with an eye informed as to its shortcomings is well worth the effort. The value-added of including *satransfer* is high, not only for the research at hand—small arms have been at the center of policy discussions and the conduit for promoting "responsible" export controls—but also for arms control research more broadly, which lacks a fundamental understanding of states' small arms export practices.

INDEPENDENT VARIABLES

The statistical model explores the relationship between arms transfers and recipients' human rights records over time and contains four additional control variables: GDP per capita as a measure of development, democracy, internal conflict, and oil production. Table B.1 summarizes the independent variables. Each of the control variables is included because it may not only have an effect on arms transfers *but also* have an effect on human rights conditions in recipient states. As a result, variables such as alliance—which do tend to have a large significant effect on arms transfers but are not theoretically or empirically linked to recipient human rights—are excluded from the model.

According to empirical research, the presence of both internal conflict[10] and oil production[11] worsens a state's human rights. Democracy[12] and more advanced economic development,[13] in contrast, are associated with better human rights. Omitting one of these variables therefore has the potential to skew the results. For example, because GDP per capita is affiliated with both positive human rights and arms transfers, its exclusion from the model risks results that overestimate the relationship between good human rights and arms transfers.

Human Rights

Arms importer human rights records are the independent variable of interest. Human rights are at the heart of evolving humanitarian standards of arms export controls, set out in codes of conduct and other statements of "responsible" arms transfer controls. Yet *whether* recipients' human rights matter in arms transfer decision making and, if so, *how* they matter are open questions. Researchers have debated the definition, measurement, and quality of human rights data.[14]

Independent variable	Source	Coding	Justification
Human rights	PTS	1 (rare or extremely exceptional human rights violations) to 5 (frequent and severe violations extended to whole population)	Included in new arms export criteria but violations may increase demand for weapons
GDP per capita	UN	Estimated from the national account aggregates and logged	May affect recipients' human rights records; greater wealth expands resources to purchase arms
Democracy	Polity IV	−10 (autocracy) to +10 (democracy)	May affect arms exports from democratic exporters; may also affect recipients' human rights.
Oil production	Centripetalism	Millions of barrels of oil produced per day per capita	Provides producers with resources with which to purchase arms and favored arms export treatment from arms suppliers
Internal conflict	Uppsala/PRIO	0 (no conflict) to 2 (full war) based on number of battle-related deaths	Increases demand for weapons, affects recipients' human rights

Most data sources focus on physical integrity rights based on annual reports published by the U.S. DOS and Amnesty International. I use the Political Terror Scale (PTS), which ranks states annually based on these reports and provides a score from 1 to 5 for each country and each year in the data set beginning with 1980 (Gibney and Dalton 1996).

PTS coding rules are detailed in Gibney and Dalton (1996), starting with level 1 for countries "under a secure rule of law" where political murder is "extraordinarily rare," torture is "rare or exceptional," and "people are not imprisoned for their views" (73). At the other end of the scale, level 5 is for countries in which leaders "place no limits on the means or thoroughness with which they pursue personal or ideological goals" and "murders, disappearances, and torture are a common part of life" for the whole population (74). I create dummy variables for each level of the PTS scale, ranging from "very good" to "very bad." Because the PTS is ordinal rather than continuous, this treatment of the data is more accurate and technically correct:[15] there is no reason to assume that the difference between level 1 and level 2 is the same as the difference between level 2 and level 3, and so on (Wooldridge 2000:221–24). The level of human rights score with no violations (1 or "very good") is removed from the statistical analysis as the reference category for the four remaining dummy variables. Because this category is dominated by wealthy democracies—which, as typically "very good" human rights performers, are less interesting to the study here—this choice does not detract from the analysis.

Like any human rights data, PTS data are "inherently subjective," yet, as the Human Security Centre notes, "[it] sheds much-needed light on a murky corner of human insecurity" (2005:79). PTS also is the most comprehensive scale in terms of years and countries and includes separate variables for U.S. DOS and Amnesty reports (Poe, Carey, and Vazquez 2001).[16] Given the focus of the analysis on government arms export decision making, I use primarily the DOS-coded data, which cover more countries than the Amnesty data and provide some insight into government perceptions of human rights performance.[17] Of course, with both of these sources, political bias may be present. Joe Foweraker and Roman Krznaric (2000) find that DOS reports may be biased against left-wing governments and Amnesty reports in favor of them. Steven Poe, Sabine Carey, and Tanya Vazquez similarly observe that in the early years of such reporting in particular, "the US . . . tended to be somewhat less harsh than Amnesty in evaluating the human rights practices of other governments" (2001:661).[18] Yet they also point out that only a low proportion of variance between the sources is explained by these biases, concluding that "we have absolutely no reason to believe that the vast majority of the differences between the reports are systematic" (670).

Gross Domestic Product per Capita

This variable, which is logged in the analysis, comes from the National Accounts Main Aggregates Database maintained by the United Nations Statistics Division (2006). GDP per capita provides a broader measure of a recipient country's wealth and is an indicator of potential resources available for arms procurement. A profit-oriented producer would presumably have a greater interest in trading with a wealthier country. More advanced economic development is also associated with better human rights.

Democracy

Democracy is an important component of the analysis: democratic importers may be more likely to adhere to international rules and norms, including greater respect for human rights.[19] Moreover, it is also thought that democracies share a closer relationship with each other in the international community, suggesting that arms trade between democracies would be higher. The variable *polity2*, taken from the Polity IV data set (Marshall and Jaggers 2005a, 2005b), indicates the level of democracy in the recipient state. Its scale of government types ranges from strongly autocratic (−10) to strongly democratic (+10) based on weighted assessments of criteria including competitiveness of political participation and executive recruitment, openness of executive recruitment, and constraints on the chief executive. Although there is a long-standing debate about how democracy is best defined and measured,[20] Polity provides the most widely accepted and most comprehensive data available on democracy (Munck and Verkuilen 2002).

Oil Production

Oil production is included in the analysis as a single variable taken from John Gerring, Strom Thacker, and Carola Moreno's (2005) Centripetalism data set, which provides data on millions of barrels of oil produced per day per capita.[21] Existing research suggests that major oil producers are privileged recipients on the arms market. This was particularly the case during the oil crisis of the 1970s, which increased the resources available to oil-producing states to buy arms and the desire of arms supplier states to sell them.[22] This relationship has endured beyond the Cold War as an influential factor in the foreign policies of major powers in the Middle East for three key reasons (Chapman and Khanna 2006; Prados 2002:9). First, oil is a lucrative resource. It can raise the income of producing states and thus increase their ability to purchase arms (Brzoska and Ohlson 1987; Pearson 1994). Second, due to insecurity and border-control issues, oil-producing states in the Persian Gulf in particular may exhibit a high demand for arms (Chapman and Khanna 2006). Finally, oil is thought to be a significant reason that major powers have sought favorable relations in the Middle East—often, it is alleged, at the expense of human rights, democratic values, and regional stability.[23] Arms transfers have long been an important means of cultivating good relationships with interested countries.

Internal Conflict

Since the end of the Cold War, the vast majority of conflicts have taken place within states and not between them. An internal conflict is defined as a conflict between a state's government and internal opposition groups, without external intervention (Gleditsch et al. 2002). Conflict increases the demand for arms. Small arms in particular are seen as a primary tool of internal conflict, although states have also supplied MCW to government and rebel allies to help tip the scale in a conflict. States engaged in internal conflicts are also likely to experience higher levels of human rights violations.

The widely used Uppsala/PRIO (Peace Research Institute Oslo) Armed Conflict Dataset (Gleditsch et al. 2002) includes both high- and low-intensity conflict at annual death thresholds lower than Correlates of War data (Human Security Centre 2005:18–20).[24] The value assigned to conflict intensity is based on the number of battle-related deaths each year: c (no conflict); 1 (minor; at least twenty-five military or civilian battle-related deaths in a year); and 2 (war; a minimum of one thousand battle-related deaths per year).[25] For the same methodological reasons just described with the human rights data, I use dummy variables for high- and low-level internal conflict in the analysis, with "no conflict" as the reference category.[26]

INTERVIEWS

The interview citations are designed to maintain the interview subjects' anonymity. Due to the sensitive political nature of the topics under discussion, all but a few subjects agreed that their general affiliation but not their name or specific agency could be used as a public reference.[27] Because the arms trade community is small and relatively tight-knit, I have refrained from listing any specific government agencies, defense companies or associations, or civil society groups, even where respondents permitted it, because doing so could make others more easily identifiable. Each interview subject is therefore coded by a number comprising the interview number; the subject's general affiliation (1 for

TABLE B.2. CASE STUDY INTERVIEWS

Country	Correlates of war code	Number of participants
Belgium	211	18
Brazil	140	2
France	220	6
Germany	255	15
Switzerland	225	9
United Kingdom	200	12
United States	002	5

Note: Participants in Switzerland were members of the international NGO and research community based in Geneva.

government official; 2 for NGO; 3 for industry; 4 for other, such as expert); the interview year; and the Correlates of War country code for the subject's national expertise/affiliation. For example, an interview number might be 60108220 (60 = interview number, 1 = affiliation, 08 = 2008, 220 = country code).

Appendix C

FULL STATISTICAL RESULTS

The statistical model used in chapter 3 focuses on the relationship between arms exports and importers' human rights records. As such, rather than including a long list of independent variables that might have an effect on arms exports, it limits the control variables in the model to those that might have a confounding effect on *both* arms exports *and* human rights. Recent work in political methodology cautions against building "garbage can" or "kitchen sink" models that include a wide array of variables that may or may not influence the outcome of interest.[1]

Instead, control variables should be carefully selected based on the theoretical relationship between the independent variable of interest and the dependent variable *as well as* between the independent variables themselves. Christopher Achen argues that without a deliberately limited set of independent control variables, the effects of variables of interest on the dependent variable will be obscured and distorted by collinearity, nonlinearities, and other problems (2002:443; see also Achen 2005). Results from models featuring unnecessary variables are often highly contingent on precise specifications and make it more difficult to explore nuances of the relationship between variables of interest and the outcome (Achen 2005; Berk 2004). To determine which control variables to include, James Lee Ray (2003) and Kelly Kadera and Sara Mitchell (2005) suggest limiting models to only those control variables that threaten to have a confounding effect on the independent variable of interest. In other words, models should contain only potentially confounding variables but not include intervening or competing variables.

Appendix B describes the variable coding and selection, including the theoretical and empirical justifications for the chosen control variables. Each independent variable is lagged one year in the regression analyses to allow for information about conditions in recipient states to reach decision makers in exporting states (Blanton 2000, 2005; Meernik, Krueger, and Poe 1998). Decision makers need time to receive government, news, and NGO reports about conditions on the ground and the opportunity to adjust arms export practices accordingly. In addition, because the data are annual, relevant changes midyear might appear only minimally in the data set, if at all.

Because the variable for MCW transfers is continuous, I use ordinary least squares regression models for all regressions with MCW as the dependent variable. The variable for SALW transfers, in contrast, is binary (dichotomous) and therefore requires logit regression models where used as the dependent variable. Because the data in both cases are cross-sectional dyadic annual data, panel-corrected standard errors must be used to avoid an understatement of the errors due to the high number of error parameters involved in panel data, including panel heteroscedasticity and temporal dependence (Beck 2001; Beck and Katz 1995).

Tables C.1 to C.4 contain the full results for the regression analyses, including the regression coefficients and standard errors (SE) for each model and time period.

TABLE C.1. INFLUENCE OF HUMAN RIGHTS ON MCW TRANSFERS (ALL SUPPLIER STATES)

	1981–1991 (SE)	1992–1997 (SE)	1998–2010 (SE)
GDP per capita	5.201**	3.820**	3.142**
	(.655)	(.434)	(.289)
Democracy	−.077	−.018	−.132
	(.138)	(.081)	(.075)
Low internal conflict	7.101**	3.871*	2.840
	(2.455)	(1.700)	(1.593)
High internal conflict	5.394	8.416**	7.750
	(3.619)	(3.061)	(4.014)
Oil production	1.008	7.955	−3.281
	(4.394)	(4.606)	(2.719)
Good human rights	4.512**	3.629**	2.674**
	(1.358)	(1.326)	(.859)
Average human rights	10.005**	4.789**	2.094**
	(1.701)	(1.487)	(.798)
Bad human rights	16.818**	6.908**	11.125**
	(3.267)	(1.556)	(1.969)
Very bad human rights	20.615**	2.711	−.044
	(4.793)	(1.83)	(1.605)
Constant	−31.198**	−25.584**	−23.541**
	(4.877)	(3.506)	(2.698)
Observations	28236	19248	37134
Dyads	2905	3521	3477
Wald Chi^2	256.67	114.69	232.04
Prob > Chi^2	0.000	0.000	0.000

*Significant at the 0.05 level.

**Significant at the 0.01 level.

Note: Coefficients for year dummies excluded from all tables to save space.

TABLE C.2. INFLUENCE OF HUMAN RIGHTS ON MCW TRANSFERS (ATT SUPPORTERS)

	1981–1991 (SE)	1992–1997 (SE)	1998–2010 (SE)
GDP per capita	4.148**	4.258**	2.935**
	(.404)	(.464)	(.243)
Democracy	.174**	−.026	−.028
	(.060)	(.079)	(.033)
Low internal conflict	5.816**	3.686*	2.988**
	(1.541)	(1.784)	(.966)
High internal conflict	2.879**	8.255**	3.175**
	(1.041)	(3.143)	(.902)
Oil production	4.680	6.903	−.080
	(3.487)	(4.948)	(2.360)
Good human rights	4.090**	4.167**	2.364*
	(1.299)	(1.415)	(.922)
Average human rights	5.710**	4.248**	1.298
	(1.307)	(1.546)	(.825)
Bad human rights	3.381**	6.120**	3.502**
	(1.248)	(1.590)	(.859)
Very bad human rights	2.024	2.531	.568
	(1.404)	(1.857)	(.891)
Constant	−26.936**	−29.387**	−22.470**
	(3.091)	(.404)	(2.433)
Observations	25670	17486	33766
Dyads	2641	3213	3161
Wald Chi^2	226.79	119.08	250.37
Prob > Chi^2	0.000	0.000	0.000

Significant at the 0.05 level.
**Significant at the 0.01 level.*

TABLE C.3. INFLUENCE OF HUMAN RIGHTS ON SALW TRANSFERS
(ALL SUPPLIER STATES)

	1981–1991 (SE)	1992–1997 (SE)	1998–2010 (SE)
GDP per capita	1.410**	1.562**	1.362**
	(.057)	(.056)	(.041)
Democracy	.084**	.076**	.066**
	(.008)	(.010)	(.008)
Low internal conflict	.366**	.336*	.312**
	(.123)	(.127)	(.091)
High internal conflict	−.077	.429*	.605**
	(.161)	(.197)	(.143)
Oil production	−1.467**	−1.417**	−2.014**
	(.409)	(.383)	(.356)
Good human rights	−.443**	.230	−.023
	(.125)	(.118)	(.085)
Average human rights	−.343**	.657**	−.193
	(.124)	(.141)	(.100)
Bad human rights	−.394*	.555**	−.310*
	(.157)	(.168)	(.121)
Very bad human rights	−.610**	−.118	−.620**
	(.193)	(.201)	(.169)
Constant	−12.593**	−12.874**	−10.936**
	(.452)	(.454)	(.364)
Observations	28236	19248	37134
Dyads	2905	3521	3477
Wald Chi^2	1223.88	1513.94	1984.55
Prob > Chi^2	0.000	0.000	0.000

*Significant at the 0.05 level.
**Significant at the 0.01 level.

TABLE C.4. INFLUENCE OF HUMAN RIGHTS ON SALW TRANSFERS (ATT SUPPORTERS)

	1981–1991 (SE)	1992–1997 (SE)	1998–2010 (SE)
GDP per capita	1.417**	1.580**	1.421**
	(.059)	(.059)	(.044)
Democracy	.083**	.076**	.065**
	(.008)	(.011)	(.008)
Low internal conflict	.417**	.317*	.364**
	(.129)	(.133)	(.096)
High internal conflict	−.103	.513*	.593**
	(.166)	(.206)	(.153)
Oil production	−1.409**	−1.416**	−1.967**
	(.425)	(.405)	(.380)
Good human rights	−.377**	.246*	−.047
	(.110)	(.125)	(.091)
Average human rights	−.276*	.665**	−.211*
	(.129)	(.149)	(.106)
Bad human rights	−.314	.526**	−.348**
	(.163)	(.177)	(.129)
Very bad human rights	−.531**	−.080	−.712**
	(.199)	(.211)	(.181)
Constant	−12.468**	−12.919**	−11.378**
	(.469)	(.476)	(.388)
Observations	25670	17486	33766
Dyads	2641	3213	3161
Wald Chi^2	1128.53	1391.09	1867.95
Prob > Chi^2	0.000	0.000	0.000

*Significant at the 0.05 level.
**Significant at the 0.01 level.

NOTES

1. INTRODUCTION AND OVERVIEW

1. For news reports, see Associated Press 2008; Baldauf and Ford 2008; Dugger 2008; Dugger and Barboza 2008; Dugger, Barboza, and Cowell 2008; Reuters 2008.

2. See chapter 3 for formal definitions of *small arms and light weapons* (such as machine guns) and *major conventional arms* (such as tanks and military aircraft). I refer to "small arms and light weapons" interchangeably by either the internationally recognized acronym SALW or the shorthand "small arms."

3. Dating back to the mid-1990s, there are simply too many newspaper stories, journal articles, and NGO reports using this terminology to begin to cite them or trace its origins.

4. The three opposed were Iran, North Korea, and Syria. There were twenty-three abstentions.

5. Article 223 of the 1957 Treaty of Rome protects members' right to produce and sell arms in the interest of their national security.

6. On this relationship, see G. Adams 1981; Cooling 1981; Dunne 1995; Eisenhower 1961; Hartung 1996; Keller 1995; Kolodziej 1979; Kurth 1971; Markusen et al. 1991; and Silverstein 2000.

7. SIPRI (2012) estimates that five countries—the United States, Russia, Germany, France, and the United Kingdom—dominate the global market in MCW, accounting

for 75 percent of global sales between 2007 and 2011. Seventy-four of the top one hundred arms companies in 2010 were from the United States and western Europe.

8. On these effects, see Boutwell and Klare 1999; Boutwell, Klare, and Reed 1995; Craft 1999; Craft and Smaldone 2002; Eavis 1999; Harkavy and Neuman 2001; Hartung 2001a; Karp 1993, 1994; Klare 1994–1995; Klare and Rotberg 1999; Musah 2002; Renner 1997; SAS 2001, 2002, 2003, 2006, 2007, 2009; Sislin and Pearson 2001; Stohl and Grillot 2009.

9. On this connection between arms and poor human rights, see, for example, Blanton 1999, 2001; Craft 1999; Craft and Smaldone 2002; Neuman 1986.

10. For the full text of the ATT, see http://www.un.org/disarmament/ATT/docs /ATT_text_(As_adopted_by_the_GA)-E.pdf.

11. A multimethod approach "aims to improve the quality of conceptualization and measurement, analysis of rival explanations, and overall confidence in the central findings of the study" (Lieberman 2005:435).

12. Chapter 3 discusses the statistical findings; appendix B provides coding details; and appendix C provides full statistical results tables.

13. Gerardo Munck suggests "matching cases on independent variables," which "serve the same purpose as statistical control" (2004:104).

14. Audie Klotz and Cecelia Lynch recommend research on both levels of analysis in order to trace more thoroughly "the spread of norms across state boundaries and into societies" (2007:95).

2. "RESPONSIBLE" ARMS TRANSFER POLICY AND THE POLITICS OF SOCIAL REPUTATION

1. Some scholars acknowledge a social dimension to international reputation (e.g., J. Busby 2008; Johnston 2008; Keohane 1984; O'Neill 2006; Paul 2009; Sharman 2006). However, the concept remains theoretically underdeveloped, and its consequences are either discounted or underexplored.

2. See Bromley 1993 for an overview of common usages of the term.

3. Many scholars conclude that reputation can lead to more frequent participation in conflicts but debate the rationality of going to war to "save face." See, for example, Crescenzi, Kathman, and Long 2007; Hugh-Jones and Zultan 2012; Lebow 1981; Mercer 1996; Press 2005; Schelling 1966; Tang 2005; Walter 2009; Wolford 2007.

4. That is, "while adversaries can get reputations for having resolve, they rarely get reputations for lacking resolve; and while allies can get reputations for lacking resolve, they rarely get reputations for having resolve" (Mercer 1996:10; see also Huth 1988).

5. This use of reputation to inform states' choices to cooperate with other states corresponds with game theoretical approaches to reputation, which observe that the "information conditions" of repeated games create the very "possibility of reputation" and can motivate compliance to acquire material gain even in the absence of formal

institutions (Alt, Calvert, and Human 1988:449; Greif 2006; Milgrom, North, and Weingast 1990).

6. J. C. Sharman (2006) engages this question only in passing. Michael Tomz (2007) does find that in the case of debtor–creditor cooperation, investors' willingness to make loans—and the terms of those loans—are connected to borrowers' payment histories. Interesting parallels can be drawn between these approaches to reputation and those of corporate management. Reputation matters in business because of its impact on an undetermined number of "future trading opportunities" and the profits attached (Kreps 1990). It is a strategic approach to spread positive information about a company and its products in order to increase its profits (Davies et al. 2003; Fombrun 1996). In fact, corporate strategies of branding and marketing linked to reputation are spreading to countries by explicit national branding efforts (Aronczyk 2013; Jones and Subotic 2011; van Ham 2008).

7. Other authors share a similar perspective: see Finnemore and Sikkink 1998; Hurd 2007; Johnston 2008; and Schimmelfennig 2001. Nicolas Jabko (2006) refers to a related approach as "strategic constructivism," in which strategic actors exploit norms and ideas in pursuit of political goals.

8. As Alastair Iain Johnston (2008) points out in the case of China, social pressures can also encourage nondemocracies engaged in international institutions to adopt policies in line with international expectations. Patterns of states ratifying human rights treaties but not complying with them lend support to this argument (Hafner-Burton and Tsutsui 2005; Hathaway 2002).

9. Legislatures are largely uninvolved in arms export decision making. Many European parliaments have called for arms export oversight, but their input is usually post hoc at best. Only in the United States, where oversight on deals over a certain dollar figure is allowed but rarely exercised, and in Sweden, where oversight committees have regular input, do legislatures have *any* regular role.

10. This concern relates primarily to elites' perceptions but can extend to that of foreign publics as well (Goldsmith and Horiuchi 2009).

11. Assigning human qualities to states—interests, identities, beliefs, the capacity to act, and so on—is standard practice in IR (Jackson 2004; Ringmar 1996; Wendt 1999, 2004; Wolfers 1962). Alexander Wendt (2004) argues that this view of "states as people" enables states to possess a collective intentionality that cannot be reduced to its individual citizens and that has associated needs and interests (see also Searle 1990; Wendt 1999). I take the common view that states can be ascribed personlike traits accounting for their collective behavior, which allows reputation to be carried by a state as an entity, but also by its leaders and diplomats.

12. A public commitment to humanitarian arms control in general, human rights treaties, nonproliferation policies, climate-change initiatives, and opposition to whaling are all additional examples of issue areas that states, international organizations, NGOs, and other international actors have associated to varying degrees with good

international citizenship. The concept itself was introduced by Australian foreign minister Gareth Evans in the 1980s and is often associated with the English School in IR theory (Wheeler and Dunne 1998).

13. International reputation here serves primarily as a motivating factor for states' *commitment* to international norms and rules. On the influence of reputation on *compliance* with international law, see Chayes and Chayes 1995; Downs and Jones 2002; R. Fisher 1981; Franck 1988; Goldsmith and Posner 2005; Guzman 2002; Henkin 1968; Norman and Trachtman 2005. The discussion of arms trade transparency (or lack thereof) later in this chapter addresses why reputation provides less of a "compliance pull," as Thomas Franck (1990) puts it.

14. Noel Kaplowitz states, "The aspects of national self-imagery which influence foreign policy behavior include how a people sees itself, what it likes and dislikes about itself, the ways in which it may want to change, how it views its history, the 'lessons' it has learned, and its conceptions of national purpose and interest" (1984:376).

15. Governments are not the only source of states' external images. Nonstate actors, such as NGOs, hoping to persuade governments to adopt certain policies or practices, may engage in their own impression-management strategies to make states look good or bad (J. Busby 2007, 2008). Domestic events outside a government's control can also influence a state's international reputation. Consider, for example, the Swiss government's embarrassment over the results of the 2009 referendum to ban minarets, a referendum that it worried would harm Switzerland's image as a country of tolerance, refuge, and respect for international law.

16. Robert Jervis defines a decision maker's image of another actor as "those of his beliefs about the other that affect his predictions of how the other will behave under various circumstances" (1970:5). Like the credibility approaches to reputation, image is important in "determining whether and how easily the state can reach its goals" (6). Unlike those approaches, however, Jervis argues that a state's image is not "completely dependent on the major actions it took" (8), making it "possible for a state to consciously influence others' images of it without paying the price of altering its basic behavior and sacrificing other goals" (10). In line with my point here, he emphasizes the psychological and subjective nature of states' images and states' ability to shape, with varied success, their desired images through "minor and relatively cheap" changes in their policy or behavior (11).

17. Christian Reus-Smit refers to this recognition as an actor's legitimacy, which describes "not just the capacity to act, but the right or entitlement to act" (2007:158). Wendt notes that "persons," especially moral and legal persons, are externally constituted by social recognition, which conveys "all the rights and privileges of that status" (2004:293, 294).

18. The American Political Science Association Task Force on U.S. Standing defines standing as "a particular kind of reputation" with "a more relative connotation in that it refers to position within a particular setting—in this case the society of states or

'international community'" (American Political Science Association 2009:4, 6). Joshua Busby (2008), in turn, defines prestige as standing. Prestige and honor are also often used interchangeably in IR as related to esteem, standing, or glory (e.g., Donelan 2007; Kagan 1998; Lebow 2008; Tsygankov and Tarver-Wahlquist 2009). Barry O'Neill, however, argues that prestige, unlike honor, depends on a group's recognition of it: "A person might possess personal honor while others do not know about that quality"; prestige, in contrast, stems from a group member's being "generally admired" and gaining influence in the group because of a good reputation (1999:193; see also O'Neill 2006).

19. Cecilia Ridgeway and Henry Walker summarize theories of social hierarchy formation and call social hierarchies "an enduring feature of human interaction and a fundamental aspect of the organization of social behavior" (1995:281).

20. Robert Gilpin, for example, notes the existence of a "hierarchy of prestige among states" linked to but distinct from material power and resting on the perceptions of other states (1981:30–31). However, soft power can also enhance reputation. For more on hard power, soft power, and standing, see American Political Science Association 2009.

21. According to Aaron Wildavsky, "Reactions [from others] are also indispensable in that the only way the self knows what it is is by feedback from others (1994:139–40). Christine Ingebritsen, for instance, argues that the increasing international scrutiny to which Scandinavia has become subjected "helps redefine its own understanding of self" (2006:107). Kristen Monroe observes that "maintaining self-esteem seems to play a key role in maintaining identity," which requires a general consistency between perceived self-image and behavior (2001:498). For more on the concept of identity as a social category and its measurement, see Abdelal et al. 2009.

22. D. B. Bromley states, "Although reputations are simplified and distorted representations of persons, they describe people's social identities. They provide an external standard or criterion against which, through social 'feedback,' we try to assess our social identities. Reconciling personal identity and social identity is a continuing problem of adjustment" (1993:11).

23. Scholars note the importance of regular interaction by diplomats in international institutions for international socialization (Adler and Barnett 1998; Checkel 2001; Johnston 2008). See also the *International Organization* special issue "International institutions and Socialization in Europe" (2005).

24. The need for dense and frequent interactions within a network to assign reputations to actors is also noted by anthropology (Bailey 1971; Colson 1974); sociology (Raub and Weesie 1990); and corporate management (Fombrun 1996). For larger groups, regimes and institutions can help to spread the information necessary for reputation to function as an enforcement mechanism, although this does not take into account the social pressure generated by interactions within a group (Ahn, Esarey, and Scholz 2009; Milgrom, North, and Weingast 1990).

25. Johnston argues that small or consensus-driven groups are more likely to lead to states' internalization of new norms but concedes that norm adoption without internalization can be a powerful social incentive in large groups where rules are majoritarian and put members' policy support on record (2008:31–32). Although majoritarian decision rules make it easier for NGOs and other actors not in the room to criticize a state's policy positions, they are not necessary to establish its reputation among the diplomats debating a policy themselves. This key audience for international reputation knows who dissents from a popular policy initiative. In fact, dissent under consensus rules may be even more controversial and subject to reputational fallout because it can single-handedly prohibit an initiative from passing (or weaken it), unlike dissent under majoritarian rules.

26. The UN Institute for Disarmament Research assembles and publishes information on states' contributions to goals set out in the 2001 UNPOA.

27. See, for example, Abdelal et al. 2009; Chayes and Chayes 1995; Johnston 2008; Keohane 1984; Simmons 2009; Wheeler 2000; Young 1992; and Zarakol 2011.

28. This dichotomy of interests and expectations can also lead to cognitive dissonance between instrumentally beneficial policies and socially beneficial policies. Leaders will try to resolve this tension within their community's existing normative framework, to the extent that a norm is defined broadly enough to make this possible (Shannon 2000).

29. Image management is common in corporate branding. Consider, for example, attempts by U.S. banks to use public-relations campaigns, personnel changes, new policies, and repayment of government loans to distance themselves from their "fat cat" reputations following the 2008 financial crisis.

30. And of consistency between policy and action to the extent that others can observe action. Without transparency, criticism of discrepancies between state policy and action can only be limited. As Nicholas Wheeler points out, "Changing norms provide actors with new public legitimating reasons to justify actions, but they do not determine that an action will take place" (2000:9). I discuss this point further in the context of states' domestic reputations and scandal sensitivity.

31. See Brooks and Wohlforth 2008; Downs and Jones 2002; R. Fisher 1981; Norman and Trachtman 2005.

32. Whether a reputation can carry across issue areas is a matter of some debate. Jonathan Mercer argues that "a general reputation has an enduring character trait that reappears in different types of situations," whereas "a specific attribution applies not across types of situations but within specific types of situations" (1996:37; see aso R. Fisher 1981). Similarly, James Lebovic and Erik Voeten posit that a good reputation in one area can help states establish good reputations in other areas (2006:868). Michael Tomz and Mark Wright (2010) find evidence of "reputational spillover" from states' default on sovereign debt to their expropriations of foreign direct investment. However, these issues may still be considered closely related within economic rela-

tions and cannot address the broader question of spillover from economic to security affairs, which Stephen Brooks and William Wohlforth contend lacks empirical support (2008:163). "Similar situations" may be defined very narrowly, suggesting that reputation is considerably more complex than other definitions might imply (e.g., Downs and Jones 2002; Norman and Trachtman 2005).

33. This perspective tends to be associated with realist views of international law (Hathaway 2002), although some liberal scholars also argue that without incorporating costly material punishments, treaty commitments may still essentially be cheap talk (Hafner-Burton 2005). In addition, once formalized into binding agreements, cheap talk can lead to expected and unexpected compliance costs (Clark 2013; Goodliffe and Hawkins 2006; Greenhill 2010; Schimmelfennig 2001; Simmons 2009).

34. This would be the general expectation of constructivism.

35. Many scholars observe similar gaps between the expectations and realities of states' follow-through on their international humanitarian commitments (e.g., Hafner-Burton 2005; Hathaway 2002; Simmons 2009; Smith-Cannoy 2012; Wheeler 2000).

36. I focus on the government as a whole and its top leaders. This focus is justified for two reasons. First, the media and public are less able to differentiate between (and take an interest in) bureaucratic versus executive responsibility. Second, governments decide whether to adopt a particular arms export policy. Top officials are often also responsible for deciding whether to approve the most controversial/political arms export applications.

37. More specifically, John Thompson labels scandals as actions, events, or circumstances in which there is (1) "the transgression of certain values, norms or moral codes"; (2) "an element of secrecy or concealment"; (3) a disapproval of the events or actions by some nonparticipants; (4) the public denunciation of the events or actions by some nonparticipants; and (5) "the disclosure and condemnation of the actions or events [that] may damage the reputation of the individuals responsible for them" (2000:13–14). See also A. King 1984; Mancuso 1998.

38. Scandal cannot simply be defined by equating it with corruption; more corruption does not predict more scandals. Instead, levels of corruption tend to remain relatively constant, whereas scandal levels and type change over time (Lowi 2004:70–71).

39. On this variation in what makes a scandal, see Dobratz and Whitfield 1992; Garment 1992; A. King 1984; Williams 1998.

40. Belgium, with its delicate governing arrangements, is a noteworthy exception. The British Arms to Iraq scandal also contributed to Labour positioning itself as a more transparent and accountable alternative in the 1997 election.

41. See Bowler and Karp 2004; Funk 1996; Meinke and Anderson 2001; Williams 1998.

42. See A. King 1984; Meinke and Anderson 2001; J. Thompson 2000; Williams 1998.

43. See Hirshberg 1993; Monroe 2001; Shannon 2000.

44. Such partnerships are often referred to as "the new diplomacy" or "new multi-lateralism." See Axworthy 1998; Malone 2002; McRae 2001; Petrova 2007.

45. For example, Amnesty International has sought to maintain neutrality from governments in order to preserve the credibility of its message and mission (Clark 2001; Dezalay and Garth 2006).

46. This suggestion goes beyond the contention that norm violators can be shamed for not keeping international commitments (J. Busby 2008:83) or because they violate norms of international society (Lebovic and Voeten 2006:869).

47. Archon Fung, Mary Graham, and David Weil (2007) pinpoint the 1980s as the start of U.S. moves toward increasing transparency in corporate governance and financial markets. Others connect the global spread of transparency to trends of democratization, globalization, and financial crisis in the 1990s (Best 2005; Florini 1998; Relly and Sabharwal 2009).

48. See Broz 2002; Chayes and Chayes 1995; Florini 1998; R. Mitchell 1998; Relly and Sabharwal 2009.

49. See Apodaca 2007; Broz 2002; Fearon 1994; Fung, Graham, and Weil 2007.

50. Jeannine Relly and Meghna Sabharwal note that authoritarian regimes have also adopted some fiscal transparency to attract international investment and aid (2009:151). However, whether transparency initiatives generally make good economic sense has been debated: see Alt and Lassen 2006; Broz 2002; Dranove et al. 2003; Florini 1998; Fung et al. 2004; Fung, Graham, and Weil 2007.

51. See J. Thompson 2000 on the rise of the "mediated scandal."

52. These commitments can be both national and multilateral. Certainly, the public has to care about arms trade practice in order for the transparency–accountability dynamic to function. Given the high volume of information available to the average media consumer and the general disinterest in arms trade policy, it is only where there is a clear disregard of fundamental national values, I argue in chapter 5, that concentrated public attention over conventional arms exports will arise.

53. Domestic defense production is important to national security: "The capacity to restock supplies or modify equipment from domestic sources is often cited as an important wartime asset. Domestic production can reduce vulnerability to boycotts or blockades. Moreover, domestic arms production and arms transfers are widely viewed as important sources of national prestige and diplomatic leverage" (Moravcsik 1991:200).

54. Joseph Grieco (1993) argues that state interests are based on their power position in the international system. States are wary of cooperative arrangements, particularly because relative gains might favor their partners.

55. This failure does not mean that realists predict an unregulated arms trade. According to Joanne Gowa (1994), states are acutely aware of the security externalities connected to improved material power capabilities brought on by foreign trade. As a

consequence, they will seek to control the flow of defense goods and technologies to ensure that only their allies receive the strategic benefits. Allies are often given preferred treatment in national export legislation, with faster decision-making processes and less intense scrutiny of applications. Such favorable terms are codified, for example, in Germany for its NATO allies as well as between the United States and Canada.

56. From 1989 to 2005, the United States was the most frequent intervener, with thirty-eight incidents of international military intervention, followed by France (thirty-three incidents) and the United Kingdom (thirteen) (Kisangani and Pickering 2007).

57. Legally binding arms embargoes may be the one exception in which international commitments effectively limit arms export practices (Erickson 2013c).

58. Although the influence of industry may to a degree wax and wane over time, the general observation from this perspective is that it remains a steady fixture of importance in security and defense-related policy making.

59. On the defense industry's influence, see G. Adams 1981; Eisenhower 1961; Kurth 1971; Markusen et al. 1991.

60. On the constructivist position, see Finnemore 1996a, 1996b; Katzenstein 1996; Klotz 1995.

61. See, for example, Hafner-Burton 2005; Hafner-Burton and Tsutsui 2005; Lebovic and Voeten 2006; Ron, Ramos, and Rodgers 2005; K. Smith 2001; Smith, Pagnucco, and Lopez 1998.

62. The determinacy with which norms influence state behavior is unclear. Constructivists suggest that "norms enable new or different behaviors; they do not ensure such behaviors" (Finnemore 1996a:158). Nevertheless, they firmly assert that "norms create patterns of behavior in accordance with their prescriptions" (Finnemore 1996b:23) and make certain behaviors more likely than others (Wendt 1999). Determining conditions for when and where norms are influential is therefore an important question for IR research (Legro 1997).

63. See Blanton 1999; Bueno de Mesquita et al. 2005; Davenport 1995; Howard and Donnelly 1986; Mitchell and McCormick 1988; Poe and Tate 1994; Rummel 1995.

64. Martha Finnemore and Kathryn Sikkink (1998) argue that instrumentalist motivations may dominate early in norm life cycles but become more deeply embedded over time.

65. On analytical eclecticism, see Abbott and Snidal 2002; Jupille, Caporaso, and Checkel 2003; Katzenstein, Keohane, and Krasner 1998; Katzenstein and Sil 2004; Sil 2000; Wildavsky 1994; Zürn and Checkel 2005.

66. Jay Goodliffe and Darren Hawkins (2006), for example, find a significant role for norms in explaining compliance with the Convention Against Torture. However, they conclude that their quantitative analysis cannot parse out whether their findings are due to rationalist mechanisms (reputational costs) or constructivist mechanisms

(state identity and socialization). Because of states' poor compliance with new arms export policies, the qualitative and quantitative evidence presented here lends itself well both to combining and to separating these mechanisms: states are socialized into policy expectations, to which they respond instrumentally out of concern for their reputation; however, they have not internalized new norms.

3. HISTORY AND CONTEMPORARY TRENDS IN CONVENTIONAL ARMS EXPORT CONTROLS

1. During the Cold War, only West Germany and the European neutrals sought explicitly to limit arms transfers to areas of instability and conflict. The United States under President Carter also had a policy (followed loosely at best) to prohibit exports to human rights violators.

2. On this optimism, see Anderson 1992; Cornish 1995; Goldring 1994–1995; Jones and Rees 1994; Kemp 1991; Klare 1991; Neuman 1993; Nolan 1991; Pierre 1997; Spear 1994.

3. UN General Assembly Resolution A/61/394 passed by a vote of 153 to 1 (the United States) on December 6, 2006. There were 24 abstentions, including Russia and China. After an unprecedented ninety-eight responses to the secretary-general's call for states' views on an ATT in 2007 (instead of the usual ten to fifteen responses for similar exercises), a Group of Governmental Experts met in 2008 to recommend a draft treaty for negotiation. I discuss the ATT process in detail in chapter 4.

4. For most governments, public reporting began only in the 1990s. The United States and a handful of states made reporting improvements during the late 1970s and 1980s. Austria, for example, began issuing reports in 1977, and Sweden followed suit in 1984 (Haug et al. 2002).

5. These problems are magnified substantially with the Eastern Bloc, which had a separate and extremely secretive system of trade (Brzoska and Ohlson 1987; Brzoska and Pearson 1994; Catrina 1988; Keller 1995; Pierre 1982).

6. In particular, China, Israel, Russia, South Africa, and Turkey.

7. SAS anticipates that Comtrade—although an extremely valuable source and the primary source for Cold War export data—generally underestimates the quantity and value of small arms transferred (2009:7).

8. On the properties and use of time-series dyadic data, see Beck and Katz 2001; Green, Kim, and Yoon 2001; G. King 2001.

9. Because the Arms Trade Data Set is intended to assess governments' arms export decision making, it does not include black-market sales (i.e., sales not authorized by the government). Although illicit arms commonly originate in the legal market, the absence of a measure of illicit sales does not affect the data or analysis here.

10. To accommodate inconsistencies in information reported (price paid/value/amount purchased), SALW transfers are coded as a dichotomous variable, taken from

raw Norwegian Initiative on Small Arms Transfers data. See appendix B for a more detailed discussion.

11. MCW data are taken from SIPRI, which uses a dollar-based standardized "trend indicator value" to measure the quality and quantity of weapons transferred. See appendix B for details.

12. The absence of data makes it impossible to assess arms export practice during earlier attempts at multilateral export controls.

13. Knowledge about Soviet arms transfer policy and practice is limited. Research finds that the Soviet Union viewed arms exports as an instrument of foreign policy in the struggle between socialism and imperialism in the Cold War superpower competition (Brzoska and Ohlson 1987:40–44; Catrina 1988:87–88).

14. The 1890 General Act for the Repression of the African Slave Trade (the Brussels Act) also contained arms clauses prohibiting arms transfers within a defined zone in Africa in order to disarm local resistance and restrict competing colonial powers' activity. Its effects in practice were mixed. See Beachey 1962; Bromley, Cooper, and Holtom 2012. For an overview of pre-twentieth-century regulations (primarily national level), see Krause and MacDonald 1993.

15. David Stone points out that the major powers, although supportive in principle, still had security and economic concerns. The United Kingdom, for example, won exemptions related to supplying armed forces needed to maintain its empire (2000:222).

16. The Nye Committee was formally the U.S. Senate Special Committee on Investigation of the Munitions Industry. For U.S. diplomatic discussions about the proposal, see *Foreign Relations of the United States Diplomatic Papers 1934* ("General, British Commonwealth" volume). At home, President Franklin Roosevelt billed it to Congress, when introducing the Nye Committee, as saving both the international community from war and strife "due in no small measure to the uncontrolled activities of the manufacturers and merchants of engines of destruction" and "the peoples of many countries" from "being taxed to the point of poverty and starvation in order to enable governments to engage in a mad race in armaments" (Roosevelt 1934:9095).

17. See Brzoska and Ohlson 1987; Keller and Nolan 1997; Klare 1984; Neuman 1986; Stanley and Pearton 1972

18. U.S. and Soviet arms transfers were also thought to have economic benefits, but their primary motivation was nevertheless political (Brzoska and Ohlson 1987:43; Pierre 1982).

19. COCOM lost its purpose with the end of the Cold War. In 1996, it was replaced by the Wassenaar Arrangement, which primarily promotes arms export transparency.

20. The United States sometimes struggled to make its allies adopt economic containment; West European states preferred to maintain trade links with their Eastern neighbors (Mastanduno 1992).

21. Arms sales also captured international attention with the UN's 1963 voluntary arms embargo against South Africa, made mandatory in 1977. The embargo was intended to isolate the Pretoria regime, denounce apartheid, and change the government's policy. However, it was neither strictly implemented nor enforced (Catrina 1988:142–44). In one example among many, the United States was accused of exporting spare parts for military use and turning a blind eye to some cases of technology acquisition and defense trade to enable monitoring of Soviet activity in the region (Klare 1981; Phythian 2000a). The embargo was one of the few mandatory UN sanctions during the Cold War and was lifted in May 1994.

22. Although policy makers introduced human rights into the discussion, public concern was for the destabilizing effect of "too many" arms exports to the developing world, not "to whom" the arms were specifically being sent.

23. On PD-13, see Ball and Leitenberg 1979; Brzoska and Ohlson 1987; Durch 2000; Hartung 1993; Hoffmann 1977–1978; Pierre 1982; Spear 1995.

24. The studies cited examine military aid rather than arms transfers as a whole (which also include the purchase of defense goods and may not include some parts of military aid). Unlike U.S. law on arms transfers more broadly, U.S. law on military aid has mandated since 1974 that a country's human rights violations should adversely affect its receipt of military aid. Although these results therefore cannot directly substitute for an analysis of arms transfer practices, they nevertheless shed some much needed light onto the role of human rights in one major exporters' military aid–giving practice during an important period of the Cold War.

25. Although David Cingranelli and Thomas Pasquarello (1985) do find that human rights modestly affect military aid to Latin America in fiscal year 1982, these findings have been contested based on their operationalization of human rights and selection of cases included in the analysis (Carleton and Stohl 1987; Mitchell and McCormick 1988).

26. Full results are reported in appendix C. The statistical analyses use ordinary least squares regressions (for the continuous MCW variable) and logit regressions (for the dichotomous SALW variable). In addition, panel-corrected standard errors must be used with the annual dyadic data to avoid an understatement of the errors due to the high number of error parameters involved in panel data, including panel heteroscedasticity and temporal dependence (Beck 2001; Beck and Katz 1995). I select control variables based on the theoretical relationship between the independent variable of interest (human rights) and the dependent variable (MCW/SALW). Results from models featuring unnecessary variables are often highly contingent on precise specifications and make it more difficult to explore nuances of the relationship between variables of interest and the outcome (Achen 2005; Berk 2004). Appendix B covers variable coding and justification for inclusion in statistical models.

27. See the sources cited in note 2 for this chapter.

28. Although still bound by bloc politics, European and other smaller producers, such as Brazil and Israel, sought to export arms to support their national arms industries, boost their balance of payments and employment, and reduce production costs (Catrina 1988; Pierre 1982; Stanley and Pearton 1972; Taylor 1994; Wentz 1987–1988). This is not to suggest that arms sales did not have economic benefits for the superpowers. In fact, arms were a significant part of Soviet foreign trade, though the Soviet Union supposedly did not intentionally seek out financial advantages from its arms exports (Brzoska and Ohlson 1987:43).

29. On this debate, see Chalmers et al. 2002; Hartley and Martin 2003; Hartung 1996; Ingram and Isbister 2004; Levine et al. 1997; S. Martin 1999; Mayhew 2005; Mintz and Huang 1991; Pierre 1982; Wentz 1987–1988.

30. See Anthony 1997; Brzoksa 2004; Durch 2000; Gold 1999; Harkavy 1994; Kapstein 1997; Keller and Nolan 1997

31. See Cornish 1995; Gold 1999; Kapstein 1997; Neuman 1993; Wulf 1993.

32. See Anthony 1997; Kapstein 1997; Neuman 1993; Wulf 1993.

33. Canada and Japan also proposed a Group of 7 (G7) working group to monitor arms transfers, but France objected to the G7 as the institutional platform. The G7 met in July 1991 and discussed, in part, the United Kingdom's arms register proposal, which was subsequently pursued under UN auspices. Mikhail Gorbachev was invited to the 1991 G7 summit, and although China was not present, it was briefed in advance on the arms control initiatives to be discussed (Phythian 2000b).

34. Human rights did return to U.S. national arms export policy in 1995 with Clinton's Presidential Decision Directive 34, which includes human rights (and other political and economic considerations) in its arms export criteria. Janne Nolan (1997) notes, however, that U.S. practices at this time did not change much from those of the Reagan and Bush administrations.

35. Countries were invited to include SALW starting in 2003.

36. Consensus rules for the 2001 UN small arms meeting made it possible for the United States to block a legally binding document that included multilateral transfer controls. I explore its position in detail in chapter 4.

37. Chapter 4 explores these major multilateral policy initiatives in detail.

38. The first sixty-seven signatory states to the ATT include Albania, Antigua and Barbuda, Argentina, Australia, Austria, Bahamas, Belgium, Belize, Benin, Brazil, Burkina Faso, Burundi, Chile, Costa Rica, Côte d'Ivoire, Croatia, Cyprus, Czech Republic, Denmark, Djibouti, Dominican Republic, Estonia, Finland, France, Germany, Greece, Grenada, Guyana, Hungary, Iceland, Ireland, Italy, Jamaica, Japan, Latvia, Liechtenstein, Lithuania, Luxembourg, Mali, Malta, Mauritania, Mexico, Montenegro, Mozambique, Netherlands, New Zealand, Norway, Palau, Panama, Portugal, South Korea, Romania, Saint Lucia, Saint Vincent and the Grenadines, Senegal, Seychelles, Slovenia, Spain, Suriname, Sweden, Switzerland, Tanzania, Togo,

Trinidad and Tobago, Tuvalu, United Kingdom, and Uruguay. The United States signed on September 25, 2013. The ATT goes into effect after fifty states deposit their instruments of ratification on December 24, 2014.

39. It can also be argued that foreign policy has always been an expression and tool of a state's values and ethics and that all that is new here is the explicit articulation and labeling by some states of their foreign policy as "ethical." This debate was most prominent under the British Labour government between 1997 and 2010.

40. The inclusion of small arms on the international agenda in connection with states' broader acceptance of international humanitarian norms was not an intentional "grafting" effort at the start, as in the landmines case (Price 1998), although the Control Arms Campaign would later do so in making its case for the ATT.

41. On these conflicts and arms control, see Eavis 1999; Goose and Smyth 1994; Hartung 2001a; HRW 2003a; Human Security Centre 2005; International Committee of the Red Cross 1999; Karp 1994; Klare 1994–1995; Misol 2004; Sislin and Pearson 2001; Wezeman 2003. See also chapter 1.

42. For a selection of contributions to this debate, see Brzoska 2001; Durch 2000; Erickson 2013c; Fruchart et al. 2007; Haass 1997; Hufbauer, Schott, and Elliot 1990; Kaempfer and Lowenberg 1995; Naylor 1999; Pape 1997; Phythian 2000a; Sislin and Pearson 2001.

43. See, for example, Blanton 1999, 2001; Boutwell and Klare 1999; Boutwell, Klare, and Reed 1995; Control Arms 2003; Craft and Smaldone 2002; Dhanapala et al. 1999; Goose and Smyth 1994; Harkavy and Neuman 2001; HRW 1999, 2003a; Human Security Centre 2005; International Committee of the Red Cross 1999; Karp 1993, 1994; Keppler 2001; Klare 1984, 1994–1995; Klare and Rotberg 1999; Maniruzzaman 1992; Misol 2004; Muggah and Berman 2001; SAS 2001, 2002, 2003, 2006, 2007, 2009; Sislin and Pearson 2001; Smith and Tasiran 2005.

44. Afghanistan and Mali were also key "affected" states. Denise Garcia (2006) provides a historic overview.

45. APL are a discrete category of weapon with limited economic or military importance. They are also inherently indiscriminate and can therefore be banned on the basis of international humanitarian law. In contrast, small and major conventional arms are broad categories of weapons with a legally recognized place in the provision of state security. Moreover, they have a significant worldwide economic base. Finally, unlike for landmines, there are both groups that advocate for and groups that oppose more restrictive controls of conventional weapons, which are not inherently indiscriminate weapons. See Brem and Rutherford 2001; D. Garcia 2006; O'Dwyer 2006.

46. See chapter 2. For materialist perspectives on compliance, see Downs, Rocke, and Barsoom 1996; Goldsmith and Posner 2005; Keohane 1984; Morrow 2007. From the normative or constructivist perspective, see Chayes and Chayes 1993; Checkel 2001; Finnemore and Toope 2001.

47. The following institutes in particular: SIPRI, the U.S. Arms Control and Disarmament Agency, and the International Institute for Strategic Studies in the United Kingdom.

48. Small arms transfers are tracked by the Norwegian Initiative on Small Arms Transfers, established in 1997.

49. The press and many NGOs do call states on questionable export deals, but these publicity incidents are typically isolated and more attention grabbing than a systematic investigation of practices over time (see chapter 5).

50. Blanton's findings are potentially important—especially given the lack of research otherwise—but, as a superpower, the United States may be an exceptional case. Its policies have often gone against the grain of world politics, whether in support of or in opposition to shared arms export restrictions. The problematic design of Blanton's Heckman models also calls her findings into question. Heckman models are subject to specific restrictions (see Achen 1986; Sartori 2003), which Blanton does not meet. Blanton 2000 uses the full model for both equations, instead of dropping at least one variable in stage 2. Blanton 2005 reverses model specification requirements by including all independent variables in the stage 2 and excluding a pair of variables (Saudi Arabia and GDP) from stage 1. She provides no explanation for her decision to reverse the model. Moreover, the dummy variable for Saudi Arabia, as Blanton's model itself acknowledges, is of little value for the selection stage and should therefore be excluded from the model entirely (all variables in stage 2 *must* be included in stage 1). Finally, GDP is a highly influential variable that can significantly change the results of an equation depending on whether it is included or not. Excluding GDP leads to a poorly specified model and misleading results.

51. Reestimated models of five-year blocks or "windows" are used for each dependent variable. The models start with 1982, the first year for the lagged independent variables, and add an additional year to each regression until a five-year window has been reached. To illustrate, the first five-year window is 1982–1986, the next is 1983–1987, and so on. There are twenty-nine consecutive five-year windows in total, ending in 2010. For recent applications of models of windows in political science, see Adolph 2004; Kayser 2007; Kwon and Pontusson 2005.

52. This result is consistent with different iterations of exporters included in the model, such as democratic exporters only and EU exporters only (subject to the EU Code since 1998).

53. Although there was a drop with "very bad" human rights in 2010, the coefficient is insignificant, and a single point is insufficient to establish whether this drop is the start of (or return to) a trend.

54. See, for example, Capie 2004; Cloud 2007; V. Garcia 2003; HRW 2002; Myerscough 2006; Waldermeirin 2007; Wright 2007.

55. Control Arms (2003), for example, argues that the United Kingdom expanded arms availability to Indonesia and relaxed arms export controls more generally in

response to U.S. arms export policy in the war on terror. Although the results for MCW transfers do not show a similar uptick for bad human rights performers, MCW export practice has generally shown less variation over time and may be slower to adapt.

56. However, recent findings suggest that legally binding export restrictions in the form of arms embargoes *do* significantly reduce SALW and MCW transfers (Erickson 2013c).

4. EXPLAINING COMMITMENT: INTERNATIONAL REPUTATION AND "RESPONSIBLE" ARMS TRANSFER POLICY

1. The United States opposed a broader mandate for the meeting, along with China, Israel, Russia, Cuba, India, and Pakistan. The latter three countries are not major exporters. By the ATT vote in 2006, only the United States was still outright opposed to shared arms transfer controls.

2. For this view, see Anders 2007; Efrat 2010; Karp 2002; Krause 2002; Miller et al. 2003; O'Dwyer 2006; Stohl and Hogendoorn 2010; Wyatt 2002.

3. All of the cases reviewed are full democracies and among the top-five small arms and/or MCW exporters. See chapter 1 for more on case selection.

4. Studies connecting arms export policy to the MIC and defense industry preferences include G. Adams 1981; Cooling 1981; Dunne 1995; Efrat 2010; Eisenhower 1961; Hartung 1996; Keller 1995; Kolodziej 1979; Kurth 1971; Markusen et al. 1991; Moravcsik 1991, 1992, 1993; Silverstein 2000.

5. Although born in the United States (Eisenhower 1961), this concept travels in Europe and elsewhere in the world (Cooling 1981; Kiss 1997; Stanley and Pearton 1972).

6. For example, the defense industry in the former Eastern Bloc enjoyed an equal—if not greater—status in domestic politics. Better conditions for defense industry employees during the Cold War "created a deep attachment to defence industrial activity," which has carried over into the difficult post–Cold War years (Kiss 1997:137).

7. See Beier and Crosby 1998; International Committee of the Red Cross 1996; Petrova 2007; Price 1998; Rutherford 2000.

8. On the French MIC, see Boyer 1996; Chatillon 1983; Graves 2000; interview 63308220; Labbé 1994; Moravcsik 1992; Stanley and Pearton 1972.

9. On the French view of the arms trade, see Chatillon 1983; J. Clarke 1981; *Défense et sécurité nationale* 2008:279, 283; Graves 2000; Guay 1998:108; interview 63308220; Kolodziej 1987; Sarkozy 2008; Scaringella 1998.

10. After Labour governments nationalized "large swaths of the British defense industry," Thatcher reprivatized companies during the 1980s (Graves 2000:60). Labour renounced its call for common ownership in 1995.

11. On the British MIC, see Bishop and Megicks 1996; Higham 1981; Jones and Rees 1994; Phythian 2000b.

12. Ian Davis (2002) provides a detailed history and description of both. See also Cooper 1997; Guay 1998; Jones and Rees 1994; Mayhew 2005; Phythian 2000b; Spear 1990.

13. On party support of the defense industry, see Cook, Foss, and Scott 2004; Jones and Rees 1994; Norton-Taylor, Lloyd, and Cook 1996.

14. The *Financial Times* called the second Al Yamamah deal "staggering both by its sheer size and by its strategic importance, not only for defence relations but also for investment and trade links between the two countries" (White and Mauthner 1988; see also "Arms and the Arabs" 1988). An investigation into the deals was suppressed in 1992, but the Serious Fraud Office opened another in 2004 to look into British Aerospace (BAE) and UK Ministry of Defense side payments. Although the deals were made during Thatcher's tenure in office, Blair stopped the inquiry in 2006, arguing that it would lead to the loss of British jobs and "a vital strategic partnership" ("Saudi Prince" 2007). In a distinct change of tone, the press responded that the defense industry is worth preserving, but "not at any price" ("The Bigger Bang" 2007). BAE paid £286 million in criminal fines in 2010 to settle investigations in the United Kingdom and the United States without admitting to bribery or corruption ("BAE Handed" 2010).

15. Interviews 32107200, 35207200, 34207200, 36307200, 39307200.

16. Interviews 35207200, 37207200, 39307200.

17. Both the Allies and the German public were largely convinced of the MIC's guilt, and the largest companies were broken apart in the early postwar years as a result (Homze 1981:76–77). The dismantling stopped by the late 1940s in response to the Soviet threat (Homze 1981:77), and a resurgence began by the 1950s (Homze 1981:79; see also Davis 2002, Pearson 1986).

18. Interview 44307255. See also Davis 2002; Freedman and Navias 1997; Moravcsik 1992; Stanley and Pearton 1972.

19. It is worth noting that much discretion surrounds the interpretation of German legal export restraints as well as a preference for coproduction arrangements with countries such as France that are subject to less-restrictive export guidelines and for selling production licenses instead of finished weapons (Brzoska 1986, 1989; Cowen 1986; Davis 2002; Graves 2000; Guay 1998; Pearson 1986; Wulf 1996).

20. The three geographic regions in Belgium—Wallonia, Flanders, and Brussels—now hold arms export–licensing competence. The Brussels share of Belgian business is extremely tiny and therefore not discussed here. Regionalization has created difficulties at the regional level—licensing and reporting mechanisms had to be developed from scratch—and problems for representation in multilateral fora at the international level. See Flemish Peace Institute 2007b.

21. Hassink 2000; interviews 20307211, 21407211, 22407211, 23407211, 31307211.

22. Over time, dual-use technology, such as visualization screens and military imaging and electronic equipment, has been the most valuable Flemish defense good (Duquet 2008; Duquet, Castryck, and Depauw 2007).

23. Interviews 21407211, 22407211, 23407211, 31307211.

24. See Guay 1998; Hartung 1996; Silverstein 2000; Wolpin 1991.

25. Arms exports were briefly emphasized as a political issue in the United States in the mid-1990s to draw out production lines and protect jobs (Hartung 1996; Nolan 1997). Yet, according to Terrence Guay, "many of the [U.S.] companies that have chosen to remain in the defense business now find themselves in a monopoly or near-monopoly position. Most contractors are generating strong cash flows, and many cost-cutting defense firms have seen their stocks rise. While defense companies' revenues have fallen sharply in the 1990s, profitability has risen" (1998:90).

26. For more on the jobs–defense industry connection, see G. Adams 1981; Hartung 1996; Markusen et al. 1991; Stanley and Pearton 1972; Wolpin 1991.

27. One NGO representative commented that some defense firms had even privately expressed an interest in establishing an international code of conduct, but the American political climate was unfavorable to make investing the resources into it worthwhile (interview 48207002).

28. Johnston attributes states' responses to new expectations to "social influence," which he claims can include "backpatting, opprobrium or shaming, social liking, status maximization, and so on" (2008:20). Social influence allows for "public conformity without private acceptance," unlike persuasion, which requires both public conformity and private acceptance (25), a dynamic strongly suggested by the gap between states' arms transfer policies and practices.

29. These institutions are the most relevant for the major arms exporters. Others include ECOWAS, the Organization of American States, and the South African Development Community.

30. I do not mean to imply here that a reputation for good international citizenship—and the enhanced social status that might accompany it—cannot also indirectly contribute to material benefits.

31. Operating under the same consensus rules, the EU agreed to the legally binding Common Position to succeed its politically binding Code of Conduct in 2008. The UN, however, had to use majoritarian voting in the General Assembly between 2006 and 2013 to pass the ATT.

32. It is worth noting that in such cases less-powerful dissenting states can often hide behind the opposition of a superpower such as the United States. Supporting states and NGOs focus their opprobrium on the superpower's opposition when it is present rather than on that of "less-significant" players.

33. Although states' obligations are essentially the same under both documents, the Common Position does make some formal additions. See M. Bromley 2012.

34. Unanimity is not always required. Some issues (although not foreign and security policy) fall under Qualified Majority Voting (majority voting weighed by member population) as designated by EU treaty law. Nevertheless, between 75 and 80 percent of decisions in the 1990s were taken unanimously, even where majoritarian rules could have been applied (Mattila and Lane 2001:40).

35. Appeasing France so that any document could pass was a central concern of the UK presidency, which worked with France in order to minimize its opposition. As a result, the 1998 Code of Conduct was not legally binding and mandated only that members report exports annually to the EU, but not that reports be made public. In fact, France strongly opposed any references to public accountability proposed by the British Labour government, which was fresh off a national election in which transparency and accountability were key issues (SIPRI 1999:39–41).

36. On the EU debate over lifting the arms embargo to China, see Erickson 2013b.

37. The EU has facilitated further policy convergence by establishing a common list of military equipment; increasing the amount of information exchanged between member states; and creating a user's guide to clarify criteria application (M. Bromley 2008:9).

38. European Parliament 2008; French Ministry of Foreign Affairs 2008; interviews 27207211, 37207200, 43107200, 61208220, 64208220.

39. Consensus rules are widely cited as the reason for the small arms conferences' lack of success (SIPRI 2007:432). As one government official said, there were just "so many damn countries" (interview 16107255), making consensus perhaps an impossibly high bar to clear.

40. News sources and informal conversations with participants suggest that China, Cuba, Egypt, India, Iran, Israel, Pakistan, and Russia also opposed a more rigorous UNPOA (Anders 2007; SIPRI 2007:432).

41. See chapter 3 for a historical overview of the emergence of the international small arms agenda as well as SAS 2001, 2002 and UN Department of Disarmament Affairs 2002 for discussions of the origins of the 2001 conference.

42. See UN Department of Disarmament Affairs 2002:79 n. 17 for a full list of invited NGOs.

43. The United States has had a reputation in the UN General Assembly both for commonly flouting the majority (Smouts 2000:48) and for being an obstructionist force on the small arms processes in particular.

44. Covering illicit small arms transfers in "all their aspects," the UNPOA is a comprehensive document acknowledging the deep complexity of the problem but also making consensus a next-to-impossible feat.

45. This group primarily included China, Cuba, Egypt, India, Iran, North Korea, Pakistan, Russia, Syria, Venezuela, and Zimbabwe. In the final ATT vote, however, only Iran, North Korea, and Syria voted in opposition.

46. Defense cooperation agreements are exempt from the treaty, for example, because of Indian lobbying. However, a ban on arms transfers to nonstate actors is not mentioned because of unresolvable disagreements between the United States (opposed) and India, Nicaragua, Russia, and others (in favor) that would have otherwise prevented treaty progress.

47. The ATT was adopted by majoritarian vote in the UN General Assembly after being blocked from consensus adoption in the final negotiation by Iran, North Korea, and Syria, which also voted against the treaty in the General Assembly. Some importing states abstained because they felt the ATT favored exporters over importers (e.g., Indonesia), whereas others abstained because they felt their substantive concerns had not been addressed (e.g., India on nonstate actors). Argentina, an ATT lead state, was the first to sign on June 3, 2013. Iceland was the first state to ratify the ATT, depositing its instrument of ratification on July 2, 2013.

48. To preserve the anonymity of the large majority of interviewees who requested it, I do not name any participants.

49. A similar point might be made about "rogue" states, whether by choice or not.

50. In particular, the United Kingdom's announcement to renew its push for an ATT in September 2006 following the 2006 UN small arms conference was met with immediate and widespread support. According to Foreign Office minister Kim Howells, "There were ambassadors literally queuing up to express their support for the proposals we announced this morning and they ranged from very small countries like Mauritius to very large countries like Canada" (Associated Press 2006).

51. Interviews 39307200, 34207200, 37207200, 58107255.

52. For more about British leadership on this issue, see Erickson 2013a.

53. For example, see Blair 1997; R. Cook 1997a, 1997b, 2002; Cooper 2000; Dunne and Wheeler 2001; Wheeler and Dunne 1998.

54. Interviews 37207200, 35207200, 40107200, 41107200 43107200.

55. Interviews 37207200, 32107200, 35207200, 39307200, 43107200.

56. One NGO representative noted that although the idea of an ATT came from NGOs, he acknowledged that the scope and form of the current ATT was "invented" by Straw and continued by his successors (interview 33207200).

57. NGOs report that in the United Kingdom they engage in "behind-the-scenes advocacy, policy recommendations, and policy-based research" and "identify points of leverage" on the issue of arms exports (interview 37207200). It is not clear whether they remain behind the scenes by choice or if doing so has been forced by lead governments seeking credit.

58. Interviews 16107255, 19407255, 45207255, 58107255.

59. One German arms trade expert reports that Germany was "disappointed with the ammunition thing and was hopeful that this would be the German thing" (interview 19407255). Promoting the ATT during Germany's 2007 EU presidency seemed like a promising opportunity for leadership, though the United Kingdom had already

claimed leadership a few years earlier. Germany has been, according to many, a more passive supporter in practice and has "missed some good opportunities to seize the field to play a prominent role" (interview 58107255).

60. Interviews 14107255, 16107255, 15107255, 58107255.

61. Interviews 10407255, 14107255, 16107255, 19407255, 58107255.

62. This comment suggests the use of "rhetorical entrapment" as an NGO strategy and perhaps an unintended consequence of states' support for "responsible" arms transfer policies and related multilateral initiatives (Schimmelfennig 2001).

63. Whether Germany's civilian power will or can persist is a matter of debate (Harnisch and Maull 2001; Hockenos 2007).

64. Or, according to some critics, French foreign policy is "long on symbolism but woefully short on substance" (Gordon 1993:134).

65. The idea that France is "destined to play leading global and European roles" has been a foundation of French foreign policy since De Gaulle (Gordon 1993:17).

66. Among French elites, consensus over France's support of and role in the EU is accepted and explained as "Mitterrand's European legacy" (Wood 1997:131). A similar argument can be made that France promotes the UN's "prestige and capabilities," strengthening its "own status and influence" in the process (Gregory 2000:170; see also Utley 2000).

67. The head of state prevails on major diplomatic questions and keeps a "direct relationship" with the minister of foreign affairs, "which enhances coordinated action" (Enjalran and Husson 1999:66).

68. France's arms trade NGO culture—or lack thereof—is detailed in chapter 5.

69. Belgian federalism provides a separation of competences but no hierarchy between the federal and regional governments, "designed to save rather than destroy national unity" (Fitzmaurice 1996:145).

70. The problems for Belgian foreign-policy making were initially more practical. Federal and regional officials were unclear how Belgium would be represented in international institutions and whether regional officials, who now implement arms export policies, would acquire equal representation alongside federal officials, who retain foreign-policy-making competences.

71. The Ministry of Foreign Affairs values its role in the EU and UN. Marc Houben attributes this attitude to Belgium's "self-image of vulnerability," which is "deeply rooted in society and widely shared by the different political parties" (2005:31). Arms export decision making aside, foreign policy and European integration are considered matters of consensus in Belgian politics (Fitzmaurice 1996).

72. The Belgian federal government signs in the name of all governments and is "very pro [arms control]" but has not put the issue to the regions for input in practice. The regions, however, reportedly "don't see a reason not to follow" (interview 21407211). External relations, including with the EU, are typically delegated to the competence of the federal government (Fitzmaurice 1996:148, 245–50).

73. Interviews 20307211, 52207211, 53207211, 56107211, 57207211.

74. This satisfaction with Belgian policy does not necessarily extend to the regions. In particular, NGOs hope that Wallonia will improve transparency measures. See also Amnesty International 2007 for broad policy objectives.

75. On this reputation, see Adam 1989; Inter Press Service 1987; Lowther 1991; Vranckx 2005.

76. Please note that conversations with U.S. government officials inform the analysis but are not for attribution.

77. This theme was certainly clear in interviews outside of the United States.

78. See the discussion of Israeli policy in chapter 6.

79. Stohl, it should be noted, was nominated by Senator Diane Feinstein (D–CA) for a spot on the 2006 U.S. delegation as the choice of the pro-control NGO community. She was turned down in favor of three NRA members, as also happened with the 2001 delegation.

80. Despite attempts over several years, I was unable to interview any representatives from the NRA or the World Forum on the Future of Sport Shooting Activity, which represents the NRA at the UN.

81. Some NRA advocates suggest that the right to bear arms is a universal human right (Schmidt 2007). Other experts, however, have contested this claim in a comparative context, finding that some states have explicitly rejected Second Amendment–like rights in their own national laws, while international law protects states' right to self-defense, not individuals' right to self-defense or to bear arms (Frey 2006; Miller et al. 2003).

82. Of course, the NRA membership—or the "pro-gun" constituency more broadly—is not homogeneous. Some members believe it should stay out of issues such as the arms trade and focus on firearm safety and hunting. Moreover, as Kristin Goss (2006) points out, its membership base is small compared to the majority of Americans who consistently support gun control.

83. A Gallup poll from early October 2009 found that although the Obama administration has not pursued a domestic gun control agenda, 55 percent of gun owners and 60 percent of Republican-leaning respondents indicated that they believed Obama would attempt to ban gun sales in his time as president (Newport 2009).

84. Following the first small arms meeting in 2001, World Forum on the Future of Sport Shooting Activity representative Thomas Mason, however, warned that some states would "seek to resurrect the issue of civilian possession of firearms" (2002:205). Since then, the UN has consistently reaffirmed civilian possession as a domestic issue outside of the scope of discussions. Yet for the NRA, there may be more to the story. As Aaron Karp observes, "[The NRA's] exclusive concern was protecting the rights of U.S. civilian gun owners to buy and sell firearms as they pleased. . . . As it learned that domestic disarmament was not part of the [UN] agenda, it grew more comfortable" (2002:190). He suggests instead that NRA leaders have used "the UN process as a whipping-boy" to feed into the distaste of "extreme supporters" to "anything con-

nected to the UN" (190). Wayne LaPierre also notes that the NRA used the issue in the 2000 election to rally support to its cause and preferred candidates as well as to solicit additional funds from its members (2006:53; see also Feldman 2007).

85. ATT preamble, available at http://www.un.org/disarmament/ATT/docs/ATT_text_(As_adopted_by_the_GA)-E.pdf.

86. For recent discussions about the origins and consequences of U.S. exceptionalism, see Chayes 2008; Fuchs and Klingemann 2008; Ignatieff 2005; Koh 2003; Kohut and Stokes 2006; Lipset 1996; Madsen 1998; Sperling 2007.

87. Both Carter and Clinton relied heavily on case-by-case exemptions despite policies that may have appeared more in line with current calls for "responsible" arms export controls.

88. Polling suggests that Obama's handling of foreign policy within the first year of his presidency quadrupled his predecessor's approval ratings among key European allies ("Transatlantic Trends" 2009).

89. A domestic backlash against the decline of U.S. world standing was palpable throughout the 2008 election process, leading the candidates to declare the need to improve U.S. reputation (Koh 2003; Kohut and Stokes 2006; "Only in America" 2008; Walt 2005). However, the ATT was unlikely to win points at home except perhaps indirectly by gaining points abroad (see chapter 5).

90. Michael Ignatieff notes that the stability of U.S. politics and institutions has led in part to its "legal isolationism" and reluctance to look to international law and foreign precedents in U.S. law (2005:8–9) as well as to a sense of self-sufficiency and lower incentive "to stabilize its own institutions with foreign treaties," in contrast to the European powers (17).

5. EXPLAINING COMPLIANCE: DOMESTIC REPUTATION AND ARMS TRADE SCANDAL

1. In 1995, Ecuador was involved in a border war with Peru. Argentina was charged as a neutral guarantor of a 1942 peace treaty between the two parties. A UN embargo prohibited arms sales to Croatia from 1991 to 1996.

2. The Argentine Senate must lift Menem's immunity before he can serve his seven-year sentence.

3. Yet 42 percent of the Argentine public were opposed to giving the UN the power to regulate the international arms trade, and only 36 percent were in favor (Chicago Council on Global Affairs and WorldPublicOpinion.org 2007).

4. With a permissive public attitude toward the arms trade and the high level of secrecy surrounding it, scandals were rare during the Cold War. The U.S. Iran–Contra Affair and the Swedish Bofors Affair are two exceptions.

5. Only Sweden and the United States allow for advance legislative scrutiny of arms export deals (those worth more than $50 million in the United States).

6. On this decline, see Baum 2002; Melanson 2000; Small 1996.

7. On the public and foreign policy, see Almond [1950] 1965; Baum 2002; Holsti 2004; Risse-Kappen 1991; Rosenau 1961; Sobel 2001; Wittkopf 1990.

8. See O'Dwyer 2006; Petrova 2007; Price 1998; Rutherford 2000.

9. Funding needs may also contribute to this difficulty. NGOs work on many issues related to SALW to keep donors interested, but this multitasking makes creating a clear, coherent, and simple message for campaigning difficult (interview 2206225).

10. For further information about the interviews, see chapter 4 and appendix B.

11. Interviews 19407255, 11407255, 17207255, 46307255.

12. As I show later in this chapter, it is typically through NGO press releases and prompting that the media pick up news stories about arms export decisions.

13. Interviews 20307211, 21407211–23407211, 26207211, 29207211, 31307211.

14. Interviews 37207200, 33207200, 36307200, 39307200, 43107200.

15. The 1970s were an unusual interlude to this trend. In his presidential campaign, Jimmy Carter responded to the U.S. public's apparent concern regarding an overabundance of arms transfers (see chapter 3). The 1970s also saw among an attentive European public a generally negative attitude toward arms transfers, but no corresponding policy changes.

16. Chicago Council on Foreign Relations 2004; Chicago Council on Global Affairs 2008; Chicago Council on Global Affairs and WorldPublicOpinion.org 2007.

17. Interviews 59108220, 60108220, 63308220, 64208220. In 2006, 77 percent of French people supported giving the UN the power to regulate the international arms trade (Chicago Council on Global Affairs and WorldPublicOpinion.org 2007). Interview participants, however, seemed unaware of such figures. One NGO representative observed that no one was really sure where the public stood on the issue and that a study would be needed to find out (interview 61208220).

18. Domestic structure comprises "the nature of the political institutions (the 'state'), basic features of the society, and the institutional and organizational arrangements linking state and society and channeling societal demands into the political system" (Risse-Kappen 1991:484).

19. I identify arms trade scandals by widespread media, NGO, and government use of the label *scandal*. See chapter 2 for a theoretical overview of the concept, literature, and the effects of scandal on democratic politics.

20. Low-level transparency exists where governments do not make publicly available their arms export reports. Although news of "irresponsible" exports can break due to investigative journalism or NGO fieldwork, it is extremely rare. See chapter 2 for a conceptual discussion of transparency.

21. Because the size, resources, and structure of national NGO communities vary by case, I define an "active pro-control NGO community" as the presence of groups engaged in sustained lobbying and public mobilization with the goal of regulating

the national arms trade. They may be home-grown groups or national affiliates of international NGOs such as Amnesty International.

22. On uneven execution of information sharing, see Abramson 2008; M. Bromley 2012; Holtom 2008; Laurance, Wagenmakers, and Wulf 2005; Lebovic 2006.

23. Transparency has also increased within the arms industry in response to pressure from company stakeholders, shareholders, NGOs, and governments. Small arms companies that are not listed on the stock market tend to be less transparent (Weidacher 2005).

24. See Phythian 2000b; Ponting 1990; Tomkins 1998; Vincent 1998.

25. The Gesetz über die Kontrolle von Kriegswaffen (known widely as the KWKG) regulates the export of "weapons of war" as defined by German law. The Aussenwirtschaftsgesetz (known as the AWG) regulates military-related technology and armaments, including dual-use technology. See Davis 2002 for a summary.

26. Richard Moose and Daniel Spiegel attribute this concern to "the end of the Vietnam war, the personal style of a Secretary of State [Kissinger], the oil price hike of 1973, and the recession" (1979:228).

27. For more on sleaze and the 1997 election, see Lee 1999; Vincent 1998; Worcester and Mortimore 1999.

28. See Aaronovitch 1996; "The Scott Report" 1996; and Stephens 1996, among many (indeed most) others.

29. On Labour's promises, see Blair 1997; Cook 1997a, 1997b; Labour Party 1997.

30. In the United Kingdom, the Campaign Against the Arms Trade had long advocated an arms trade ban. However, it has taken a back seat in the current debate as a result of other groups' willingness to compromise (regulate, not ban). Anna Stavrianakis argues that the main NGOs in the current debate are "reformist" rather than "transformist," upholding "the close relationship between arms capital and the state" and seeking to "[regulate] away [the arms trade's] worst excesses within the existing system" rather than to overhaul it radically (2010:9).

31. Interviews 32107200, 37207200, 40107200, 41107200, 42107200, 43107200.

32. Broek 1997, Control Arms 2004, Oxfam 1998, 2002, and Saferworld 2007 are examples of NGO reports seeking to improve arms export practices, which have also picked up a following in the press.

33. See also UK House of Commons 1999, debate on November 3, and 2000, debate on May 4, among others.

34. See the All-Party Parliamentary Group on International Corporate Responsibility website at http://appg-icr.org/.

35. Interviews 35207200, 37207200, 38207200, 393072C0.

36. The exception has been support for more liberal East–West trade as a part of *Ostpolitik* (Davis 2002:159).

37. The 1982 guidelines (Cowen 1986:269) held until new guidelines reflecting the 1998 EU Code of Conduct were adopted in Germany in January 2000. Current criteria

include provisions to disqualify applicants who are located in areas of tension, are engaged in an armed conflict, or show "reasonable grounds to suspect serious human rights violations." For the full text of the new guidelines, see http://www.bmwi.de/DE/Themen/Aussenwirtschaft/aussenwirtschaftsrecht.html.

38. The domestic economy is typically the point of greatest concern for Germans (Klein and Kuhlmann 2000). In periods of economic trouble and high unemployment, this concern can translate into tolerance for more arms transfers (Brzoska 1989; Davis 2002). Even then, however, governments have sought to avoid criticism by maintaining "the public image of a restrictive arms transfer policy" (Brzoska 1989:171).

39. Of course, this aspect of German identity can easily clash with its identity as an export-oriented economic powerhouse with respect to the arms trade (Davis 2002).

40. Alternative sources of information included reports in the foreign press from other intelligence sources, data collection and publication from open sources by organizations such as SIPRI, and individual groups' efforts in Germany to monitor port activity. The BUKO Kampagne: Stoppt den Rüstungsexport (Campaign to Stop Arms Exports), which sought to ban the arms trade completely, especially engaged in data collection and dissemination strategies.

41. Of course, common standards of export control today are meant in part to keep suppliers from following this coproduction strategy. Germany nevertheless supports these policies, recognizing their importance for its international reputation (see chapter 4).

42. Chemical weapons and dual-use technologies present a useful comparison. In the early 1990s, scandal emerged with knowledge that Germany had supplied Iraq with chemical weapons and infrastructure in the 1980s (Phythian 1997). The government immediately responded with legal reform to place stricter controls on dual-use technology (Davis 2002; Müller et al. 1994). Scandal accelerated the reform process by authorities "[a]nxious to repair the tainted reputation of Germany" (Müller et al. 1994:4).

43. Activist Andrea Kolling notes that the German government got around the "areas of tension" criterion by declaring in 1984 that there was no Indonesian war against East Timor (1997:58).

44. "Support for NATO" means support both for Turkey as a NATO ally and for the United States, whose policy supported Ankara and labeled the Kurdish Workers' Party a terrorist organization.

45. In the 1992 Schleswig-Holstein election, this candidate—CDU leader Ottfried Hennig—did not take the majority from the SPD. Yet both parties lost ground to right-wing extremist parties (May 1992).

46. On Stoltenberg, see Casdorff 1992; M. Fisher 1992; Kinzer 1992; "Unter dem Druck" 1992. Stoltenberg had also been implicated in covert transfers of supplies of former East German arms to Israel—an area of tension in the Middle East—in 1991, a factor that certainly increased public distaste for his continued role as head of the Defense Ministry (M. Fisher 1992; "Kritik an Stoltenberg" 1992).

47. Interviews 14107255, 17207255, 19407255, 44307255, 45207255.

48. For a sample of overview pieces on German civilian power, see Harnisch and Maull 2001 as well as Hockenos 2007.

49. See Gaetner 1987 and Pontaut 1987 for the articles that (re)broke the would-be scandal.

50. All interviewees pointed out the lack of an active arms trade NGO community in France. Its absence is considered symptomatic of an absence of an established French NGO lobbying culture more broadly. Although foreign development and aid groups are prominent, the proliferation of NGO activity in domestic politics on foreign-policy issues is more recent and a point of contention in French politics (S. Cohen 2004).

51. On French arms supplies to Rwanda, see Alusala 2004; Austin 1995; Braeckman 1994; Callamard 1999; Dorn, Matloff, and Matthews 1999; HRW 1994; Melvern 2000, 2004.

52. See Patrick De Saint-Exupéry's (1998a, 1998b, 1998c, 1998d) four-part series in *Le Figaro* in January 1998 and Rousselin 1998. The reports accused France of complicity in the genocide and openly criticized the content and conduct of France's Africa policy. See also *Le Figaro* in general from March 30 to April 3, 1998.

53. For the Quilès Commission report, see http://www.assemblee-nationale.fr/dossiers/rwanda/r1271.asp.

54. The Rwandan government has been dissatisfied with French responses to the scandal and has since made allegations that France played an active role in the 1994 genocide ("Report Done" 2007; "Rwanda Accuses France" 2008).

55. Note later in the chapter similar public sentiments in the United States during the Iran–Contra Affair.

56. The Rwanda Affair did, however, expose major flaws in France's Africa policy and helped to instigate reform (Utley 2002). And although the arms trade angle remained untouched, it later spurred French activism to control illicit small arms flows in Africa (interview 60108220; Utley 2002).

57. Primarily Amnesty, Agir-Ici–Oxfam, Comité Catholique contre la faim et pour le développement, l'Observatoire des transfers d'armements, and Secours Catholique—Caritas France.

58. Boland I prohibited the use of funds "for the purpose of overthrowing the Government of Nicaragua or provoking military exchange between Nicaragua and Honduras" (qtd. in Draper 1991:18). Boland II "prohibited any military or paramilitary support for the Nicaraguan contras for the period of October 3, 1984 to December 19, 1985" (Draper 1991:23–24) and remained in effect into 1986.

59. The plan was to focus questions on "North's diversion scheme and [shy] away from the larger issues of administration policy toward Iran and the Contras" (Kornbluh and Byrne 1993:310). Attorney General Edwin Meese testified in 1989, "I was concerned that the two major policy issues within the Administration at the time

would be merged together and that this would—could complicate the ability of the President in both of the issues" and might constitute an impeachable offense if revealed by a source outside the administration (qtd. in Draper 1991:521).

60. On these possible repercussions of Iran–Contra, see, for example, Barnes 1987; R. Busby 1999; Cohen and Mitchell 1988; Draper 1991; Kornbluh and Byrne 1993; Thelen 1996; Trager 1988; Walsh 1997; Wroe 1991.

61. For the full reports, see http://www.gwu.edu/~nsarchiv/NSAEBB/NSAEBB365/index.htm.

62. Note the ongoing covert arms transfers (primarily dual-use technologies for biological and chemical warfare) to Iraq during this time, also against U.S. law and policy. However, it was a matter of debate "just how much of a scandal Iraqgate was," and the lack of any newfound accountability following Iran–Contra was clear (Jentleson 1994:9; see also Kornbluh and Byrne 1993).

63. To the extent that some NRA leaders are interested, they argue that governments should supply *more* arms to areas of conflict and genocide (LaPierre 2006).

64. The U.S. NGO community focused on domestic gun control has not worked on export policy. NGOs advocating arms export controls (among other issues) include Amnesty U.S., the Federation of American Scientists, HRW, the Quakers, and a few think tanks, such as the former Center for Defense Information.

65. On the "supergun," see Lowther 1991; Naylor 1999; Toolis 1990.

66. Bull sent U.S.- and Canadian-made shell casings to PRB because Canadian law did not require end-user certificates for "inert" shells to going European countries. The manufacturer "in turn could arm the shells and sell them to anywhere that [the much less restrictive] Belgian law would allow" (Lowther 1991:107).

67. Cools's death initially appeared connected to the supergun. However, investigations concluded in 1995 that "the personal secretary to the senior minister of the Wallonian regional government had been using his office as a cover for a gang stealing securities, credit cards and paintings." Cools had pushed for an investigation, and in response the official hired an assassin (Naylor 1999:308–9, 311).

68. Past restrictions in arms trade to recipients engaged in conflict or internal repression were policy, not law (Inter Press Service 1987).

69. See also Adam 1989; Inter Press Service 1987; Vranckx 2005.

70. Reports indicated that the Flemish Volksunie Party refused to authorize Belgian arms sales to Saudi Arabia (Agence France Presse 1991a), which caused a split between Flemish- and French-speaking ministers in the coalition and dissolved Parliament (Agence France Press 1991b).

71. Prominent and active NGOs include Amnesty Flanders and Wallonia, International Peace Information Service, Network Vlaanderen, Oxfam–Solidarity Belgium, and research groups such as the Groupe de recherche et d'information sur la paix et la sécurité (Research and Information Group on Peace and Security) and the Flemish Peace Institute.

72. The Code states, "Before any Member State grants a license which has been denied by another Member State or States for an essentially identical transaction within the last three years, it will first consult the Member State or States which issued the denial(s). If following consultations, the Member State nevertheless decides to grant a license, it will notify the Member State or States issuing the denial(s), giving a detailed explanation of its reasoning" (Operative Provision no. 3). For the full text of the Code, see http://www.consilium.europa.eu/uedocs/cmsUpload/08675r2en8.pdf.

73. Flemish Green Party (Groen) health minister Magda Aelvoet resigned.

74. The section heading refers to the 2003 regionalization of export controls (Otte and Verschelden 2006).

75. See also interviews 21407211, 24107211, 27207211, 52207211, 55107211.

76. Interviews 29207211, 21407211, 27207211; Mampaey 2002:13.

77. Export denials noted in the Flemish press following regionalization include exports to Chile, Ethiopia, Saudi Arabia, Suriname, Tanzania, Turkey, and Venezuela (Brinckman 2005; Verschelden 2006a, 2006b).

78. In the case of Liberia, the Belgian government noted that Belgium had been granted an exemption by the UN in order to supply local police under UN auspices (Brinckman 2005).

79. This is not to say that NGOs have *no* access to the Walloon government. One official notes that the government sometimes has contact with NGOs in addition to meetings with companies (interview 55107211).

6. CONCLUSIONS AND IMPLICATIONS

1. See, for example, Amnesty International 2010; Blanton 1999, 2001; Boutwell, Klare, and Reed 1995; Craft and Smaldone 2002; Eavis 1999; Goose and Smyth 1994; Harkavy and Neuman 2001; Hartung 2001a; Karp 1993, 1994; Klare and Rotberg 1999; Musah 2002; Neuman 1986; Sislin and Pearson 2001; Verwimp 2006.

2. Attention to arms exporters in the post–Cold War scholarly literature is limited, perhaps because of sparse media attention or a widely shared mindset that not much has changed over time or both.

3. The United States was the sole vote against the ATT process until late 2009, a move that contributed to its obstructionist international reputation. I attribute U.S. opposition primarily to its long-term reluctance to concede to external export constraints and exceptionalist attitude toward international institutions. See chapter 4.

4. Israel was ranked seventh among recipients and tenth among MCW exporters from 2002 to 2006 (SIPRI 2007:418, 422). SAS lists Israel in the lower end of the top-thirty small arms exporters (2006:71).

5. On postapartheid South Africa's search for international legitimacy, see Becker 2010.

6. South Africa developed its defense industrial base during the apartheid era. It is now a midsize MCW exporter, ranked twentieth from 2002 to 2006 (SIPRI 2007). It is also in the lower end of the top-thirty SALW exporters (SAS 2006).

7. South Africa released annual arms trade reports from 1995 to 2002, which were subject to civil society criticism on specific cases (e.g., sales to Rwanda and Pakistan). Legislative reform in 2002 required annual export reports, but none was presented from 2003 to 2006. In response, NGOs "expressed concerns that South Africa may be returning to apartheid era secrecy." Reports for 2003–2006 were released in 2007 but were viewed as too late to allow any real critique or action (Lamb 2007).

8. Known South African arms exports to human rights violators from 2000 to 2004 include those to China, Colombia, Indonesia, Nigeria, Pakistan, Saudi Arabia, Uganda, and Zimbabwe (Nathan 2005:371; SAS 2007:98–107).

9. International Action Network on Small Arms (IANSA) affiliates include Amnesty International, Centre for Conflict Resolution, Coalition for Peace in Africa–Action Support Centre, Congolese Association for Peace and Development, Gun Free South Africa, Institute for Security Studies, the Peace and Security Program at the University of Witwatersrand, and SaferAfrica.

10. Brazil ranked thirty-third in MCW exports from 2002 to 2006 (SIPRI 2007:418).

11. Pro-gun groups do not dominate Brazilian politics on this issue as the NRA does in the United States. IANSA lists a number of active, established pro-control affiliates: Movimento Paz Espirito Santo, Desarme.org, Viva Rio, Children and Youth in Organised Armed Violence, and Instituto Sou da Paz. Many pro-control groups are more focused on domestic than international issues. Viva Rio and Sou da Paz are involved in both.

12. Matthew Baum sees a similar trend of broadening public attention to political issues through soft news, which can frame them as "compelling human dramas" and capture the imagination of a public that would ordinarily not be tuned into or interested in such events (2002:91).

13. See Schimmelfennig 2001; Wheeler 2000.

14. Edward Kwakwa (2003) observes that separating the interests of the United States and the interests of the international community requires the exclusion of U.S. *social* interests, which affect its reputation and social standing.

15. This is a primary reason ICBL leaders chose to pursue the landmine treaty outside of the UN. Similarly, the EU consented to the politically binding Code of Conduct for Arms Exports in 1998 because of French opposition to a legally binding document (France withdrew its opposition to legalization in 2008).

16. Research generally finds that norms will diffuse more easily when there is a cultural match between international and domestic norms (Checkel 1999). Leaders' choice of framing, the use of naming and shaming, and the wielding of social and material incentives to adopt norms can also affect norm diffusion (Finnemore and Sikkink 1998; Nadelmann 1990; Price 1998), as can norm-taking states' domestic

structures (Checkel 1999). Norm adoption by "critical states" can also speed and spread the process (Finnemore and Sikkink 1998; Florini 1996; Nadelmann 1990), as happened with British support for "responsible" arms export controls.

17. See http://www.un.org/disarmament/ATT/docs/ATT_text_(As_adopted_by _the_GA)-E.pdf.

APPENDIX B. DATA SOURCES AND CODING

1. Although thirteen states were absent for the UN General Assembly vote on Document A/67/L.58, all exporter states in the data set were present. Of the twenty-three formal abstentions, only China and Russia abstained among the exporters included in the data set. Only three states formally voted against the ATT (Iran, North Korea, and Syria), none of which are major exporters and are therefore included in the data set only as importer states.

2. No database provides a comprehensive combined figure for annual SALW and MCW transfers disaggregated by recipient outside of U.S. commercial arms sales.

3. SIPRI is the only public source for annual conventional arms trade disaggregated export–import data for non-U.S. exporters. Although there is little quantitative work on the conventional arms trade, researchers often use SIPRI data to illustrate trends in the trade. Post–Cold War examples include Durch 2000; Erickson 2013b, 2013c; Golde and Tishler 2004; Harkavy 1994; Khanna 1992; Kinsella 1994; Sanjian 1998; Wulf 1993.

4. I thank Mark Bromley at SIPRI for providing me with the initial data from the SIPRI Arms Transfer Database in 2006 (see SIPRI 2006). The current version of this database is now available at http://www.sipri.org.

5. Re-exports authorized by the original recipient state should appear with its transfer data.

6. For a complete description of SIPRI's TIV calculation methodology, see SIPRI 2007:429–30.

7. SIPRI argues that identifying an accurate and reliable price figure for weapons is impossible for three reasons: "First, in many cases no reliable data on the value of a transfer are available. Second, even if the value of a transfer is known, in almost every case it is the total value of a deal, which may include not only the weapons themselves but also other items related to these weapons . . . as well as support systems . . . and items related to the integration of the weapon in the arms forces. Third, even if the value of a transfer is known, important details about the financial arrangements of the transfer (e.g., credit or loan conditions and discounts) are often unavailable" (2007:429).

8. I accessed NISAT in spring 2006, fall 2011, and summer 2013 from http://nisat. prio.org. See NISAT n.d.

9. SAS calls UN Comtrade "the most comprehensive source of comparable data on the international trade in small arms" (2003:99). However, Comtrade relies on

voluntary submissions by governments and tends to be incomplete in the area of SALW, a particularly sensitive export. SAS concludes that Comtrade data "[appear] to be the strongest on the exports and imports of western countries, principally North America and western Europe" (99).

10. See, for example, Forsythe 2006; Krain 1997; Lopez 1986:90; Poe and Tate 1994.

11. The presence of oil may cause a government to repress its citizens to protect its access to the resource (HRW 2003b; Ross 2004); fund repressive regimes, thus allowing them to stay in power (Chen 2007; HRW 2003b); attract companies that may violate human rights (Forsythe 2006; UN Economic and Social Council 2006); and cause other states to turn a blind eye to a government's repressive practices in order to retain access to an important resource (Chen 2007; Forsythe 2006).

12. See, for example, Blanton 1999; Bueno de Mesquita et al. 2005; Davenport 1995; Howard and Donnelly 1986; Mitchell and McCormick 1988; Poe and Tate 1994; Rummel 1995.

13. See, for example, Davenport 1995; Davenport and Armstrong 2004; Mitchell and McCormick 1988; Poe and Tate 1994; Wolpin 1986.

14. See, for example, Banks 1986; Carleton and Stohl 1987; Cingranelli and Richards 1999a, 1999b; Goldstein 1986; Hafner-Burton and Ron 2009; Human Security Centre 2005; Poe, Carey, and Vazquez 2001; and Stohl et al. 1986.

15. Sabine Carey (2007) also uses this approach.

16. The primary advantage of the Cingranelli–Richards data is that they allow researchers to disaggregate types of physical integrity violations. However, this level of detail is too fine-grained for a study of arms export practice. See Hafner-Burton and Ron 2009 for comparisons between the Cingranelli–Richards data and PTS data.

17. The correlation between variables from the two sources is nevertheless high (0.808).

18. To illustrate, 54 percent of Amnesty-coded dyad-years fall from 3 to 5 on the PTS in contrast to 45 percent of DOS-coded dyad-years.

19. Nevertheless, Emilie Hafner-Burton and James Ron note that although democracies "are better protectors of human rights," measures of human rights are not highly correlated with measures of democracy, suggesting that countries can be both democratic and abusive (2009:379, 365).

20. See, for example, Bollen and Paxton 2000; Collier and Levitsky 1997; Collier and Mahon 1993; Diamond 2002; Foweraker and Krznaric 2000; Munck and Verkuilen 2002; Schaffer 1998; Schmitter and Karl 1991.

21. Gerring, Thacker, and Moreno (2005) take their measure from Macartan Humphreys (2005). Because their data end in 2000, the years 2001–2010 are calculated based on the sources used by Humphreys to generate the original variable.

22. See, for example, Ball and Leitenberg 1979; Brzoska and Ohlson 1987; Cahn et al. 1977; Catrina 1988; Chan 1980; Chatillon 1983; Klare 1984; Kolodziej 1987.

23. See Cahn et al. 1977; Chatillon 1983; Klare 1984; Phythian 1997.

24. For a discussion of the difficulties of coding conflict data and the merits and drawbacks of various data sets, see Hegre and Sambanis 2006; Human Security Centre 2005; and Sambanis 2004.

25. Correlates of War data traditionally include only this high-level intensity of conflict (one thousand battle-related deaths per year)

26. Only 12.89 percent of dyad-years in the data set are engaged in low- or high-level internal conflict.

27. With the exception of U.S. government contacts, who require that conversations be for background purposes only and therefore cannot be cited here.

APPENDIX C. FULL STATISTICAL RESULTS

1. See, for example, Achen 2002, 2005; Kadera and Mitchell 2005; Ray 2003, 2005. For a more general discussion, see Berk 2004.

REFERENCES

Aaronovitch, David. 1996. "The Scott Report: Contempt and Content for a Crime Without Punishment." *The Independent*, February 16. Retrieved August 3, 2008, from Factiva.

Abbott, Kenneth W. and Duncan Snidal. 2002. "Values and Interests: International Legalization in the Fight Against Corruption." *Journal of Legal Studies* 31:S141–78.

Abdelal, Rawi, Yoshiko M. Herrera, Alastair Iain Johnston, and Rose McDermott. 2009. "Identity as a Variable." In *Measuring Identity: A Guide for Social Scientists*, edited by Rawi Abdelal, Yoshiko M. Herrera, Alastair Iain Johnston, and Rose McDermott, 17–32. New York: Cambridge University Press.

Abramson, Jeff. 2008. "UN Register Captures Expanded Small Arms Trade." *Arms Control Today*, October. Retrieved January 8, 2009, from http://www.armscontrol .org.

Achen, Christopher H. 1986. *The Statistical Analysis of Quasi-Experiments*. Berkeley: University of California Press.

——. 2002. "Toward a New Political Methodology: Microfoundations and ART." *Annual Review of Political Science* 5:423–50.

——. 2005. "Let's Put Garbage-Can Regressions and Garbage-Can Probits Where They Belong." *Conflict Management and Peace Science* 22 (4): 327–39.

Adam, Bernard. 1989. "La Belgique, plaque tournante du traffic d'armes." In *L'Europe des armes: Trafics et exportations vers le tiers monde*, 35–44. Brussels: Collection GRIP-Informations.

Adams, Christopher. 2004. "War 'Weakened Human Rights Policy.'" *Financial Times*, April 15. Retrieved March 24, 2007, from LexisNexis Academic.

Adams, Gordon. 1981. *The Politics of Defense Contracting: The Iron Triangle*. New Brunswick, NJ: Transaction Books.

Adler, Emanuel and Michael Barnett, eds. 1998. *Security Communities*. New York: Cambridge University Press.

Adolph, Christopher Alan. 2004. "The Dilemma of Discretion: Career Ambitions and the Politics of Central Banking." Ph.D. diss., Harvard University.

Agence France Presse. 1991a. "Belgian Government Expected to Resign." September 29. Retrieved March 3, 2007, from LexisNexis Academic.

——. 1991b. "Belgian Parliament to Be Dissolved on Thursday." October 16. Retrieved March 3, 2007, from LexisNexis Academic.

——. 2014. "German Government to Cancel Saudi Tank Deal: Report." April 13. Retrieved July 19, 2014, from LexisNexis Academic.

Ahn, T. K., Justin Esarey, and John T. Scholz. 2009. "Reputation and Cooperation in Voluntary Exchanges: Comparing Local and Central Institutions." *Journal of Politics* 71 (2): 398–413.

Almond, Gabriel A. [1950] 1965. *The American People and Foreign Policy*. New York: Praeger.

Alt, James E., Randall L. Calvert, and Brian D. Human. 1988. "Reputation and Hegemonic Stability: A Game-Theoretic Analysis." *American Political Science Review* 82 (2): 445–66.

Alt, James E. and David Dreyer Lassen. 2006. "Transparency, Political Polarization, and Political Budget Cycles in OECD Countries." *American Journal of Political Science* 50 (3): 530–50.

Alusala, Nelson. 2004. "The Arming of Rwanda, and the Genocide." *African Security Review* 13 (2). Retrieved July 26, 2007, from http://www.iss.co.za.

American Bar Association. 2013. *White Paper on the Proposed Arms Trade Treaty and the Second Amendment*. Washington, DC: Center for Human Rights.

American Political Science Association. 2009. *U.S. Standing in the World: Causes, Consequences, and the Future*. Long Report of the Task Force on US Standing in World Affairs. Washington, DC: American Political Science Association.

Amnesty International. 2007. "Mémorandum en vue des elections legislatives 10 juin 2007." Amnesty International Belgium.

——. 2010. *Killer Facts: The Impact of the Irresponsible Arms Trade on Lives, Rights, and Livelihoods*. London: Amnesty International Publications.

Anders, Holger. 2007. "The UN Process on Small Arms: All Is Not Lost." *Arms Control Today*, March. Retrieved April 14, 2007, from http://www.armscontrol.org.

Anderson, David G. 1992. "The International Arms Trade: Regulating Conventional Arms Transfers in the Aftermath of the Gulf War." *American University International Law Review* 7 (4): 749–805.

Anthony, Ian. 1994. "Current Trends and Developments in the Arms Trade." *Annals of the American Academy of Political and Social Science* 535:29–42.

——. 1997. "The Conventional Arms Trade." In *Cascade of Arms: Managing Conventional Weapons Proliferation*, edited by Andrew J Pierre, 15–41. Cambridge, MA: World Peace Foundation; Washington, DC: Brookings Institutions Press.

Apodaca, Clair. 2007. "The Whole World Could Be Watching: Human Rights and the Media." *Journal of Human Rights* 6 (2): 147–64.

Apodaca, Clair and Michael Stohl. 1999. "United States Human Rights Policy and Foreign Assistance." *International Studies Quarterly* 43 (1): 185–98.

"Argentine Foreign Minister Says Relations with Peru 'Upset' by Arms Scandal." 1996. *BBC Summary of World Broadcasts*, May 14. Retrieved July 3, 2008, from LexisNexis Academic.

"Arms and the Arabs." 1988. *The Times*, July 12. Retrieved March 18, 2007, from LexisNexis Academic.

Aronczyk, Melissa. 2013. *Branding the Nation: The Global Business of National Identity*. New York: Oxford University Press.

Associated Press. 2006. "Britain Renews Push for Arms Trade Treaty." *International Herald Tribune*, September 14. Retrieved April 24, 2007, from http://www.iht.com.

——. 2008. "US Seeks to Block Zimbabwe-Bound Chinese Arms." *New York Times*, April 22. Retrieved April 22, 2008, from http://www.nytimes.com.

——. 2011. "1991 Report Said Reagan Not Liable in Arms Deal." *New York Times*, November 25. Retrieved November 26, 2011, from http://www.nytimes.com.

Austin, Kathi L. 1995. "Rwanda/Zaire: Rearming with Impunity: International Support for the Perpetrators of the Rwandan Genocide." *Human Rights Watch Arms Project* 7 (4). Retrieved June 19, 2006, from http://www.hrw.org.

Axelrod, Robert. 1984. *The Evolution of Cooperation*. New York: Basic Books.

Axworthy, Lloyd. 1998. "Towards a New Multilateralism." In *To Walk Without Fear: The Global Movement to Ban Landmines*, edited by Maxwell A. Cameron, Robert J. Lawson, and Brian W. Tomlin, 448–59. New York: Oxford University Press.

"BAE Handed £286m Criminal Fines." 2010. *BBC News*, February 5. Retrieved March 4, 2010, from http://newsvote.bbc.co.uk.

Bailes, Alyson. 2004. Preface to *The European Union Code of Conduct on Arms Exports: Improving the Annual Report*, v–vi. Stockholm International Peace Research Institute (SIPRI) Policy Paper no. 8. Solna, Sweden: SIPRI

Bailey, F. G. 1971. "Gifts and Poison." In *Gifts and Poison: The Politics of Reputation*, 1–25. New York: Schocken Books.

Baldauf, Scott and Peter Ford. 2008. "China Slammed for Arming Zimbabwe's Mugabe." *Christian Science Monitor*, April 23. Retrieved April 25, 2008, from http://www.csmonitor.com.

Ball, Nicole and Milton Leitenberg. 1979. "The Foreign Arms Sales Policy of the Carter Administration." *Alternatives* 4 (4): 527–56.

Banks, David L. 1986. "The Analysis of Human Rights Data Over Time." *Human Rights Quarterly* 8 (4): 654–80.

Barnes, Fred. 1987. "Wake-Up Call." *The New Republic*, October 26: 10–11.

Bauer, Sibylle and Mark Bromley. 2004. *The European Union Code of Conduct on Arms Exports: Improving the Annual Report*. Stockholm International Peace Research Institute (SIPRI) Policy Paper no. 8. Solna, Sweden: SIPRI.

Baum, Matthew A. 2002. "Sex, Lies, and War: How Soft News Brings Foreign Policy to the Inattentive Public." *American Political Science Review* 96 (1): 91–109.

Beachey, R. W. 1962. "The Arms Trade in East Africa in the Late Nineteenth Century." *Journal of African History* 3 (3): 451–67.

Beck, Nathaniel. 1983. "Time-Varying Parameter Regression Models." *American Journal of Political Science* 27 (3): 557–600.

——. 2001. "Time-Series-Cross-Section Data: What Have We Learned in the Past Few Years?" *Annual Review of Political Science* 4:271–93.

Beck, Nathaniel and Jonathan N. Katz. 1995. "What to Do (and Not to Do) with Time-Series Cross-Section Data." *American Political Science Review* 89 (3): 634–47.

——. 2001. "Throwing Out the Baby with the Bath Water: A Comment on Green, Kim, and Yoon." *International Organization* 55 (2): 487–95.

Becker, Derick. 2010. "The New Legitimacy and International Legitimation: Civilization and South African Foreign Policy." *Foreign Policy Analysis* 6:133–46.

Beier, J. Marshall and Ann Denholm Crosby. 1998. "Harnessing Change for Continuity: The Play of Political and Economic Forces Behind the Ottawa Process." In *To Walk Without Fear: The Global Movement to Ban Landmines*, edited by Maxwell A. Cameron, Robert J. Lawson, and Brian W. Tomlin, 269–91. New York: Oxford University Press.

Belgian Chamber of Representatives. 2002. *Motions. Plenary Session, August 29*. Doc. 50 025/390. 50th Leg., 4th sess. Brussels: Central Press.

Bell, Susan. 2001. "France Wakes Up to Spreading Scandal." *Scotland on Sunday*, January 28. Retrieved August 6, 2008, from LexisNexis Academic.

Berk, Richard A. 2004. *Regression Analysis: A Constructive Critique*. Thousand Oaks, CA: Sage.

Besley, Timothy. 2006. *Principled Agents? The Political Economy of Good Government*. New York: Oxford University Press.

Best, Jacqueline. 2005. *The Limits of Transparency: Ambiguity and the History of International Finance*. Ithaca: Cornell University Press.

"The Bigger Bang." 2007. *The Economist*, June 14, 15–16. Retrieved June 14, 2007, from Economist.com.

Bishop, Paul and Phil Megicks. 1996. "Defense Spending and the UK Service Sector." *Defense Analysis* 12 (3): 347–69.

Blair, Tony. 1997. "The Principles of a Modern British Foreign Policy." Speech at the Lord Mayor's Banquet, November 10, Guildhall, London. Retrieved June 5, 2007, from http://www.fco.gov.uk.

Blanton, Shannon Lindsey. 1999. "Instruments of Security or Tools of Repression? Arms Imports and Human Rights Conditions in Developing Countries." *Journal of Peace Research* 36 (2): 233–44.

——. 2000. "Promoting Human Rights and Democracy in the Developing World: U.S. Rhetoric Versus U.S. Arms Exports." *American Journal of Political Science* 44 (1): 123–31.

——. 2001. "The Role of Arms Transfers in the Quest for Human Security." *Journal of Political and Military Sociology* 29 (2): 240–58.

——. 2005. "Foreign Policy in Transition? Human Rights, Democracy, and U.S. Arms Exports." *International Studies Quarterly* 49 (4): 647–67.

Bob, Clifford. 2012. *The Global Right Wing and the Clash of World Politics.* New York: Cambridge University Press.

Bollen, Kenneth A. and Pamela Paxton. 2000. "Subjective Measures of Liberal Democracy." *Comparative Political Studies* 33 (1): 58–86.

Boulding, Kenneth E. 1956. *The Image.* Ann Arbor: University of Michigan Press.

Boutwell, Jeffrey and Michael T. Klare, eds. 1999. *Light Weapons and Civil Conflict: Controlling the Tools of Violence.* Lanham, MD: Rowman & Littlefield.

Boutwell, Jeffrey, Michael T. Klare, and Laura W. Reed, eds. 1995. *Lethal Commerce: The Global Trade in Small Arms and Light Weapons.* Cambridge, MA: American Academy of Arts and Sciences.

Bowler, Shaun and Jeffrey A. Karp. 2004. "Politicians, Scandal, and Trust in Government." *Political Behavior* 26 (3): 271–87.

Boyer, Yves. 1996. "French Arms Trade and the EC." In *The European Arms Trade*, edited by Martin S. Navias and Susan Willett, 47–56. New York: Nova Science.

Braeckman, Colette. 1994. *Qui a armé le Rwanda? Chronique d'une tragédie annoncée.* Les Dossiers du Groupe de recherche et d'information sur la paix et la sécurité (GRIP). Brussels: GRIP.

Brem, Stefan and Ken Rutherford. 2001. "Walking Together or Divided Agenda? Comparing Landmines and Small-Arms Campaigns." *Security Dialogue* 32 (2): 169–86.

Brinckman, Bart. 2005. "Arms Policy Most Transparent in Europe—Weapons from Antwerp Policy Went to Liberia." *De Standaard*, October 14. Reprinted in "Belgian Flemish Government Releases Half-Yearly Arms Export Statistics." *BBC*

Worldwide Monitoring, October 14. Retrieved March 3, 2007, from LexisNexis Academic.

Broek, Martin, ed. 1997. *Indonesia: Arms Trade to a Military Regime*. Amsterdam: European Network Against Arms Trade Secretariat.

Bromley, D. B. 1993. *Reputation, Image, and Impression Management*. New York: Wiley.

Bromley, Mark. 2008. *The Impact on Domestic Policy of the EU Code of Conduct on Arms Exports: The Czech Republic, the Netherlands, and Spain*. Stockholm International Peace Research Institute (SIPRI) Policy Paper no. 21. Solna, Sweden: SIPRI.

——. 2012. *The Review of the EU Common Position on Arms Exports: Prospects for Strengthened Controls*. Non-Proliferation Papers no. 7. N.p.: EU Non-Proliferation Consortium.

Bromley, Mark, Neil Cooper, and Paul Holtom. 2012. "The UN Arms Trade Treaty: Arms Export Controls, the Human Security Agenda, and the Lessons of History." *International Affairs* 88 (5): 1029–48.

Brooks, Stephen G. and William C. Wohlforth. 2008. *World out of Balance: International Relations and the Challenge of American Primacy*. Princeton: Princeton University Press.

Broz, J. Lawrence. 2002. "Political System Transparency and Monetary Commitment Regimes." *International Organization* 56 (4): 861–87.

Brzoska, Michael. 1986. *Rüstungsexportpolitik: Lenkung, Kontrolle und Einschränkung bundesdeutscher Rüstungsexporte in die Dritte Welt*. Frankfurt am Main: Haag und Herchen.

——. 1989. "The Erosion of Restraint in German Arms Transfer Policy." *Journal of Peace Research* 26 (2): 165–77.

——, ed. 2001. *Smart Sanctions: The Next Steps*. Baden-Baden: Nomos.

——. 2004. "The Economics of Arms Imports After the End of the Cold War." *Defence and Peace Economics* 15 (2): 111–23.

Brzoska, Michael and Thomas Ohlson. 1987. *Arms Transfers to the Third World, 1971–85*. New York: Oxford University Press.

Brzoska, Michael and Frederic S. Pearson. 1994. *Arms and Warfare: Escalation, De-escalation, and Negotiation*. Columbia: University of South Carolina Press.

Bueno de Mesquita, Bruce, George W. Downs, Alastair Smith, and Feryal Marie Cherif. 2005. "Thinking Inside the Box: A Closer Look at Democracy and Human Rights." *International Studies Quarterly* 49:439–57.

Bull, Hedley. 1977. *The Anarchical Society*. New York: Columbia University Press.

Burley, Anne-Marie. 1992. "Law Among Liberal States: Liberal Internationalism and the Act of State Doctrine." *Columbia Law Review* 92 (8): 1907–96.

Burns, Christopher. 1998. "France Supplied Arms to Hutu Govt During 1994 Genocide." *AAP Newsfeed*, January 12. Retrieved June 1, 2006, from LexisNexis.

Busby, Joshua William. 2007. "Bono Made Jesse Helms Cry: Jubilee 2000, Debt Relief, and Moral Action in International Politics." *International Studies Quarterly* 51:247–75.

——. 2008. "The Hardest Problem in the World: Leadership in the Climate Regime." In *Cooperating Without America: Theories and Case Studies of Non-hegemonic Regimes*, edited by Stefan Brem and Kendall Stiles, 71–104. New York: Routledge.

Busby, Robert. 1999. *Reagan and the Iran–Contra Affair: The Politics of Presidential Recovery.* New York: St. Martin's Press.

Cahn, Anne Hessing, Joseph J. Kruzel, Peter M. Dawkins, and Jacques Huntzinger. 1977. *Controlling Future Arms Trade.* New York: McGraw-Hill.

Callamard, Agnès. 1999. "French Policy in Rwanda." In *The Path of a Genocide: The Rwanda Crisis from Uganda to Zaire*, edited by Howard Adelman and Astri Suhrke, 157–83. New Brunswick, NJ: Transaction.

Capie, David. 2004. "Between a Hegemon and a Hard Place: The 'War on Terror' and Southeast Asian–US Relations." *Pacific Review* 17 (2): 223–48.

Capitanchik, David and Richard C. Eichenberg. 1983. *Defence and Public Opinion.* Chatham House Papers no. 20. London: Routledge & Kegan Paul.

Carey, Sabine C. 2007. "European Aid: Human Rights Versus Bureaucratic Inertia?" *Journal of Peace Research* 44 (4): 447–64.

Carleton, David and Michael Stohl. 1987. "The Role of Human Rights in U.S. Foreign Assistance Policy: A Critique and Reappraisal." *American Journal of Political Science* 31 (4): 1002–18.

Carlman, Åsa. 1998. *Arms Trade from the EU: Secrecy vs Transparency.* Stockholm: Swedish Peace and Arbitration Society.

Carter, Jimmy. 1976. Speech to the Foreign Policy Association, New York City, June 23. Excerpts from speech reprinted in the *New York Times*, June 24. Retrieved July 2, 2014 from ProQuest.

Casdorff, Stephan-Andreas. 1992. "Bonn: Der Rücktritt von Gerhard Stoltenberg." *Süddeutsche Zeitung*, April 1. Retrieved February 10, 2007, from LexisNexis Academic.

Castryck, Geert, Sara Depauw, and Nils Duquet. 2007. *Profile of Foreign Trade in Military Material and the Defence-Related Industry in Flanders.* Brussels: Flemish Peace Institute.

Catrina, Christian. 1988. *Arms Transfers and Dependence.* New York: Taylor & Francis.

Chalmers, Malcolm, Neil V. Davies, Keith Hartley, and Chris Wilkinson. 2002. "The Economic Costs and Benefits of UK Defence Exports." *Fiscal Studies* 23 (3): 343–67.

Chan, Steve. 1980. "The Consequences of Expensive Oil on Arms Transfers." *Journal of Peace Research* 17 (3): 235–46.

Chapman, Duane and Neha Khanna. 2006. "The Persian Gulf, Global Oil Resources, and International Security." *Contemporary Economic Policy* 24 (4): 507–19.

Chatillon, Georges. 1983. "La France et le tiers monde: Problèmes d'armements." *Défense nationale* 39:73–96.

Chayes, Abram and Antonia Handler Chayes. 1993. "On Compliance." *International Organization* 47 (2): 175–205.

——. 1995. *The New Sovereignty: Compliance with International Regulatory Agreements.* Cambridge, MA: Harvard University Press.

Chayes, Antonia. 2008. "How American Treaty Behavior Threatens National Security." *International Security* 33 (1): 45–81.

Checkel, Jeffrey T. 1999. "Norms, Institutions, and National Identity in Contemporary Europe." *International Studies Quarterly* 43 (1): 83–114.

——. 2001. "Why Comply? Social Learning and European Identity Change." *International Organization* 55 (3): 553–88.

Chen, Matthew E. 2007. "Chinese National Oil Companies and Human Rights." *Orbis* 51 (1): 41–54.

Chicago Council on Foreign Relations. 2004. *Global Views 2004: American Public Opinion and Foreign Policy.* Chicago: Chicago Council on Foreign Relations.

Chicago Council on Global Affairs. 2008. *Global Views 2008—Foreign Policy Report.* Chicago: Chicago Council on Global Affairs.

Chicago Council on Global Affairs and WorldPublicOpinion.org. 2007. *World Public Opinion 2007.* Chicago: Chicago Council on Global Affairs.

Chirac, Jacques. 2005. Speech at the Paris International Conference on Microfinance, June 20, Paris. Retrieved February 1, 2010, from http://www.elysee.fr.

Chong, Dennis. 1992. "Social Incentives and the Preservation of Reputation in Public-Spirited Collective Action." *International Political Science Review* 12 (2): 171–98.

Chrobok, Vera. 2004. "Germany." In *Disposal of Surplus Small Arms: A Survey of Policies and Practices in OSCE Countries*, edited by Sami Faltas and Vera Chrobok, 41–55. Retrieved July 7, 2014, from http://www.smallarmssurvey.org/fileadmin/docs/E-Co-Publications/SAS-BICC-2004-OSCE-surplus-small-arms.pdf.

Cingranelli, David L. and Thomas E. Pasquarello. 1985. "Human Rights Practices and the Distribution of U.S. Foreign Aid to Latin American Countries." *American Journal of Political Science* 29 (3): 539–63.

Cingranelli, David L. and David L. Richards. 1999a. "Measuring the Level, Pattern, and Sequence of Government Respect for Physical Integrity Rights." *International Studies Quarterly* 43 (2): 407–17.

——. 1999b. "Respect for Human Rights After the End of the Cold War." *Journal of Peace Research* 36 (5): 511–34.

Clark, Ann Marie. 2001. *Diplomacy of Conscience: Amnesty International and Changing Human Rights Norms.* Princeton: Princeton University Press.

——. 2013. "The Normative Context of Human Rights Criticism: Treaty Ratification and UN Mechanisms." In *The Persistent Power of Human Rights: From Commitment to Compliance*, edited by Thomas Risse, Stephen C. Ropp, and Kathryn Sikkink, 125–44. New York: Cambridge University Press.

Clarke, Duncan. 1995. "Israel's Unauthorized Arms Transfers." *Foreign Policy*, Summer, 89–109.

Clarke, Jeffrey. 1981. "Land Armament in France: The Tradition of 'Etatism.'" In *War, Business, and World Military-Industrial Complexes*, edited by Benjamin Franklin Cooling, 33–50. Port Washington, NY: National University Publications.

Clinton, Hillary Rodham. 2009. "US Support for the Arms Trade Treaty." October 14. Retrieved October 16, 2009, from http://www.state.gov.

Cloud, David S. 2007. "U.S. Set to Offer Huge Arms Deal to Saudi Arabia." *New York Times*, July 28. Retrieved July 31, 2007, from http://www.nytimes.com.

Cohen, Mike. 2011. "South Africa Gives Panel Probing Arms Deal Sweeping Powers." *Businessweek*, October 27. Retrieved November 12, 2011, from http://www.businessweek.com.

Cohen, Samy. 2004. *A Model of Its Own? State–NGO Relations in France.* U.S.–France Analysis series. Washington, DC: Brookings Institution.

Cohen, William S. and George J. Mitchell. 1988. *Men of Zeal: A Candid Inside Story of the Iran–Contra Hearings.* New York: Viking.

Collier, David and Steven Levitsky. 1997. "Democracy with Adjectives: Conceptual Innovation in Comparative Research." *World Politics* 49 (3): 430–51.

Collier, David and James E. Mahon. 1993. "Conceptual 'Stretching' Revisited: Adapting Categories in Comparative Analysis." *American Political Science Review* 87 (4): 845–55.

Colson, Elizabeth. 1974. *Tradition and Contract: The Problem of Order.* Chicago: Aldine.

Control Arms. 2003. *Shattered Lives: The Case for Tough International Arms Control.* London: Amnesty International and Oxfam International.

——. 2004. *Lock, Stock, and Barrel: How British Arms Components Add Up to Deadly Weapons.* London: Oxfam GB.

Cook, Nick, Christopher F. Foss, and Richard Scott. 2004. "Feast and Famine: Breaking the Cycle." *Jane's Defence Weekly*, August 25, 20–28.

Cook, Robin. 1997a. "Details of the Government's Announcement of a Strategic Review of UK Export Licensing." In *Strategic Review of UK Export Licensing Controls*, 1997. URN no. 97/1029. Retrieved March 19, 2007, from http://www.dti.gov.uk.

——. 1997b. "Robin Cook's Speech on the Government's Ethical Foreign Policy: The Speech by Robin Cook That Started It All." *Guardian Unlimited*, May 12. Retrieved January 9, 2007, from http://www.guardian.co.uk.

——. 1999. "Examination of Witnesses, Select Committee on Defence, UK House of Commons, November 3." Retrieved July 6, 2014, from http://www.publications.parliament.uk/pa/cm199899/cmselect/cmdfence/541/9110301.htm.

——. 2002. "Putting Principle Into Practice: The Role of Human Rights in Foreign Policy." *Cambridge Review of International Affairs* 15 (1): 45–51.

Cooling, Benjamin Franklin, ed. 1981. *War, Business, and World Military-Industrial Complexes*. Port Washington, NY: National University Publications.

Cooper, Neil. 1997. *The Business of Death: Britain's Arms Trade at Home and Abroad*. New York: Tauris Academic Studies.

——. 2000. "Arms Exports, New Labour, and the Pariah Agenda." *Contemporary Security Policy* 21 (3): 54–77.

——. 2006. "What's the Point of Arms Transfer Controls?" *Contemporary Security Policy* 27:118–37.

Cornish, Paul. 1995. *The Arms Trade and Europe*. London: Royal Institute of International Affairs.

Cowen, Regina H. E. 1986. *Defense Procurement in the Federal Republic of Germany: Politics and Organization*. Boulder, CO: Westview Press.

Craft, Cassady. 1999. *Weapons for Peace, Weapons for War: The Effect of Arms Transfers on War Outbreak, Involvement, and Outcomes*. New York: Routledge.

Craft, Cassady and Joseph P. Smaldone. 2002. "The Arms Trade and the Incidence of Political Violence in Sub-Saharan Africa, 1967–97." *Journal of Peace Research* 39 (6): 693–710.

Crescenzi, Mark J. C. 2007. "Reputation and Interstate Conflict." *American Journal of Political Science* 51 (2): 382–96.

Crescenzi, Mark J. C., Jacob D. Kathman, and Stephen B. Long. 2007. "Reputation, History, and War." *Journal of Peace Research* 44 (6): 651–67.

Crutzen, Nicolas. 2003. *Question juridiques sur la régionalisation des licences d'armes*. Rapport du Groupe de recherche et d'information sur la paix et la sécurité (GRIP) (2003/4). Brussels: GRIP.

Davenport, Christian. 1995. "Multi-dimensional Threat Perception and State Repression: An Inquiry Into Why States Apply Negative Sanctions." *American Journal of Political Science* 39 (3): 683–713.

Davenport, Christian and David A. Armstrong II. 2004. "Democracy and the Violation of Human Rights: A Statistical Analysis from 1976 to 1996." *American Journal of Political Science* 48 (3): 538–54.

Davies, Gary, Rosa Chun, Rui Vinhas da Silva, and Stuart Roper. 2003. *Corporate Reputation and Competitiveness*. London: Routledge.

Davis, Ian. 2002. *The Regulation of Arms and Dual-Use Exports*. New York: Oxford University Press.

De Cock, Jorn. 2003. "Government Skirts Round Arms Supplies." *De Standaard*, July 9. Reprinted as "Belgian Government Accord Foreign Policy Influenced by Row with US." *BBC Monitoring International Reports*. July 9. Retrieved March 3, 2007, from LexisNexis Academic.

Défense et sécurité nationale: Le Livre blanc. 2008. Paris: Odile Jacob/La documentation française.

Dempsey, Judy. 2012. "Europe Deals Arms While Defending Rights." *New York Times*, March 5. Retrieved March 5, 2012, from http://www.nytimes.com.

De Saint-Exupéry, Patrick. 1998a. "France–Rwanda: Un Genocide sans importance." *Le Figaro*, January 12.

——. 1998b. "France–Rwanda: Des Silences d'etat." *Le Figaro*, January 14.

——. 1998c. "France–Rwanda: Le Syndrome de Fachoda." *Le Figaro*, January 13.

——. 1998d. "France–Rwanda: Le Temps de l'hypocrisie. *Le Figaro*, January 15.

"Deutsche Gewehre im Himalaja Heckler & Koch will Gewehre nach Nepal exportieren." 2002. *Berliner Zeitung*, March 6. Retrieved February 10, 2007, from LexisNexis Academic.

Deutsche Presse-Agentur. 1995. "Argentina Violated U.N. Arms Embargo Against Croatia, Paper Says." November 29. Retrieved July 3, 2008, from LexisNexis Academic.

Dezalay, Yves and Bryant Garth. 2006. "From the Cold War to Kosovo: The Rise and Renewal of the Field of International Human Rights." *Annual Review of Law and Social Science* 2:231–55.

Dhanapala, Jayantha, Mitsuro Donowaki, Swadesh Rana, and Lora Lumpe, eds. 1999. *Small Arms Control: Old Weapons, New Issues*. United Nations Institute for Disarmament Research. Brookfield, VT: Ashgate.

Diamond, Larry. 2002. "Thinking about Hybrid Regimes." *Journal of Democracy* 13 (2): 21–35.

Dobratz, Betty A. and Stephanie Whitfield. 1992. "Does Scandal Influence Voters' Party Preference? The Case of Greece During the Papandreou Era." *European Sociological Review* 8 (2): 167–80.

Dombey, Daniel. 2002. "Belgian Minister Defends Sale of Arms to Nepal." *Financial Times*, August 27. Retrieved March 31, 2007, from LexisNexis Academic.

Donelan, Michael. 2007. *Honor in Foreign Policy: A History and Discussion*. New York: Palgrave Macmillan.

Donnay, Françoise. 2002. "Les exportations d'armes vers le Népal sont-elles conforms à la loi de 1991? Adversaires et partisans de ces exportations s'affrontent sur les lacunes et imprécisions de la loi." In *Les Exportations d'armes de la Belgique*, edited by Bernard Adam, Sara Bayes, Georges Berghezan, Ilhan Berkol, Françoise Donnay,

Luc Mampaey, and Michel Wéry, 28–34. Rapport du Groupe de recherche et d'information sur la paix et la sécurité (GRIP) (2002/4). Brussels: GRIP.

Donnelly, Jack. 1986. "International Human Rights: A Regime Analysis." *International Organization* 40 (3): 599–642.

Dorn, A. Walter, Jonathan Matloff, and Jennifer Matthews. 1999. *Preventing the Bloodbath: Could the UN Have Predicted and Prevented the Rwandan Genocide?* Peace Studies Program Occasional Paper no. 24, November. Ithaca: Cornell University. Retrieved August 3, 2007, from http://www.ciaonet.org.

Downs, George W. and Michael A. Jones. 2002. "Reputation, Compliance, and International Law." *Journal of Legal Studies* 31:S95–S114.

Downs, George W., David M. Rocke, and Peter N. Barsoom. 1996. "Is the Good News About Compliance Good News About Cooperation?" *International Organization* 50 (3): 379–406.

Doyle, Michael W. 1986. "Liberalism and World Politics." *American Political Science Review* 80 (4): 1151–69.

Dranove, David, Daniel Kessler, Mark McClellan, and Mark Satterthwaite. 2003. "Is More Information Better? The Effects of 'Report Cards' on Health Care Providers." *Journal of Public Economy* 111 (3): 555–88.

Draper, Theodore. 1991. *A Very Thin Line: The Iran–Contra Affairs.* New York: Hill and Wang.

Duggan, Mark and Steven D. Levitt. 2000. *Winning Isn't Everything: Corruption in Sumo Wrestling.* National Bureau of Economic Research (NBER) Working Paper no. 7798. Cambridge, MA: NBER.

Dugger, Celia W. 2008. "Zimbabwe Arms Shipped by China Spark Uproar." *New York Times,* April 19. Retrieved April 19, 2008, from http://www.nytimes.com.

Dugger, Celia W. and David Barboza. 2008. "Zimbabwe Arms Delivery May Turn Back." *New York Times,* April 23. Retrieved April 23, 2008, from http://www.nytimes.com.

Dugger, Celia W., David Barboza, and Alan Cowell. 2008. "Zimbabwe-Bound Ship Heads Back to China." *New York Times,* April 25. Retrieved April 24, 2008, from http://www.nytimes.com.

Dunne, J. Paul. 1995. "The Defense Industrial Base." In *Handbook of Defense Economics,* vol. 1, edited by Keith Hartley and Todd Sandler, 399–430. Amsterdam: Elsevier Science.

Dunne, Tim and Nicholas J. Wheeler. 2001. "Blair's Britain: A Force for Good in the World?" In *Ethics and Foreign Policy,* edited by Karen E. Smith and Margot Light, 167–84. New York: Cambridge University Press.

Duquet, Nils. 2008. *Flemish Arms Trade and Trade in Dual-Use Goods in 2007.* Brussels: Flemish Peace Institute.

Duquet, Nils, Geert Castryck, and Sara Depauw. 2007. *Flemish Foreign Arms Trade 2006.* Brussels: Flemish Peace Institute.

Durch, William J. 2000. *Constructing Regional Security: The Role of Arms Transfers, Arms Control, and Reassurance*. New York: Palgrave.

Eavis, Paul. 1999. "Awash with Light Weapons." *The World Today* 55 (4): 19–21.

Echikson, William. 1987. "French Leaders on Both Sides Play Down Iran 'Scandal.'" *Christian Science Monitor*, November 10. Retrieved August 8, 2008, from LexisNexis.

Eckstein, Harry. 1975. "Case Study and Theory in Political Science." In *Handbook of Political Science*, edited by Fred I. Greenstein and Nelson W. Polsby, 79–138. Reading, MA: Addison-Wesley.

Efrat, Asif. 2010. "Toward Internationally Regulated Goods: Controlling the Trade in Small Arms and Light Weapons." *International Organization* 64 (1): 97–131.

Eisenhower, Dwight D. 1961. "Military-Industrial Complex Speech." In Avalon Project, *Public Papers of the Presidents, Dwight D. Eisenhower*, Yale Law School. Retrieved July 16, 2007, from http://www.yale.edu/lawweb/avalon/presiden/speeches/eisenhower001.htm.

Enjalran, Paulette and Philippe Husson. 1999. "France: The Ministry of Foreign Affairs: 'Something New, but Which Is the Legitimate Continuation of Our Past'" (Paul Claudel—*Le soulier de satin*). In *Foreign Ministries: Change and Adaptation*, edited by Brian Hocking, 59–74. New York: St. Martin's Press.

Erickson, Jennifer L. 2013a. "Leveling the Playing Field: Cost Diffusion and the Promotion of 'Responsible' Arms Export Norms." Paper presented at the International Studies Association Annual Meeting, San Francisco, April 3–6.

——. 2013b. "Market Imperative Meets Normative Power: Human Rights and European Arms Transfer Policy." *European Journal of International Relations* 19 (2): 208–33.

——. 2013c. "Stopping the Legal Flow of Weapons: Compliance with Arms Embargoes, 1981–2004." *Journal of Peace Research* 50 (2): 159–74.

——. Forthcoming. "Saint or Sinner? Human Rights and US Support for the Arms Trade Treaty." *Political Science Quarterly*.

European Parliament. 2008. "Resolution of 4 December 2008 on the EU Code of Conduct on Arms Exports." Retrieved February 13, 2008, from http://www.europarl.europa.eu.

Eyre, Dana P. and Mark C. Suchman. 1996. "Status, Norms, and the Proliferation of Conventional Weapons: An Institutional Theory Approach." In *The Culture of National Security: Norms and Identity in World Politics*, edited by Peter J. Katzenstein, 79–113. New York: Columbia University Press.

Fearon, James D. 1994. "Domestic Political Audiences and the Escalation of International Disputes." *American Political Science Review* 88 (3): 577–92.

Feldman, Richard. 2007. *Ricochet: Confessions of a Gun Lobbyist*. Hoboken, NJ: Wiley.

Fidler, Stephen. 2006. "UK Arms Makers to Join Call for Treaty." *Financial Times*, June 20.

Finch, Phillip. 1983. *God, Guts, and Guns*. New York: Seaview/Putnam.

Finnemore, Martha. 1996a. "Constructing Norms of Humanitarian Intervention." In *The Culture of National Security: Norms and Identity in World Politics*, edited by Peter J. Katzenstein, 153–85. New York: Columbia University Press.

——. 1996b. *National Interests in International Society*. Ithaca: Cornell University Press.

Finnemore, Martha and Kathryn Sikkink. 1998. "International Norm Dynamics and Political Change." *International Organization* 52 (4): 887–917.

Finnemore, Martha and Stephen J. Toope. 2001. "Alternatives to 'Legalization': Richer Views of Law and Politics. *International Organization* 55 (3): 743–58.

Fisher, Marc. 1992. "German Defense Minister Resigns Amid Arms Scandal." *Washington Post*, April 1. Retrieved February 10, 2007, from LexisNexis Academic.

Fisher, Roger. 1981. *Improving Compliance with International Law*. Charlottesville: University Press of Virginia.

Fitzmaurice, John. 1996. *The Politics of Belgium: A Unique Federalism*. Boulder, CO: Westview Press.

Flemish Peace Institute. 2006. *Transparency in Reporting on the Flemish Foreign Arms Trade*. Advice, November 13. Brussels: Flemish Peace Institute.

——. 2007a. *The Decline of Flemish Arms Exports in 2005: Testing Hypotheses*. Background Paper, October 5. Brussels: Flemish Peace Institute.

——. 2007b. *Enhancing Cooperation to Strengthen Export Controls*. Advice, January 23. Brussels: Flemish Peace Institute.

——. 2007c. *Peace in Flanders: Attitudes and Commitments of Flemish People Regarding Peace and Violence*. Report, July. Brussels: Flemish Peace Institute.

Fligstein, Neil and Jason McNichol. 1998. "The Institutional Terrain of the European Union." In *European Integration and Supranational Governance*, edited by Wayne Sandholtz and Alec Stone Sweet, 59–91. New York: Oxford University Press.

Florini, Ann. 1996. "The Evolution of International Norms." *International Studies Quarterly* 40:363–89.

——. 1998. "The End of Secrecy." *Foreign Policy*, no. 111 (Summer): 50–63.

Fombrun, Charles J. 1996. *Reputation: Realizing Value from the Corporate Image*. Boston: Harvard Business School Press.

Forsythe, David P. 1987. "Congress and Human Rights in U.S. Foreign Policy: The Fate of General Legislation." *Human Rights Quarterly* 9 (3): 382–404.

——. 2006. *Human Rights in International Relations*. 2nd ed. New York: Cambridge University Press.

Fortna, Virginia Page. 2003. "Scraps of Paper? Agreements and the Durability of Peace." *International Organization* 57 (2): 337–72.

Foster, Jonathan, Els Cleemput, and Sarah Lambert. 1991. "Murder Linked to Iraqi 'Supergun.' Belgian Murder Linked to Supergun.' *The Independent*, August 5. Retrieved January 26, 2009, from LexisNexis Academic.

Foweraker, Joe and Roman Krznaric. 2000. "Measuring Liberal Democratic Performance: An Empirical and Conceptual Critique." *Political Studies* 48 (4): 759–87.

France Denies Arms Exports. 1998. *Financial Times*, January 13. Retrieved March 31, 2007, from Access World News.

Franck, Thomas M. 1988. "Legitimacy in the International System." *American Journal of International Law* 82 (4): 705–59.

——. 1990. *The Power of Legitimacy Among Nations*. New York: Oxford University Press.

Freedman, Lawrence and Martin Navias. 1997. "Western Europe." In *Cascade of Arms: Managing Conventional Weapons Proliferation*, edited by Andrew J. Pierre, 151–71. Washington, DC: Brookings Institution Press; Cambridge, MA: World Peace Foundation.

French Ministry of Foreign Affairs. 2008. "An EU Code of Conduct on Arms Exports Adopted (December 8)." Retrieved February 13, 2008, from http://diploma tie.gouv.fr.

"French Move to Boost Exports." 1998. *Jane's Defence Weekly*, May 20, 15.

Frey, Barbara A. 2006. *Final Report: Prevention of Human Rights Violations Committed with Small Arms and Light Weapons*. Submitted in accordance with Sub-Commission Resolution 2002/25. A/HRC/Sub.1/58/27. New York: United Nations General Assembly.

Fruchart, Damien, Paul Holtom, Siemon T. Wezeman, Daniel Strandow, and Peter Wallensteen. 2007. *United Nations Arms Embargoes: Their Impact on Arms Flows and Target Behaviour*. Solna: Stockholm International Peace Research Institute; Uppsala: Uppsala University.

Fuchs, Dieter and Hans-Dieter Klingemann. 2008. "American Exceptionalism or Western Civilization?" In *The End of the West? Crisis and Change in the Atlantic Order*, edited by Jeffrey Anderson, G. John Ikenberry, and Thomas Risse, 247–62. Ithaca: Cornell University Press.

Fung, Archon, David Weil, Mary Graham, and Elena Fagotto. 2004. *The Political Economy of Transparency: What Makes Disclosure Policies Effective?* Ash Institute for Democratic Governance and Innovation, John F. Kennedy School of Government. OP-03-04. Cambridge, MA: Harvard University.

Fung, Archon, Mary Graham, and David Weil. 2007. *Full Disclosure: The Perils and Promise of Transparency*. New York: Cambridge University Press.

Funk, Carolyn L. 1996. "The Impact of Scandal on Candidate Evaluations: An Experimental Test of the Role of Candidate Traits." *Political Behavior* 18 (1): 1–24.

Gaetner, Gilles. 1987. "Luchaire: Les Obus rebondissent." *L'Express*, no. 1895 (November 6): 22–23.

Garcia, Denise. 2006. *Small Arms and Security: New Emerging International Norms.* New York: Routledge.

——. 2011. *Disarmament Diplomacy and Human Security: Regimes, Norms, and Moral Progress in International Relations.* New York: Routledge.

Garcia, Victoria. 2003. "U.S. Military Aid for Allies in a War Against Iraq." Center for Defense Information, March 13. Retrieved October 30, 2006, from http://www.cdi.org.

Garment, Suzanne. 1992. *Scandal: The Culture of Mistrust in American Politics.* Updated ed. New York: Anchor Books.

Gee, Jack. 2000. "Mitterrand Caught in Gun Scandal." *Sunday Express,* December 31. Retrieved August 6, 2008, from LexisNexis.

George, Alexander L. and Andrew Bennett. 2005. *Case Studies and Theory Development in the Social Sciences.* Cambridge, MA: MIT Press.

Gelb, Leslie H. 1976–1977. "Arms Sales." *Foreign Policy* 25:3–23.

German Minister for Economics. 1993. *Antwort der Bundesregierung: Rüstungsexport-Kontrollpolitik.* Drucksache 12/4241 (February 1). Deutscher Bundestag 12. Wahlperiode. Bonn.

Gerring, John, Strom C. Thacker, and Carola Moreno. 2005. "Centripetal Democratic Governance: A Theory and Global Inquiry." *American Political Science Review* 99 (4): 567–81.

Gibney, Mark and Matthew Dalton. 1996. "The Political Terror Scale." *Policy Studies and Developing Nations* 4:73–84.

Gilpin, Robert. 1981. *War and Change in World Politics.* New York: Cambridge University Press.

Gleditsch, Nils Petter, Peter Wallensteen, Mikael Eriksson, Margareta Sollenberg, and Håvard Strand. 2002. "Armed Conflict 1946–2001: A New Dataset." *Journal of Peace Research* 39 (5): 615–37.

Goffman, Erving. 1959. *The Presentation of Self in Everyday Life.* New York: Anchor Books.

Gold, David. 1999. "The Changing Economics of the Arms Trade." In *Arming the Future: A Defense Industry for the 21st Century,* edited by Ann R. Markusen and Sean S. Costigan, 249–68. New York: Council on Foreign Relations Press.

Golde, Saar and Asher Tishler. 2004. "Security Needs, Arms Exports, and the Structure of the Defense Industry: Determining the Security Level of Countries." *Journal of Conflict Resolution* 48 (5): 672–98.

Goldring, Natalie J. 1994–1995. "Toward Restraint: Controlling the International Arms Trade." *Harvard International Review* 17 (1). Retrieved February 18, 2007, from Academic Search Premier.

Goldsmith, Benjamin and Yusaku Horiuchi. 2009. "Spinning the Globe? U.S. Public Diplomacy and Foreign Public Opinion." *Journal of Politics* 71 (3): 863–75.

Goldsmith, Jack L. and Eric A. Posner. 2005. *The Limits of International Law*. New York: Oxford University Press.

Goldstein, Robert Justin. 1986. "The Limitations of Using Quantitative Data in Studying Human Rights Abuses." *Human Rights Quarterly* 8 (4): 607–27.

Goodliffe, Jay and Darren G. Hawkins. 2006. "Explaining Commitment: States and the Convention Against Torture." *Journal of Politics* 68 (2): 358–71.

Goose, Stephen D. and Frank Smyth. 1994. "Arming Genocide in Rwanda." *Foreign Affairs* 73 (5): 86–96.

Gordon, Philip H. 1993. *A Certain Idea of France: French Security Policy and the Gaullist Legacy*. Princeton: Princeton University Press.

Goss, Kristin A. 2006. *Disarmed: The Missing Movement for Gun Control in America*. Princeton: Princeton University Press.

Gouteux, Jean-Paul. 1998. *Un génocide secret d'état· La France et le Rwanda 1990–1997*. Paris: Éditions socials.

Gowa, Joanne. 1994. *Allies, Adversaries, and International Trade*. Princeton: Princeton University Press.

Grant, Wyn. 2000. *Pressure Groups and British Politics*. New York: St. Martin's Press.

Graves, James L. 2000. *The Post–Cold War Armored Vehicle Industries in Britain, Germany, and France*. Westport, CT: Greenwood Press.

Gray, Colin S. 1992. *House of Cards: Why Arms Control Must Fail*. Ithaca: Cornell University Press.

Green, Donald P., Soo Yeon Kim, and David H. Yoon. 2001. "Dirty Pool." *International Organization* 55 (2): 441–68.

Greene, Owen. 2002. "The 2001 UN Conference: A Useful Step Forward?" *SAIS Review* 22 (1): 195–201.

Greenhill, Kelly M. 2010. *Weapons of Mass Migration: Forced Displacement, Coercion, and Foreign Policy*. Ithaca: Cornell University Press.

Greenhouse, Steven. 1987. "An Iran Affair Is Emerging in France." *New York Times*, November 2. Retrieved February 24, 2007, from ProQuest Historical Newspapers.

Gregory, Shaun. 2000. *French Defence Policy Into the Twenty-First Century*. New York: St. Martin's Press.

Greif, Avner. 2006. *Institutions and the Path to the Modern Economy: Lessons from Medieval Trade*. New York: Cambridge University Press.

Grieco, Joseph M. 1993. "Anarchy and the Limits of Cooperation." In *Neorealism and Neoliberalism: The Contemporary Debate*, edited by David A. Baldwin, 116–40. New York: Columbia University Press.

Grimmett, Richard F. and Paul K. Kerr. 2012. *Conventional Arms Transfers to Developing Nations, 2004–2011*. Washington, DC: Congressional Research Service.

Grossmann, Angela and Hartwig Hummel. 1997. "Einleitung: Deutschland in der UNO—ein vernachlässigtes Thema der außenpolitischen Debatte." In *UN-williges Deutschland: Der WEED-Report zur deutschen UNO-Politik*, 11–25. Bonn: Dietz.

Guay, Terrence R. 1998. *At Arm's Length: The European Union and Europe's Defence Industry*. New York: St. Martin's Press.

Gummett, Philip. 1999. "The Politics, Economics, and Ethics of Arms Exports." In *Security, Strategy, and the Global Economics of Defence Production*, edited by David G. Haglund and S. Neil MacFarlane, 107–18. Montreal: McGill-Queen's University Press.

——. 2000. "New Labour and Defence." In *New Labour in Power*, edited by David Coates and Peter Lawler, 268–80. New York: Manchester University Press.

Guzman, Andrew T. 2002. "A Compliance-Based Theory of International Law." *California Law Review* 90 (6): 1823–87.

Haass, Richard N. 1997. "Sanctioning Madness." *Foreign Affairs* 76 (6): 74–85.

Hafner-Burton, Emilie M. 2005. "Trading Human Rights: How Preferential Trade Agreements Influence Government Repression." *International Organization* 59 (3): 593–629.

Hafner-Burton, Emilie M. and James Ron. 2009. "Seeing Double: Human Rights Through Qualitative and Quantitative Eyes." *World Politics* 61 (2): 360–401.

Hafner-Burton, Emilie M. and Kiyoteru Tsutsui. 2005. "Human Rights in a Globalizing World: The Paradox of Empty Promises." *American Journal of Sociology* 110 (5): 1373–411.

Haftendorn, Helga. 1971. *Militärhilfe und Rüstungsexporte der BRD*. Gütersloh, Germany: Bertelsmann Universitätsverlag.

Hampson, Fen Osler and Holly Reid. 2003. "Coalition Diversity and Normative Legitimacy in Human Security Negotiations." *International Negotiation* 8:7–42.

Harkavy, Robert E. 1994. "The Changing International System and the Arms Trade." *Annals of the American Academy of Political and Social Science* 535:11–28.

Harkavy, Robert E. and Stephanie G. Neuman. 2001. *Warfare and the Third World*. New York: Palgrave.

Harnisch, Sebastian and Hanns W. Maull, eds. 2001. *Germany as a Civilian Power? The Foreign Policy of the Berlin Republic*. New York: Manchester University Press.

Hartley, Keith, and Stephen Martin. 2003. "The Economics of UK Arms Exports." In *Arms Trade, Security, and Conflict*, edited by Paul Levine and Ron Smith, 5–20. New York: Routledge.

Hartung, William D. 1993. "Why Sell Arms? Lessons from the Carter Years." *World Policy Journal* 10 (1): 57–64.

——. 1996. *Welfare for Weapons Dealers: The Hidden Costs of the Arms Trade*. World Policy Papers. New York: World Policy Institute, New School for Social Research.

——. 2001a. "The New Business of War: Small Arms and the Proliferation of Conflict." *Ethics and International Affairs* 15 (1): 79–96.

——. 2001b. "Stop Arming the World." *Bulletin of the Atomic Scientists* 57 (1): 34–36. Retrieved November 14, 2006, from http://www.thebulletin.org.

Hassink, Robert. 2000. "Regional Involvement in Defense Industry Restructuring in Belgium and the Netherlands." *International Regional Science Review* 23 (1): 81–90.

Hathaway, Oona A. 2002. "Do Human Rights Treaties Make a Difference?" *Yale Law Journal* 111:1935–2042.

Haug, Maria, Martin Langvandslien, Lora Lumpe, and Nicolas Marsh. 2002. *Shining a Light on Small Arms Exports: The Record of State Transparency.* Small Arms Survey: Occasional Paper no. 4. Geneva: Small Arms Survey with the Norwegian Initiative on Small Arms Transfers.

Hayes-Renshaw, Fiona. 2002. "The Council of Ministers." In *The Institutions of the European Union*, edited by John Peterson and Michael Shackleton, 68–95. New York: Oxford University Press.

Hébert, Jean-Paul. 1998. "La Réforme de la politique de défense et l'industrie française d'armement." In *La Réforme de la politique française de défense*, edited by Pierre Dabezies and Jean Klein, 125–45. Paris: Economica.

Hegre, Håvard and Nicholas Sambanis. 2006. "Sensitivity Analysis of Empirical Results on Civil War Onset." *Journal of Conflict Resolution* 50 (4): 508–35.

Henkin, Louis. 1968. *How Nations Behave: Law and Foreign Policy.* New York: Praeger.

Henley, Jon. 2001. "French Arms Scandal Implicates Politicians." *The Guardian*, January 10. Retrieved August 6, 2008, from LexisNexis.

Higham, Robin. 1981. "Complex Skills and Skeletons in the Military-Industrial Relationship in Great Britain." In *War, Business, and World Military-Industrial Complexes*, edited by Benjamin Franklin Cooling, 8–32. Port Washington, NY: National University.

Hirshberg, Matthew S. 1993. "The Self-Perpetuating National Self-Image: Cognitive Biases in Perceptions of International Relations." *Political Psychology* 14 (1): 77–98.

Hoagland, Jim. 1987. "Iran Scandal, French Style." *Washington Post*, November 4. Retrieved August 6, 2008, from LexisNexis.

Hockenos, Paul. 2007. "Is Germany Still a Civilian Power? Three Authors Examine German Foreign Policy in the Berlin Republic." *Internationale Politik* 8 (2): 102–6.

Hoffmann, Stanley. 1977–1978. "The Hell of Good Intentions." *Foreign Policy* 29:3–26.

Hollinger, Peggy. 2009. "Paris Pressed to Reveal Secrets on Arms Sales." *Financial Times*, October 29. Retrieved November 2, 2009, from http://www.ft.com.

Holsti, Ole R. 2004. *Public Opinion and American Foreign Policy.* Rev. ed. Ann Arbor: University of Michigan Press.

Holtom, Paul. 2008. *Transparency in Transfers of Small Arms and Light Weapons: Reports to the United Nations Register of Conventional Arms, 2003–2006.* Stockholm International Peace Research Institute (SIPRI) Policy Paper no. 22. Solna, Sweden: SIPRI.

Homze, Edward M. 1981. "The German MIC." In *War, Business, and World Military-Industrial Complexes,* edited by Benjamin Franklin Cooling, 51–83. Port Washington, NY: National University.

Honneth, Axel. 1995. *The Struggle for Recognition: The Moral Grammar of Social Conflicts.* Translated by Joel Anderson. Cambridge, MA: MIT Press.

Houben, Marc. 2005. *International Crisis Management: The Approach of European States.* New York: Routledge.

Howard, Rhoda E. and Jack Donnelly. 1986. "Human Dignity, Human Rights, and Political Regimes." *American Political Science Review* 80 (3): 801–17.

Huberman, Bernardo A., Christoph H. Loch, and Ayse Önçüler. 2004. "Status as a Valued Resource." *Social Psychology Quarterly* 67 (1): 103–14.

Hufbauer, Gary C., Jeffrey J. Schott, and Kimberly A. Elliot. 1990. *Economic Sanctions Reconsidered: History and Current Policy.* 2nd ed. Washington, DC: Institute for International Economics.

Hugh-Jones, David and Ro'i Zultan. 2012. "Reputation and Cooperation in Defense." *Journal of Conflict Resolution* 57 (2): 327–55.

Human Rights Watch (HRW). 1994. *Arming Rwanda: The Arms Trade and Human Rights: Abuses in the Rwandan War.* Human Rights Watch Arms Project, vol. 6, no. 1. New York: HRW.

——. 1999. "Arms Transfers to Abusive End-Users." In *HRW World Report 1999.* New York: HRW. Retrieved January 23, 2007, from http://www.hrw.org.

——. 2002. *Dangerous Dealings: Changes to US Military Assistance After September 11.* United States, vol. 14, no. 1 (G). New York: HRW.

——. 2003a. *Small Arms and Human Rights: The Need for Global Action.* An HRW briefing paper for the UN Biennial Meeting on Small Arms. New York: HRW.

——. 2003b. *Sudan, Oil, and Human Rights.* New York: HRW.

Human Security Centre. 2005. *The Human Security Report 2005: War and Peace in the 21st Century.* New York: Oxford University Press.

Humphreys, Macartan. 2005. "Natural Resources, Conflict, and Conflict Resolution: Uncovering the Mechanisms." *Journal of Conflict Resolution* 49 (4): 508–37.

Hurd, Ian. 2007. *After Anarchy: Legitimacy and Power in the United Nations Security Council.* Princeton: Princeton University Press.

Hurrell, Andrew. 1993. "International Society and the Study of Regimes: A Reflective Approach." In *Regime Theory and International Relations,* edited by Volker Rittberger, 49–72. New York: Oxford University Press.

Huth, Paul K. 1988. *Extended Deterrence and the Prevention of War.* New Haven: Yale University Press.

Ignatieff, Michael. 2005. "Introduction: American Exceptionalism and Human Rights." In *American Exceptionalism and Human Rights,* edited by Michael Ignatieff, 1–26. Princeton: Princeton University Press.

Ikenberry, G. John. 2001. *After Victory: Institutions, Strategic Restraint, and the Rebuilding of Order After Major Wars.* Princeton: Princeton University Press.

Ingebritsen, Christine. 2006. *Scandinavia in World Politics.* Lanham, MD: Rowman & Littlefield.

Ingram, Paul and Roy Isbister. 2004. *Escaping the Subsidy Trap: Why Arms Exports Are Bad for Britain.* London: BASIC, Saferworld, Oxford Research Group.

International Committee of the Red Cross (ICRC). 1996. *Anti-personnel Landmines: Friend or Foe? A Study of the Military Use and Effectiveness of Anti-personnel Mines.* Geneva: ICRC.

——. 1999. *Arms Availability and the Situation of Civilians in Armed Conflict: A Study Presented by the ICRC.* ICRC Publication 1999 Ref. 0734. Geneva: ICRC. Retrieved September 13, 2006, from http://www.icrc.org.

"International Organizations and Socialization in Europe." 2005. Special issue of *International Organization* 59 (4).

Inter Press Service. 1987. "Belgium: Tough New Laws Proposed for Arms Shipments." February 11. Retrieved March 3, 2007, from LexisNexis Academic.

Jabko, Nicolas. 2006. *Playing the Market: A Political Strategy for Uniting Europe, 1985–2005.* Ithaca: Cornell University Press.

Jackson, Patrick Thaddeus. 2004. "Forum Introduction: Is the State a Person? Why Should We Care?" *Review of International Studies* 30:255–58.

Jacobson, Phillip. 1987a. "Knives Out for Mitterrand: French Arms Scandal." *The Times,* November 6. Retrieved August 6, 2008, from LexisNexis.

——. 1987b. "Mitterrand's Close Circle Touched by Iran Arms Scandal." *London Times,* December 23. Retrieved August 6, 2008, from LexisNexis.

Jentleson, Bruce W. 1994. *With Friends Like These: Reagan, Bush, and Saddam 1982–1990.* New York: Norton.

Jervis, Robert. 1970. *The Logic of Images in International Relations.* Princeton: Princeton University Press.

Johnston, Alastair Iain. 2008. *Social States: China in International Institutions, 1980–2000.* Princeton: Princeton University Press.

Jones, Ian and G. Wyn Rees. 1994. "Britain and Post–Cold War Arms Transfers." *Contemporary Security Policy* 15 (1): 109–26.

Jones, Shannon and Jelena Subotic. 2011. "Fantasies of Power: Performing Europeanization on the European Periphery." *European Journal of Cultural Studies* 14 (5): 542–57.

Jupille, Joseph, James A. Caporaso, and Jeffrey T. Checkel. 2003. "Integrating Institutions: Rationalism, Constructivism, and the Study of the European Union." *Comparative Political Studies* 36 (1–2): 7–40.

Kadera, Kelly M. and Sara McLaughlin Mitchell. 2005. "Manna from Heaven or Forbidden Fruit? The (Ab)Use of Control Variables in Research on International Conflict." *Conflict Management and Peace Science* 22 (4): 273–75.

Kaempfer, William H. and Anton D. Lowenberg. 1995. "The Problems and Promise of Sanctions." In *Economic Sanctions: Panacea or Peacebuilding in a Post–Cold War World?* edited by David Cortright and George A. Lopez, 61–71. Boulder, CO: Westview Press.

Kagan, Donald. 1998. "Honor, Interest, and the Nation-State." In *Honor Among Nations: Intangible Interests and Foreign Policy,* edited by Elliot Abrams, 1–16. Washington, DC: Ethics and Public Policy Center.

Kaplowitz, Noel. 1984. "Psychopolitical Dimensions of International Relations: The Reciprocal Effects of Conflict Strategies." *International Studies Quarterly* 28 (4): 373–406.

Kapstein, Ethan B. 1997. "Advanced Industrialized Countries." In *Cascade of Arms: Managing Conventional Weapons Proliferation,* edited by Andrew J. Pierre, 75–88. Cambridge, MA: World Peace Foundation; Washington, DC: Brookings Institution Press.

Karp, Aaron. 1993. "Arming Ethnic Conflict." *Arms Control Today* 23 (7): 8–13.

——. 1994. "The Arms Trade Revolution: The Major Impact of Small Arms." *Washington Quarterly* 17 (4). Retrieved February 18, 2007, from LexisNexis.

——. 2002. "Laudable Failure." *SAIS Review* 22 (1): 177–93.

Katzenstein, Peter J. 1996. Introduction to *The Culture of National Security: Norms and Identity in World Politics,* edited by Peter J. Katzenstein, 1–32. New York: Columbia University Press.

Katzenstein, Peter J., Robert O. Keohane, and Stephen D. Krasner. 1998. "*International Organization* and the Study of World Politics." *International Organization* 52 (4): 645–85.

Katzenstein, Peter J. and Rudra Sil. 2004. "Rethinking Asian Security: A Case for Analytical Eclecticism." In *Rethinking Security in East Asia: Identity, Power, and Efficiency,* edited by J. J. Suh, Peter J. Katzenstein, and Allen Carlson, 1–33. Stanford: Stanford University Press.

Kayser, Mark Andreas. 2007. "Partisan Waves: International Sources of Electoral Choice." Unpublished paper.

Kearns, Graham. 1980. *Arms for the Poor: President Carter's Policies on Arms Transfers to the Third World.* Canberra: Australian National University.

Keller, William W. 1995. *Arm in Arm: The Political Economy of the Global Arms Trade.* New York: Basic Books.

Keller, William W. and Janne E. Nolan. 1997. "The Arms Trade: Business as Usual?" *Foreign Policy* 109:113–25.

Kemp, Geoffrey. 1991. *The Control of the Middle East Arms Race*. Washington, DC: Carnegie Endowment for International Peace.

Kemp, Geoffrey and Steven Miller. 1979. "The Arms Transfer Phenomenon." In *Arms Transfers and American Foreign Policy*, edited by Andrew J. Pierre, 15–97. New York: New York University Press.

Keohane, Robert O. 1984. *After Hegemony: Cooperation and Discord in the World Political Economy*. Princeton: Princeton University Press.

——. 1998. "When Does International Law Come Home?" *Houston Law Review* 35 (3): 699–713.

Keppler, Elise. 2001. "Preventing Human Rights Abuses by Regulating Arms Brokering: The U.S. Brokering Amendment to the Arms Export Control Act." *Berkeley Journal of International Law* 19 (2): 381–411.

Khanna, Sushil. 1992. "International Trade and Debt: India in the Eighties." *Social Scientist* 20 (1–2): 47–62.

King, Anthony. 1984. *Sex, Money, and Power: Political Scandals in Great Britain and the United States*. Essex Papers in Politics and Government no. 14. Essex, UK: Department of Government, University of Essex.

King, Gary. 2001. "Proper Nouns and Methodological Propriety: Pooling Dyads in International Relations Data." *International Organization* 55 (2): 497–507.

Kinsella, David. 1994. "Conflict in Context: Arms Transfers and Third World Rivalries During the Cold War." *American Journal of Political Science* 38 (3): 557–81.

Kinzer, Stephen. 1992. "Turks Got Tanks, and German Minister Must Quit." *New York Times*, April 1. Retrieved January 22, 2009, from http://www.nytimes.com.

Kisangani, Emizet F. and Jeffrey Pickering. 2007. *International Military Intervention, 1989–2005*. Interuniversity Consortium for Political and Social Research no. 21282. Retrieved May 26, 2010, from http://www.icpsr.umich.edu.

Kiss, Yudit. 1997. *The Defence Industry in East–Central Europe: Restructuring and Conversion*. New York: Oxford University Press.

Klare, Michael T. 1981. "Evading the Embargo: Illicit U.S. Arms Transfers to South Africa." *Journal of International Affairs* 35 (1): 15–28.

——. 1984. *American Arms Supermarket*. Austin: University of Texas Press.

——. 1991. "Gaining Control: Building a Comprehensive Arms Restraint System." *Arms Control Today*, June, 9–13.

——. 1994–1995. "Awash in Armaments." *Harvard International Review* 17 (1). Retrieved February 18, 2007, from Academic Search Premier.

Klare, Michael and Robert I. Rotberg. 1999. *The Scourge of Small Arms*. World Peace Foundation Reports no. 23. Cambridge, MA: World Peace Foundation; Washington, DC: Fund for Peace.

Klein, Paul and Jürgen Kuhlmann. 2000. "Germany and Its Armed Forces in Transition." In *Military and Society in 21st Century Europe: A Comparative Analysis*, edited by Jürgen Kuhlmann and Jean Callaghan, 183–226. Piscataway, NJ: Transaction.

Kleine-Brockhoff, Mortiz and Dewi Kurniawati. 2003. "Dunkle Wege deutscher Waffen Indonesier schieß am liebsten mit MPs von Heckler & Koch." *Der Tagesspiegel*, December 18. Retrieved February 20, 2007, from http://www.tagesspiegel.de.

Kleinfield, N. R. 2008. "Politics, and Scandal, as Usual." *New York Times*, March 11. Retrieved March 11, 2008, from http://www.nytimes.com.

Klinghoffer, Arthur Jay. 1998. *The International Dimension of Genocide in Rwanda*. New York: New York University Press.

Klotz, Audie. 1995. *Norms in International Relations: The Struggle Against Apartheid*. Ithaca: Cornell University Press.

Klotz, Audie and Cecelia Lynch. 2007. *Strategies for Research in Constructivist International Relations*. Armonk, NY: M. E. Sharpe.

Koh, Harold Hongju. 1990. *The National Security Constitution: Sharing Power After the Iran–Contra Affair*. New Haven: Yale University Press.

——. 1998. "The 1998 Frankel Lecture: Brining International Law Home." *Houston Law Review* 35 (3): 623–81.

——. 2003. "On American Exceptionalism." *Stanford Law Review* 55:1479–527.

Kohut, Andrew and Bruce Stokes. 2006. *America Against the World: How We Are Different and Why We Are Disliked*. New York: Times Books.

Kolling, Andrea. 1997. "Germany: Arming the Indonesian Regime of Terror." In *Indonesia: Arms Trade to a Military Regime*, edited by Martin Broek, 55–58. Amsterdam: European Network Against Arms Trade Secretariat.

Kolodziej, Edward A. 1979. "Arms Transfers and International Politics: The Interdependence of Independence." In *Arms Transfers in the Modern World*, edited by Stephanie G. Neuman and Robert E. Harkavy, 3–26. New York: Praeger.

——. 1987. *Making and Marketing Arms: The French Experience and Its Implications for the International System*. Princeton: Princeton University Press.

Kornbluh, Peter and Malcolm Byrne, eds. 1993. *The Iran–Contra Scandal: The Declassified History*. A National Security Archive Documents Reader. New York: New Press.

Krain, Matthew. 1997. "State-Sponsored Mass Murder: The Onset and Severity of Genocides and Politicides." *Journal of Conflict Resolution* 41 (3): 331–60.

Krasner, Stephen D. 1983. "Structural Causes and Regime Consequences: Regimes as Intervening Variables." In *International Regimes*, edited by Stephen D. Krasner, 1–21. Ithaca: Cornell University Press.

Krause, Keith. 2002. "Multilateral Diplomacy, Norm Building, and UN Conferences: The Case of Small Arms and Light Weapons." *Global Governance* 8 (2): 247–63.

Krause, Keith and Mary K. MacDonald. 1993. "Regulating Arms Sales Through World War II." In *Encyclopedia of Arms Control and Disarmament*, vol. 2, edited by Richard D. Burns, 707–24. New York: Scribner's.

Kreps, David M. 1990. "Corporate Culture and Economic Theory." In *Perspectives on Positive Political Economy*, edited by James E. Alt and Kenneth A. Shepsle, 90–143. New York: Cambridge University Press.

"Kritik an Stoltenberg von Union und FDP." 1992. *Süddeutsche Zeitung*, March 30. Retrieved February 10, 2007, from LexisNexis Academic.

Krook, Mona Lena and Jacqui True. 2012. "Rethinking the Life Cycles of International Norms: The United Nations and the Global Promotion of Gender Equality." *European Journal of International Relations* 18 (1): 103–27.

Kroslak, Daniela. 2007. *The Role of France in the Rwandan Genocide*. London: Hurst.

Kurth, James R. 1971. "A Widening Gyre: The Logic of American Weapons Procurement." *Public Policy* 19 (3): 373–404.

Kwakwa, Edward. 2003. "The International Community, International Law, and the United States: Three in One, Two Against One, or One and the Same?" In *United States Hegemony and the Foundations of International Law*, edited by Michael Byers and Georg Nolte, 25–56. New York: Cambridge University Press.

Kwon, Hyeok Yong and Jonas Pontusson. 2005. "The Rise and Fall of Government Partisanship: Dynamics of Social Spending in OECD Countries, 1962–2000." Unpublished paper.

La Balme, Natalie. 2000. "Constraint, Catalyst, or Political Tool? The French Public and Foreign Policy." In *Decisionmaking in a Glass House: Mass Media, Public Opinion, and American and European Foreign Policy in the 21st Century*, edited by Brigitte L. Nacos, Robert Y. Shapiro, and Pierangelo Isernia, 265–78. Lanham, MD: Rowman & Littlefield.

Labbé, Marie-Hélène. 1994. "French Export Control Policy." In *International Cooperation on Nonproliferation Export Controls: Prospects for the 1990s and Beyond*, edited by Gary K. Bertsch, Richard T. Cupitt, and Steven Elliott-Gower, 201–19. Ann Arbor: University of Michigan Press.

Labour Party. 1997. "New Labour Because Britain Deserves Better: 1997 Labour Party Manifesto." Retrieved August 4, 2008, from http://www.labour-party.org.uk.

Lafer, Celso. 2000. "Brazilian International Identity and Foreign Policy: Past, Present, and Future." *Daedalus* 129 (2): 207–38.

Lamb, Guy. 2007. "The Transparency and Accountability of South Africa's Arms Trade." *ISS Today*, August 6, Institute for Strategic Studies. Retrieved March 19, 2009, from http://www.iss.co.za.

LaPierre, Wayne. 2006. *The Global War on Your Guns: Inside the U.N. Plan to Destroy the Bill of Rights*. Nashville, TN: Nelson Current.

Larson, Deborah Welch. 1997. "Trust and Missed Opportunities in International Relations." *Political Psychology* 18 (3): 701–34.

Laurance, Edward J., Hendrik Wagenmakers, and Herbert Wulf. 2005. "Managing the Global Problems Created by the Conventional Arms Trade: An Assessment of the United Nations Register of Conventional Arms." *Global Governance* 11 (2): 225–46.

Lawler, Peter. 2000. "New Labour's Foreign Policy." In *New Labour in Power,* edited by David Coates and Peter Lawler, 281–99. New York: Manchester University Press.

League of Nations. 1925. *Proceedings of the Conference for the Supervision of the International Trade in Arms and Ammunition and in Implements of War.* A.13.1925.IX. Geneva: League of Nations.

Lebovic, James H. 2006. "Democracies and Transparency: Country Reports to the UN Register of Conventional Arms, 1992–2001." *Journal of Peace Research* 43 (5): 543–62.

Lebovic, James H. and Erik Voeten. 2006. "The Politics of Shame: The Condemnation of Country Human Rights Practices in the UNCHR." *International Studies Quarterly* 50 (4): 861–88.

Lebow, Richard Ned. 1981. *Between Peace and War: The Nature of International Crisis.* Baltimore: Johns Hopkins University Press.

——. 2008. *A Cultural Theory of International Relations.* New York: Cambridge University Press.

Lee, Geoff. 1999. "Sleaze: Standards in Public Life." In *Political Issues in Britain Today,* edited by Bill Jones, 5th ed., 281–306. New York: Manchester University Press.

Legro, Jeffrey W. 1997. "Which Norms Matter? Revisiting the 'Failure' of Internationalism." *International Organization* 51 (1): 31–63.

Levine, Paul, Ron Smith, Lucrezia Reichlin, and Patrick Rey. 1997. "The Arms Trade: Winners and Losers." *Economic Policy* 12 (25): 335–70.

Lewis, J. A. C. 2004. "Holding a Steady Course." *Jane's Defence Weekly,* June 16, 75–82.

Leyland, Peter. 2007. *The Constitution of the United Kingdom: A Contextual Analysis.* Portland, OR: Hart.

Lieberman, Evan S. 2005. "Nested Analysis as a Mixed-Method Strategy for Comparative Research." *American Political Science Review* 99 (3): 435–52.

Lipset, Seymour Martin. 1996. *American Exceptionalism: A Double-Edged Sword.* New York: Norton.

Lopez, George A. 1986. "National Security Ideology as an Impetus to State Violence and State Terror." In *Government Violence and Repression: An Agenda for Research,* edited by Michael Stohl and George A. Lopez, 73–95. New York: Greenwood Press.

Lowi, Theodore J. 2004. "Power and Corruption: Political Competition and the Scandal Market." In *Public Affairs: Politics in the Age of Sex Scandals,* edited by

Paul Apostolidis and Juliet A. Williams, 69–100. Durham, NC: Duke University Press.

Lowther, William. 1991. *Arms and the Man: Dr. Gerald Bull, Iraq, and the Supergun.* Novato, CA: Presidio.

Lumpe, Lora. 1999a. "Curbing the Proliferation of Small Arms and Light Weapons." *Security Dialogue* 30 (2): 151–64.

——. 1999b. "Transparency in the Legal Small Arms Trade." Paper prepared for the Swiss Government Workshop on Small Arms, Geneva. Retrieved January 8, 2009, from http://www.prio.no.

Lumsdaine, David Halloran. 1993. *Moral Vision in International Politics: The Foreign Aid Regime, 1949–1989.* Princeton: Princeton University Press.

Lutz, Ellen L. and Kathryn Sikkink. 2000. "International Human Rights Law and Practice in Latin America." *International Organization* 54 (3): 633–59.

MacFarquhar, Neil. 2008. "2 Vetoes Quash U.N. Sanctions on Zimbabwe." *New York Times,* July 12. Retrieved July 12, 2008, from http://www.nytimes.com.

Madsen, Deborah L. 1998. *American Exceptionalism.* Jackson: University Press of Mississippi.

Mahley, Donald A. 2012. Statement by Ambassador Donald Mahley, U.S. Representative to the Arms Trade Treaty Conference, at the UN Conference on the Arms Trade Treaty. July 12. Retrieved July 9, 2013, from http://usun.state.gov/briefing /statements/194950.htm.

Malone, David. 2002. "The New Diplomacy at the United Nations: How Substantive?" In *Enhancing Global Governance: Towards a New Diplomacy,* edited by Andrew F. Cooper, John English, and Ramesh Thakur, 38–54. New York: United Nations University Press.

Mampaey, Luc. 2002. "La Belgique et le commerce des armes de 1996 à 2001: Quelques chiffres." In *Les Exportations d'armes de la Belgique,* edited by Bernard Adam, Sara Bayes, Georges Berghezan, Ilhan Berkol, Françoise Donnay, Luc Mampaey, and Michel Wéry, 8–21. Rapport du Groupe de recherche et d'information sur la paix et la sécurité (GRIP) (2002/4). Brussels: GRIP.

——. 2003. "Les exportations d'armes de la Belgique: Synthèse en chiffres, 1996 à 2002." *Note d'Analyse,* August 6. Retrieved March 12, 2007, from http://www.grip .org.

Mancuso, Maureen. 1998. "Politicising Ethics: Scandal and the American Experience." In *Ethics and Political Practice: Perspectives on Legislative Ethics,* edited by Noel Preston and Charles Sampford, wth C-A. Bois, 66–80. New York: Routledge.

Maniruzzaman, Talukder. 1992. "Arms Transfers, Military Coups, and Military Rule in Developing States." *Journal of Conflict Resolution* 36 (4): 733–55.

Marín-Bosch, Miguel. 1998. *Votes in the UN General Assembly.* Boston: Kluwer Law International.

Markham, James M. 1987a. "Arms Scandal Puts Mitterrand on Defensive." *New York Times*, November 8. Retrieved February 24, 2007, from ProQuest Historical Newspapers.

——. 1987b. "Furor Growing in France on Arms-Sale Case." *New York Times*, November 5. Retrieved August 6, 2008, from http://www.nytimes.com.

Markovits, Andrei S. and Mark Silverstein, eds. 1988. *The Politics of Scandal: Power and Processes in Liberal Democracies*. New York: Holmes & Meier.

Markusen, Ann, Peter Hall, Scott Campbell, and Sabina Deitrick. 1991. *The Rise of the Gunbelts: The Military Remapping of Industrial America*. New York: Oxford University Press.

Marsh, Nicholas. 2002. "Two Sides of the Same Coin? The Legal and Illegal Trade in Small Arms." *Brown Journal of World Affairs* 9 (1): 217–28.

——. 2005. "The Methodology Used in Creating a Comtrade Based Dataset of Small Arms Transfers." Memoradum for the Norwegian Initiative on Small Arms Transfers and the International Peace Research Institute, Oslo. September 28.

Marshall, Monty G. and Keith Jaggers. 2005a. *Polity IV Project: Political Regime Characteristics and Transitions, 1800–2003*. College Park: University of Maryland.

——. 2005b. *Polity IV Project: Political Regime Characteristics and Transitions, 1800–2004*. College Park: University of Maryland.

Martin, Laurence and John Garnett. 1997. *British Foreign Policy: Challenges and Choices for the 21st Century*. Chatham House Papers. Herndon, VA: Pinter.

Martin, Lisa L. 1992. *Coercive Cooperation: Explaining Multilateral Economic Sanctions*. Princeton: Princeton University Press.

Martin, Stephen. 1999. "The Subsidy Savings from Reducing UK Arms Exports." *Journal of Economic Studies* 26 (1): 15–37.

Mason, Thomas L. 2002. "A Free Trade Perspective from the Firearms Community." *SAIS Review* 22 (1): 203–6.

Mastanduno, Michael. 1992. *Economic Containment: CoCom and the Politics of East–West Trade*. Ithaca: Cornell University Press.

Mattila, Mikko and Jan-Erik Lane. 2001. "Why Unanimity in the Council? A Roll Call Analysis of Council Voting." *European Union Politics* 2 (1): 31–52.

May, Diane. 1992. "The Schleswig-Holstein Land Election of 5 April 1992." *German Politics* 1 (2): 282–84.

Mayhew, Emma. 2005. "A Dead Giveaway: A Critical Analysis of New Labour's Rationales for Supporting Military Exports." *Contemporary Security Policy* 26 (1): 62–83.

McNulty, Mel. 2000. "French Arms, War, and Genocide in Rwanda." *Crime, Law, and Social Change* 33:105–29.

McRae, Rob. 2001. "International Relations and the New Diplomacy." In *Human Security and the New Diplomacy: Protecting People, Promoting Peace*, edited by Rob McRae and Don Hubert, 250–59. Montreal: McGill-Queen's University Press.

Meernik, James, Eric L. Krueger, and Steven C. Poe. 1998. "Testing Models of U.S. Foreign Policy: Foreign Aid During and After the Cold War." *Journal of Politics* 60 (1): 63–85.

Meinke, Scott R. and William D. Anderson. 2001. "Influencing from Impaired Administrations: Presidents, White House Scandals, and Legislative Leadership." *Legislative Studies Quarterly* 26 (4): 639–59.

Melanson, Richard A. 2000. *American Foreign Policy Since the Vietnam War: The Search for Consensus from Nixon to Clinton.* 3rd ed. Armonk, NY: M. E. Sharpe.

Melvern, Linda. 2000. *A People Betrayed: The Role of the West in Rwanda's Genocide.* New York: Zed Books.

——. 2004. *Conspiracy to Murder: The Rwandan Genocide.* New York: Verso.

Mercer, Jonathan. 1996. *Reputation and International Politics.* Ithaca: Cornell University Press.

Milgrom, Paul R., Douglass C. North, and Barry R. Weingast. 1990. "The Role of Institutions in the Revival of Trade: The Law Merchant, Private Judges, and the Campagne Fairs." *Economics and Politics* 2 (1): 1–23.

Miller, Davina. 1996. "The Scott Report and the Future of British Defense Sales." *Defense Analysis* 12 (3): 359–69.

Miller, Derek, Wendy Cukier, Helena Vázquez, and Charlotte Watson. 2003. *Regulation of Civilian Possession of Small Arms and Light Weapons.* Biting the Bullet Briefing no. 16. London: International Alert, Saferworld, and the University of Bradford.

Miller, Manjari Chatterjee. 2013. *Wronged by Empire: Post-imperial Ideology and Foreign Policy in India and China.* Stanford: Stanford University Press.

Milner, Helen V. 1997. *Interests, Institutions, and Information: Domestic Politics and International Relations.* Princeton: Princeton University Press.

Mintz, Alex and Chi Huang. 1991. "Guns Versus Butter: The Indirect Link." *American Journal of Political Science* 35 (3): 738–57.

Misol, Lisa. 2004. "Weapons and War Crimes: The Complicity of Arms Suppliers." In *Human Rights Watch World Report 2004.* New York: Human Rights Watch. Retrieved September 13, 2006, from http://www.hrw.org.

Mitchell, Neil J. and James M. McCormick. 1988. "Economic and Political Explanations of Human Rights Violations." *World Politics* 40 (4): 476–98.

Mitchell, Ronald B. 1998. "Sources of Transparency: Information Systems in International Regimes." *International Studies Quarterly* 42 (1): 109–30.

Monroe, Kristen Renwick. 2001. "Morality and a Sense of Self: The Importance of Identity and Categorization for Moral Action." *American Journal of Political Science* 45 (3): 491–507.

Moose, Richard M. and Daniel L. Spiegel. 1979. "Congress and Arms Transfers." In *Arms Transfers and American Foreign Policy*, edited by Andrew J. Pierre, 228–60. New York: New York University Press.

Moravcsik, Andrew. 1991. "1992 and the Future of the European Armaments Indus-try." In *Emerging Dimensions of European Security Policy*, edited by Wolfgang F. Danspeckgruber, 199–220. Boulder, CO: Westview Press.

——. 1992. "Arms and Autarky in Modern European History." In *Defense and Dependence in a Global Economy*, edited by Raymond Vernon and Ethan B. Kapstein, 23–45. Washington, DC: Congressional Quarterly Inc.

——. 1993. "Armaments Among Allies: European Weapons Collaboration, 1975–1985." In *Double-Edged Diplomacy: International Bargaining and Domestic Politics*, edited by Peter B. Evans, Harold K. Jacobson, and Robert D. Putnam, 128–67. Berkeley: University of California Press.

——. 1997. "Taking Preferences Seriously: Liberalism and International Relations Theory." *International Organization* 51 (4): 513–53.

Morrow, James D. 2007. "When Do States Follow the Laws of War?" *American Political Science Review* 101 (3): 559–72.

Morton, David. 2006. "Gunning for the World." *Foreign Policy*, January–February, 58–67. .

Muggah, Robert and Eric Berman. 2001. *Humanitarianism Under Threat: The Humanitarian Impacts of Small Arms and Light Weapons*. Small Arms Survey (SAS) Special Report. Geneva: SAS and Centre for Humanitarian Dialogue.

Mulholland, David. 2003. "Export Drive." *Jane's Defence Weekly*, October 29, 22–27.

——. 2005. "Feeling the Squeeze." *Jane's Defence Weekly*, March 30, 20–28.

Müller, Harald, Matthias Dembinski, Alexander Kelle, and Annette Schaper. 1994. *From Black Sheep to White Angel? The New German Export Control Policy*. Peace Research Institute Frankfurt (PRIF) Reports no. 32. Frankfurt: PRIF.

Munck, Gerardo L. 2004. "Tools for Qualitative Research." In *Rethinking Social Inquiry: Diverse Tools, Shared Standards*, edited by Henry E. Brady and David Collier, 105–21. Lanham, MD: Rowman & Littlefield.

Munck, Gerardo L. and Jay Verkuilen. 2002. "Conceptualizing and Measuring Democracy: Evaluating Alternative Indices." *Comparative Political Studies* 35 (1): 5–34.

Musah, Abdel-Fatau. 2002. "Small Arms: A Time Bomb Under West Africa's Democratization Process." *Brown Journal of World Affairs* 9 (1): 239–49.

Myerscough, Rhea. 2006. "Putting the Cart Before the Horse: United States Resumes Military Assistance to Indonesia." Center for Defense Information, May 18. Retrieved October 30, 2006, from http://www.cdi.org.

Naaz, Farah. 2000. "Israel's Arms Industry." *Strategic Analysis* 23 (12). Retrieved May 6, 2010, from http://www.ciaonet.org.

Nadelmann, Ethan A. 1990. "Global Prohibition Regimes: The Evolution of Norms in International Society." *International Organization* 44 (4): 479–526.

Nassauer, Otfried and Christopher Steinmetz. 2005. *"Made in Germany" Inside: Komponenten—die vergessenen Rüstungsexporte*. Executive Summary. Berlin: Oxfam Deutschland and Berliner Informationszentrums für Transatlantische Sicherheit.

Nathan, Laurie. 2005. "Consistencies and Inconsistencies in South African Foreign Policy." *International Affairs* 81 (2): 361–72.

Naylor, R. T. 1999. *Economic Warfare: Sanctions, Embargo Busting, and Their Human Cost*. Boston: Northeastern University Press.

Negrine, Ralph. 1997. "The Inquiry's Media Coverage." In *Under the Scott-Light: British Government Seen Through the Scott Report*, edited by Brian Thompson and F. F. Ridley, 27–40. New York: Oxford University Press.

Neuman, Stephanie G. 1986. *Military Assistance in Recent Wars: The Dominance of the Superpowers*. New York: Praeger.

——. 1993. "Controlling the Arms Trade: Idealistic Dream or Realpolitik?" *Washington Quarterly* 16 (3). Retrieved October 28, 2006, from LexisNexis.

Newport, Frank. 2009. "Many Gun Owners Think Obama Will Try to Ban Gun Sales." Gallup, October 20. Retrieved January 27, 2010, from http://www.gallup.com.

"News Agency Says Arms Affair Beginning to Affect International Image." 1996. *BBC Summary of World Broadcasts*, May 15. Retrieved July 3, 2008, from LexisNexis Academic.

Nolan, Janne E. 1991. "The Global Arms Market After the Gulf War: Prospects for Control." *Washington Quarterly* 14 (3). Retrieved September 27, 2006, from LexisNexis.

——. 1997. "United States." In *Cascade of Arms: Managing Conventional Weapons Proliferation*, edited by Andrew J. Pierre, 131–49. Washington, DC: Brookings Institution Press; Cambridge, MA: World Peace Foundation.

Norman, George and Joel P. Trachtman. 2005. "The Customary International Law Game." *American Journal of International Law* 99 (3): 541–80.

Norton-Taylor, Richard, Mark Lloyd, and Stephen Cook. 1996. *Knee Deep in Dishonour: The Scott Report and Its Aftermath*. London: Victor Gollancz.

Norton-Taylor, Richard and John McGrath. 1995. "Half the Picture." In *Truth Is a Difficult Concept: Inside the Scott Inquiry*, by Richard Norton-Taylor with Mark Lloyd, 213–74. London: A Guardian Book.

Norwegian Initiative on Small Arms Transfers (NISAT). n.d. NISAT Database of Authorised Transfers of Small Arms and Light Weapons. Accessed at various times in 2006, 2011, and 2013 from http://nisat.prio.org.

Nye, Joseph S. 2004. *Soft Power: The Means to Success in World Politics*. New York: PublicAffairs.

O'Dwyer, Diana. 2006. "First Landmines, Now Small Arms? The International Campaign to Ban Landmines as a Model for Small Arms Advocacy." *Irish Studies in International Affairs* 17:77–97.

O'Neill, Barry. 1999. *Honor, Symbols, and War.* Ann Arbor: University of Michigan Press.

——. 2006. *Nuclear Weapons and National Prestige.* Cowles Foundation Discussion Paper no. 1560. New Haven: Yale University Press.

"Only in America." 2008. *The Economist,* April 24. Retrieved November 26, 2008, from http://www.economist.com.

Otte, Anja. 2003. "Senate Approves Regionalization of Arms Exports." *De Standaard,* July 30. Reprinted in *BBC Worldwide Monitoring,* July 31. Retrieved March 3, 2007, from LexisNexis Academic.

Otte, Anja and Wouter Verschelden. 2006. "Moerman Should Resolve Her Own Problems." *De Standaard,* May 16. Reprinted in "Flemish Minister's Arms Export Proposal Meets with Little Support." *BBC Worldwide Monitoring,* May 16. Retrieved March 3, 2007, from LexisNexis Academic.

Oxfam. 1998. *Out of Control: The Loopholes in UK Controls on the Arms Trade.* London: Oxfam GB.

——. 2002. *The Spoils of Peace: How Can Tighter Arms Export Controls Benefit Both the Poor and British Industry?* Oxfam Briefing Paper no. 13. London: Oxfam GB.

Oxford English Dictionary. 1989. 2nd ed. New York: Oxford University Press. Accessed April 4, 2008, at OED online.

Pape, Robert A. 1997. "Why Economic Sanctions Do Not Work." *International Security* 22 (2): 90–136.

Parlement Wallon. 2007. *Rapport au Parlement Wallon sur l'application de la loi 05 Aout 1991, modifiee par les lois du 25 et 26 Mars 2003 relatives a l'importation, a l'exportation et au transit d'armes, de munitions et de materiel devant servir specialement a un usage militaire et de la technologie y afferente: Rapport annuel 2006.* Namur, Belgium: Parlement Wallon.

Paul, T. V. 2009. *The Tradition of Non-use of Nuclear Weapons.* Stanford: Stanford University Press.

Pearson, Frederic S. 1983. "The Question of Control in British Defence Sales Policy." *International Affairs* 59 (2): 211–38.

——. 1986. "'Necessary Evil': Perspectives on West German Arms Transfer Policies." *Armed Forces and Society* 12 (4): 525–52.

——. 1994. *The Global Spread of Arms: Political Economic of International Security.* Boulder, CO: Westview Press.

Peel, Quentin. 1993. "Bonn Attacked on Arms Exports." *Financial Times,* February 16. Retrieved January 31, 2007, from LexisNexis Academic.

Peterson, M. J. 2006. *The UN General Assembly.* New York: Routledge.

Petrova, Margarita Hristoforova. 2007. "Leadership Competition and the Creation of Norms: A Cross-National Study of Weapons Restrictions." Ph.D. diss., Cornell University.

Phythian, Mark. 1997. *Arming Iraq: How the U.S. and Britain Secretly Built Saddam's War Machine*. Boston: Northeastern University Press.

——. 2000a. "The Illicit Arms Trade: Cold War and Post–Cold War.: *Crime, Law, and Social Change* 33 (1–2): 1–52.

——. 2000b. *The Politics of British Arms Sales Since 1964*. New York: Manchester University Press.

Pierre, Andrew J. 1982. *The Global Politics of Arms Sales*. Princeton: Princeton University Press.

——. 1997. "Toward an International Regime for Conventional Arms Sales." In *Cascade of Arms: Managing Conventional Weapons Proliferation*, edited by Andrew J. Pierre, 369–436. Washington, DC: Brookings Institution Press.

Pilkington, Colin. 1998. *Issues in British Politics*. New York: St. Martin's Press.

Poe, Steven C., Sabine C. Carey, and Tanya C. Vazcuez. 2001. "How Are These Pictures Different? A Quantitative Comparison of the US State Department and Amnesty International Human Rights Reports, 1976–1995." *Human Rights Quarterly* 23:650–77.

Poe, Steven C. and C. Neal Tate. 1994. "Repression of Human Rights to Personal Integrity in the 1980s: A Global Analysis." *American Political Science Review* 88 (4): 853–72.

Pontaut, Jean-Marie. 1987. "Affaire Luchaire: Le Rapport explosif." *Le Pont*, no. 789 (November 2): 19.

Ponting, Clive. 1990. *Secrecy in Britain*. Cambridge, MA: Blackwell.

Powell, G. Bingham, Jr., and Guy D. Whitten. 1993. "A Cross-National Analysis of Economic Voting: Taking Account of the Political Context." *American Journal of Political Science* 37 (2): 391–414.

Prados, Alfred B. 2002. *Saudi Arabia: Current Issues and U.S. Relations*. Issue Brief for Congress no. IB93113. Washington, DC: Congressional Research Service.

Press, Daryl G. 2005. *Calculating Credibility: How Leaders Assess Military Threats*. Ithaca: Cornell University Press.

Price, Richard. 1998. "Reversing the Gun Sights: Transnational Civil Society Targets Land Mines." *International Organization* 52 (3): 613–44.

Raub, Werner and Jeroen Weesie. 1990. "Reputation and Efficiency in Social Interactions: An Example of Network Effects." *American Journal of Sociology* 96 (3): 626–54.

Ray, James Lee. 2003. "Explaining Interstate Conflict and War: What Should Be Controlled for?" *Conflict Management and Peace Science* 20 (2): 1–31.

——. 2005. "Constructing Multivariate Analyses (of Dangerous Dyads)." *Conflict Management and Peace Science* 22 (4): 277–92.

Relly, Jeannine E. and Meghna Sabharwal. 2009. "Perceptions of Transparency of Government Policymaking: A Cross-National Study." *Government Information Quarterly* 26:148–57.

Renner, Michael. 1997. *Small Arms, Big Impact: The Next Challenge of Disarmament.* Worldwatch Paper no. 137. Washington, DC: Worldwatch Institute.

"Report Done on France's Alleged Role in Genocide." 2007. *Mail & Guardian Online,* November 16. Retrieved November 19, 2007, from http://www.mg.co.za.

Reus-Smit, Christian. 2007. "International Crises of Legitimacy." *International Politics* 44:157–74.

Reuters. 2008. "Zambia Seeks to Block Arms for Zimbabwe." *New York Times,* April 22. Retrieved July 28, 2008, from http://www.nytimes.com.

Ridgeway, Cecilia L. and Henry A. Walker. 1995. "Status Structures." In *Sociological Perspectives on Social Psychology,* edited by Karen S. Cook, Gary Alan Fine, and James S. House, 281–310. Needham Heights, MA: Allyn and Bacon.

Ringmar, Erik. 1996. "On the Ontological Status of the State." *European Journal of International Relations* 2 (4): 439–66.

Risse-Kappen, Thomas. 1991. "Public Opinion, Domestic Structure, and Foreign Policy in Liberal Democracies." *World Politics* 43 (4): 479–512.

——, ed. 1995a. *Bringing Transnational Relations Back In: Non-state Actors, Domestic Structures, and International Institutions.* New York: Cambridge University Press.

——. 1995b. "Democratic Peace—Warlike Democracies? A Social Constructivist Interpretation of the Liberal Argument." *European Journal of International Relations* 1 (4): 491–517.

Robbins, Keith. 1997. "Britishness and British Foreign Policy." UK Foreign Commonwealth Office Annual Lecture, London, May 14. Retrieved June 5, 2007, from http://www.fco.gov.uk.

Rodman, David. 2007. *Arms Transfers to Israel: The Strategic Logic Behind American Military Assistance.* Portland, OR: Sussex Academic Press.

Ron, James, Howard Ramos, and Kathleen Rodgers. 2005. "Transnational Information Politics: NGO Human Rights Reporting, 1986–2000." *International Studies Quarterly* 49:557–87.

Roosevelt, Franklin D. 1934. Message to the Senate, May 18. *Congressional Record: Proceedings and Debates,* 73rd Cong., 2nd sess., Vol. 78, Part 8. Washington, DC: US Government Printing Office.

Rosenau, James N. 1961. *Public Opinion and Foreign Policy: An Operational Formulation.* New York: Random House.

Ross, Michael L. 2004. "How Do Natural Resources Influence Civil War? Evidence from Thirteen Cases." *International Organization* 68:35–67.

Rossel-Cambier, Koen. 1997. "Sustainable Disarmament for Sustainable Development." Address by the secretary of state for development co-operation attached to the prime minister of Belgium at the conference "Controlling the Global Trade in Light Weapons," American Academy of Arts and Sciences, Washington, DC, December 12. Retrieved January 9, 2008, from http://www.iansa.org.

Roussel, Violaine. 2002. "Changing Definitions of Risk and Responsibility in French Political Scandals." *Journal of Law and Society* 29 (3): 461–86.

Rousselin, Pierre. 1998. "La France et le Rwanda: Les Mécomptes de la cohabitation." *Le Figaro*, January 15. Retrieved August 6, 2008, from LexisNexis.

Rubenberg, Cheryl A. 1989. *Israel and the American National Interest: A Critical Examination.* Urbana: University of Illinois Press.

Rummel, R. J. 1995. "Democracy, Power, Genocide, and Mass Murder." *Journal of Conflict Resolution* 39 (1): 3–26.

Rutherford, Kenneth R. 2000. "The Evolving Arms Control Agenda: Implications of the Role of NGOs in Banning Antipersonnel Landmines." *World Politics* 53 (1): 74–114.

"Rwanda Accuses France Over 1994 Genocide." 2008. *France 24*, August 5. Retrieved August 7, 2008, from http://www.france24.com.

Saferworld. 2007. *The Good, the Bad, and the Ugly: A Decade of Labour's Arms Exports.* London: Saferworld.

——. 2011. "UK Arms Export Review Misses the Target." News article, July 22. Retrieved July 26, 2011, from http://www.saferworld.org.uk.

Sambanis, Nicholas. 2004. "What Is Civil War? Conceptual and Empirical Complexities of an Operational Definition." *Journal of Conflict Resolution* 48 (6): 814–58.

Sanjian, Gregory S. 1998. "Cold War Imperatives and Quarrelsome Clients: Modeling US and USSR Arms Transfers to India and Pakistan." *Journal of Conflict Resolution* 42 (1): 97–127.

Sariibrahimoglu, Lale. 1994. "Germans Put New Ban on Arms Transfers." *Jane's Defence Weekly*, April 16, 11.

Sarkozy, Nicolas. 2008. "Déclaration de M. Nicolas Sarkozy, Président de la République, approuvant le projet de loi relatif à la programmation militaire pour les années 2009 à 2014 et portant diverses dispositions concernant la defense." Public Speeches, October 29, Paris. Retrieved February 1, 2010, from http://discours.vie-publique.fr.

Sartori, Anne E. 2002. "The Might of the Pen: A Reputational Theory of Communication in International Disputes." *International Organization* 56 (1): 121–49.

——. 2003. "An Estimator for Some Binary-Outcome Selection Models Without Exclusion Restrictions." *Political Analysis* 11 (2): 111–38.

"Saudi-Arabien bestätigt Panzergeschäft." 2011. *Die Zeit*, December 7. Retrieved December 14, 2011, from http://www.zeit.de.

"Saudi Prince 'Received Arms Cash.'" 2007. *BBC News*, June 7. Retrieved June 7, 2007, from http://news.bbc.co.uk.

Scaringella, Jean-Louis. 1998. *Les Industries de défense en Europe.* Paris: Economica.

Schaffer, Frederic C. 1998. *Democracy in Translation: Understanding Politics in an Unfamiliar Culture.* Ithaca: Cornell University Press.

Schelling, Thomas C. 1966. *Arms and Influence.* New Haven: Yale University Press.

Schimmelfennig, Frank. 2001. "The Community Trap: Liberal Norms, Rhetorical Action, and the Eastern Enlargement of the European Union." *International Organization* 55 (1): 47–80.

Schmidt, Christopher J. 2007. "An International Right to Keep and Bear Arms." *William and Mary Bill of Rights Journal* 15:982–1020.

Schmitter, Philippe C. and Terry Lynn Karl. 1991. "What Democracy Is . . . and Is Not." *Journal of Democracy* 2 (3): 75–88.

Schroeder, Matt. 2005. "Transparency and Accountability in Arms Export Systems: The United States as a Case Study." *Disarmament Forum*, no. 3: 29–37.

"The Scott Report." 1996. *The Economist*, February 24. Retrieved August 3, 2008, from Factiva.

Searle, John R. 1990. "Collective Intensions and Actions." In *Intentions in Communication*, edited by Philip R. Cohen, Jerry Morgan, and Martha E. Pollack, 401–15. Cambridge, MA: MIT Press.

Shannon, Vaughn P. 2000. "Norms Are What States Make of Them: The Political Psychology of Norm Violation." *International Studies Quarterly* 44 (2): 293–316.

Shapiro, Andrew J. 2012. "Briefing on Department of State Efforts to Expand Defense Trade, June 14." Retrieved July 9, 2013, from http://www.state.gov/r/pa/prs/ps/2012/06/192408.htm.

Sharman, J. C. 2006. *Havens in a Storm: The Struggle for Global Tax Regulation.* Ithaca: Cornell University Press.

Sil, Rudra. 2000. "The Foundations of Eclecticism: The Epistemological Status of Agency, Culture, and Structure in Social Theory." *Journal of Theoretical Politics* 12 (3): 353–87.

Silverstein, Ken. 2000. *Private Warriors.* New York: Verso.

Simmons, Beth A. 1998. "Compliance with International Agreements." *Annual Review of Political Science* 1:75–93.

——. 2009. *Mobilizing for Human Rights: International Law in Domestic Politics.* New York: Cambridge University Press.

Sislin, John and Frederic S. Pearson. 2001. *Arms and Ethnic Conflict.* Lanham, MD: Rowman & Littlefield.

Slaughter, Anne-Marie. 1995. "International Law in a World of Liberal States." *European Journal of International Law* 6 (1): 1–39.

Slonin, Shlomo. 1987. "Origins of the 1950 Tripartite Declaration on the Middle East." *Middle East Studies* 23 (2): 135–49.

Small, Melvin. 1996. *Democracy and Diplomacy: The Impact of Domestic Politics on US Foreign Policy, 1789–1994.* Baltimore: Johns Hopkins University Press.

Small Arms Survey (SAS). 2001. *Small Arms Survey 2001: Profiling the Problem.* New York: Oxford University Press.

——. 2002. *Small Arms Survey 2002: Counting the Human Cost*. New York: Oxford University Press.

——. 2003. *Small Arms Survey 2003: Development Denied*. New York: Oxford University Press.

——. 2006. *Small Arms Survey 2006: Unfinished Business*. New York: Oxford University Press.

——. 2007. *Small Arms Survey 2007: Guns and the City*. New York: Oxford University Press.

——. 2009. *Small Arms Survey 2009: Shadows of War*. New York: Oxford University Press.

Smith, Jackie, Ron Pagnucco, and George A. Lopez. 1998. "Globalizing Human Rights: The Work of Transnational Human Rights NGOs in the 1990s." *Human Rights Quarterly* 20 (2): 379–412.

Smith, Karen E. 2001. "The EU, Human Rights, and Relations with Third Countries: 'Foreign Policy' with an Ethical Dimension?" In *Ethics and Foreign Policy*, edited by Karen E. Smith and Margot Light, 185–204. New York: Cambridge University Press.

Smith, Ron P. and Ali Tasiran. 2005. "The Demand for Arms Imports." *Journal of Peace Research* 42 (2): 167–81.

Smith-Cannoy, Heather. 2012. *Insincere Commitments: Human Rights Treaties, Abusive States, and Citizen Activism*. Washington, DC: Georgetown University Press.

Smouts, Marie-Claude. 2000. "The General Assembly: Grandeur and Decadence." In *The United Nations at the Millennium: The Principal Organs*, edited by Paul Taylor and A. J. R. Groom, 21–60. New York: Continuum.

Soares de Lima, Maria Regina and Mônica Hirst. 2006. "Brazil as an Intermediate State and Regional Power: Action, Choice, and Responsibilities." *International Affairs* 82 (1): 21–40.

Sobel, Richard. 2001. *The Impact of Public Opinion on U.S. Foreign Policy Since Vietnam*. New York: Oxford University Press.

Southall, David P. and Bernadette A. M. O'Hare. 2002. "Empty Arms: The Effect of the Arms Trade on Mothers and Children." *British Medical Journal*, December 21–28: 1457–61.

Spear, Joanna. 1990. "Britain and Conventional Arms Transfer Restraint." In *UK Arms Control in the 1990s*, edited by Mark Hoffman, 170–89. New York: Manchester University Press.

——. 1994. "On the Desirability and Feasibility of Arms Transfer Regime Formation." *Contemporary Security Policy* 15 (3): 84–111.

——. 1995. *Carter and Arms Sales: Implementing the Carter Administration's Arms Transfer Restraint Policy*. New York: St. Martin's Press.

Sperling, James. 2007. "United States: The Unrelenting Search for an Existential Threat in the Twenty-First Century." In *Global Security Governance: Competing Perceptions of Security in the 21st Century*, edited by Emil J. Kirchner and James Sperling, 161–95. New York: Routledge.

Squires, Peter. 2000. *Gun Culture or Gun Control? Firearms, Violence, and Society.* New York: Routledge.

Stanley, John and Maurice Pearton. 1972. *The International Trade in Arms.* London: Chatto & Windus.

Stavrianakis, Anna. 2008. *The Façade of Arms Control: How the UK's Export Licensing System Facilitates the Arms Trade.* Goodwin Paper no. 6. Retrieved March 11, 2010, from http://www.caat.org.uk.

——. 2010. *Taking Aim at the Arms Trade: NGOs, Global Civil Society, and the World Military Order.* London: Zed Books.

Stephens, Philip. 1996. "An Obsession with Secrecy." *Financial Times*, February 16. Retrieved August 3, 2008, from Factiva.

Stockholm International Peace Research Institute (SIPRI). 1971. *The Arms Trade with the Third World.* Stockholm: Almqvist & Wiksell.

——. 1999. *SIPRI Yearbook 1999: Armaments, Disarmament, and International Security.* New York: Oxford University Press.

——. 2006. The SIPRI Military Expenditure Database. Retrieved April–June 2006 from http://www.sipri.org.

——. 2007. *SIPRI Yearbook 2007: Armaments, Disarmament, and International Security.* New York: Oxford University Press.

——. 2012. *SIPRI Yearbook 2012: Armaments, Disarmament, and International Security.* New York: Oxford University Press.

Stohl, Michael, David Carleton, and Steven E. Johnson. 1984. "Human Rights and U.S. Foreign Assistance from Nixon to Carter." *Journal of Peace Research* 21 (3): 215–26.

Stohl, Michael, David Carleton, George Lopez, and Stephen Samuels. 1986. "State Violations of Human Rights: Issues and Problems of Measurement." *Human Rights Quarterly* 8 (4): 592–606.

Stohl, Rachel. 2006. *US Small Arms and Global Transfer Principles.* Working Paper 06-1. Waterloo, Canada: Project Ploughshares.

Stohl, Rachel and E. J. Hogendoorn. 2010. *Stopping the Destructive Spread of Small Arms.* Washington, DC: Center for American Progress.

Stohl, Rachel and Suzette Grillot. 2009. *The International Arms Trade.* Malden, MA: Polity.

Stone, David R. 2000. "Imperialism and Sovereignty: The League of Nations' Drive to Control the Global Arms Trade." *Journal of Contemporary History* 35 (2): 213–30.

Straw, Jack. 2005. "Securing a Global Arms Trade Treaty." Speech given at the Institute of Civil Engineers, London, March 15. Retrieved April 24, 2007, from http://www.fco.gov.uk.

Swanson, Norman R. 1998. "Money and Output Viewed Through a Rolling Window." *Journal of Monetary Economics* 41:455–73.

Tajfel, Henri and John C. Turner. 1986. "The Social Identity Theory of Intergroup Behavior." In *Psychology of Intergroup Relations*, 2nd ed., edited by Stephen Worchel and William G. Austin, 7–24. Chicago: Nelson-Hall.

Tang, Shiping. 2005. "Reputation, Cult of Reputation, and International Conflict." *Security Studies* 14 (1): 34–62.

Tanner, Stephen. 2001. "Ministerial Ethics and the Media." In *Motivating Ministers to Morality*, edited by Jenny Fleming and Ian Holland, 159–70. Burlington, VT: Ashgate.

Tarbuck, Emily. 2013. "Argentina's Arms Trafficking Scandal: Inside Menem's Trial." *Argentina Independent*, June 26. Retrieved July 10, 2013, from http://www.argentinaindependent.com.

Tardy, Thierry. 2007. "France: Between Exceptionalism and Orthodoxy." In *Global Security Governance: Competing Perceptions of Security in the 21st Century*, edited by Emil J. Kirchner and James Sperling, 25–45. New York: Routledge.

Taylor, Trevor. 1994. "Conventional Arms: The Drives to Export." In *The Defence Trade: Demand, Supply, and Control*, edited by Trevor Taylor and Ryukichi Imai, 95–123. London: Royal Institute for International Affairs.

Tesser, Abraham and Jennifer Campbell. 1980. "Self-Definition: The Impact of Relative Performance and Similarity of Others." *Social Psychology Quarterly* 43 (3): 341–47.

"That Damned Elusive Mitterrand." 1987. *The Economist*, November 14. Retrieved August 6, 2008, from LexisNexis.

Thelen, David. 1996. *Becoming Citizens in the Age of Television: How Americans Challenged the Media and Seized Political Initiative During the Iran–Contra Debate*. Chicago: University of Chicago Press.

Thompson, Brian. 1997. Introduction to *Under the Scott-Light: British Government Seen Through the Scott Report*, edited by Brian Thompson and F. F. Ridley, 1–8. New York: Oxford University Press.

Thompson, John B. 2000. *Political Scandal: Power and Visibility in the Media Age*. Cambridge, UK: Polity Press.

Thréard, Yves. 2011. "L'Honneur retrouvé de Pierre Falcone." *Le Figaro*, April 30. Retrieved July 10, 2013, from http://www.lefigaro.fr.

Tinsley, Becky. 2004. "France's Secret Dirty Wars." *New Statesman*, June 28. Retrieved August 5, 2008, from http://www.newstatesman.com.

Tomkins, Adam. 1998. *The Constitution After Scott: Government Unwrapped*. New York: Oxford University Press.

Tomz, Michael. 2007. *Reputation and International Cooperation: Sovereign Debt Across Three Centuries*. Princeton: Princeton University Press.

Tomz, Michael and Mark L. J. Wright. 2010. "Sovereign Theft: Theory and Evidence About Sovereign Default and Expropriation." In *The Natural Resources Trap: Private Investment Without Public Commitment*, edited by William Hogan and Federico Sturzenegger, 69–110. Cambridge, MA: MIT Press.

Toolis, Kevin. 1990. "The Man Behind Iraq's Supergun." *New York Times*, August 26. Retrieved January 26, 2009, from LexisNexis Academic.

Trager, Oliver, ed. 1988. *The Iran–Contra Arms Scandal: Foreign Policy Disaster*. An Editorials on File Book. New York: Facts on File.

Transatlantic Trends. 2009. *Key Findings 2009*. Washington, DC: German Marshall Fund of the United States.

Tsygankov, Andrei P. and Matthew Tarver-Wahlquist. 2009. "Duelling Honors: Power, Identity, and the Russia–Georgia Divide." *Foreign Policy Analysis* 5:307–26.

UK House of Commons. 1988–2006. *Hansard Debates* (UK House of Commons daily debates). Retrieved March 2007 and August 2008 from http://www.publications.parliament.uk.

United Nations. 1997. *Report of the Panel of Governmental Experts on Small Arms*. A/52/298. New York: United Nations.

United Nations Department of Disarmament Affairs. 2002. *The United Nations Disarmament Year Book 2001*. Vol. 26. New York: United Nations.

United Nations Economic and Social Council. 2006. *Promotion and Protection of Human Rights: Interim Report of the Special Representative of the Secretary-General on the Issue of Human Rights and Transnational Corporations and Other Business Enterprises*. E/CN.4/2006/97. New York: United Nations.

United Nations General Assembly. 2007. *Towards an Arms Trade Treaty: Establishing Common International Standards for the Import, Export, and Transfer of Conventional Arms: Report of the Secretary-General*. A/62/278 (Part I). New York: United Nations.

United Nations Office for Disarmament Affairs. 2012. *Transparency in Armaments: Reporting to the United Nations Register of Conventional Arms*. Fact Sheet. New York: UN Office for Disarmament Affairs.

United Nations Statistics Division. 2006. National Accounts Main Aggregates Database. Updated 2012. Retrieved May 1, 2006, from http://unstats.un.org.

Unter dem Druck der Öffentlichkeit. 1992. *Süddeutsche Zeitung*, April 1. Retrieved February 10, 2007, from LexisNexis Academic.

US Department of State (DOS). 2001. *Background Paper: Can Small Arms and Light Weapons Be Controlled?* Fact Sheet, June 2. Washington, DC: Bureau

of Political-Military Affairs. Retrieved November 17, 2006, from http://www
.state.gov.

US General Accounting Office (GAO). 2000. *US Efforts to Control the Availability of Small Arms and Light Weapons. Report to the Honorable Dianne Feinstein, US Senate.* GAO/NSIAD-00–141. Washington, DC: US GAO.

U.S. Senate, Committee on Foreign Relations. 1979. *Prospects for Multilateral Arms Export Restraint: A Staff Report.* 96th Cong., 1st Sess. Washington, DC: U.S. Government Printing Office.

Utley, Rachel. 2000. *The French Defence Debate: Consensus and Continuity in the Mitterrand Era.* New York: St. Martin's Press.

——. 2002. "'Not to Do Less but to Do Better . . . ': French Military Policy in Africa." *International Affairs* 78 (1): 129–46.

Uviller, H. Richard and William G. Merkel. 2002. *The Militia and the Right to Arms, or How the Second Amendment Fell Silent.* Durham, NC: Duke University Press.

Van Ham, Peter. 2008. "Place Branding: The State of the Art." *Annals of the American Academy of Political and Social Science* 616:126–49.

Verbruggen, Didier, Peter Danssaert, Johan Peleman, and Tomas Baum. 2005. *Wapentrafieken in de regio van de grote meren: Tanzania.* International Peace Information Service (IPIS) Dossier 145. Antwerp: IPIS.

Verschelden, Wouter. 2006a. "Drop in Flemish Arms Exports." *De Standaard*, May 16. Reprinted in "Belgium Reports Fall in Flemish Arms Exports, Details Rejected Deals." *BBC Worldwide Monitoring*, May 16. Retrieved March 3, 2007, from Lexis-Nexis Academic.

——. 2006b. "Weapons to Israel Not Kosher." *De Standaard*, October 26. Reprinted in "Belgium's Flemish MPs Condemn Military Sales Reaching Israel." *BBC Worldwide Monitoring*, October 26. Retrieved March 3, 2007, from LexisNexis Academic.

Verwimp, Philip. 2006. "Machetes and Firearms: The Organization of Massacres in Rwanda." *Journal of Peace Research* 43 (1): 5–22.

Vincent, David. 1998. *The Culture of Secrecy: Britain, 1832–1998.* New York: Oxford University Press.

Von Hammerstein, Konstantin, Ralf Neukirch, Gordon Repinski, Holger Stark, Gerald Traufetter, and Klaus Wiegrefe. 2012. "Die Merkel-Doktrin." *Der Spiegel* 49: 20–27.

Vranckx, An. 2005. *European Arms Exports to Latin America—an Inventory.* International Peace Information Service (IPIS) Background Report, March. Brussels: IPIS.

Waldermeirin, Patti. 2007. "Bush Faces Hurdle on Arms Deal." *Financial Times*, July 30. Retrieved July 31, 2007, from http://www.ft.com.

Walsh, Lawrence E. 1997. *Firewall: The Iran–Contra Conspiracy and Cover-Up*. New York: Norton.

Walt, Stephen M. 2005. *Taming American Power: The Global Response to US Primacy*. New York: Norton.

Walter, Barbara F. 2009. *Reputation and Civil War: Why Separatist Conflicts Are so Violent*. New York: Cambridge University Press.

Waltz, Kenneth N. 1979. *Theory of International Politics*. Reading, MA: Addison-Wesley.

Waltz, Susan. 2007. *US Policy on Small Arms Transfers: A Human Rights Perspective*. Human Rights and Human Welfare Working Paper no. 43. Denver: University of Denver.

Webster, Paul. 1987a. "Amused and Silent: The French President's Response to the Carefully Timed Iran Arms Deal Allegations." *Guardian*, November 6. Retrieved August 6, 2008, from LexisNexis.

——. 1987b. "Irangate Scandal Rocks Paris." *Guardian*, November 2. Retrieved August 6, 2008, from LexisNexis.

——. 1988. "Iran Scandal Brings Paris Arms Crisis to a Head: French Weapons Industry Rethinks Its Traditional Reliance on Exports." *Guardian*, January 4. Retrieved August 6, 2008, from LexisNexis.

Weidacher, Reinhilde. 2005. *Behind a Veil of Secrecy: Military Small Arms and Light Weapons Production in Western Europe*. Small Arms Survey Occasional Paper no. 16. Geneva: Small Arms Survey.

Wendt, Alexander. 1999. *Social Theory of International Politics*. New York: Cambridge University Press.

——. 2004. "The State as Person in International Theory." *Review of International Studies* 30:289–316.

Wentz, William George. 1987–1988. "The United States Is Moving Further from Fostering Multilateral Restraint of Conventional Arms Sales." *Dickinson Journal of International Law* 6:343–75.

Wezeman, Pieter D. 2003. *Conflicts and Transfers of Small Arms*. Report for SIPRI Conflicts and Transfers of Small Arms Project. Solna, Sweden: Stockholm International Peace Research Institute.

Wheeler, Nicholas J. 2000. *Saving Strangers: Humanitarian Intervention in International Society*. New York: Oxford University Press.

Wheeler, Nicholas J. and Tim Dunne. 1998. "Good International Citizenship: A Third Way for British Foreign Policy." *International Affairs* 74 (4): 847–70.

Whetten, David A. 1997. "Theory Development and the Study of Corporate Reputation." *Corporate Reputation Review* 1 (1): 26–34.

White, David and Robert Mauthner. 1988. "Britain's Arms Sale of the Century." *Financial Times*, July 9. Retrieved March 18, 2007, from LexisNexis Academic.

Whitney, Craig R. 1998. "Panel Finds French Errors in Judgment on Rwanda." *New York Times*, December 20. Retrieved August 5, 2008, from http://www.nytimes.com.

Wildavsky, Aaron. 1994. "Why Self-Interest Means Less Outside of a Social Context: Cultural Contributions to a Theory of Rational Choices." *Journal of Theoretical Politics* 6 (2): 131–59.

Williams, Robert. 1998. *Political Scandals in the USA*. Edinburgh, UK: Keele University Press.

Wittkopf, Eugene R. 1990. *Faces of Internationalism: Public Opinion and American Foreign Policy*. Durham, NC: Duke University Press.

Wolfers, Arnold. 1962. *Discord and Collaboration: Essays on International Politics*. Baltimore: Johns Hopkins University Press.

Wolford, Scott. 2007. "The Turnover Trap: New Leaders, Reputation, and International Conflict." *American Journal of Political Science* 51 (4): 772–88.

Wolpin, Miles. 1986. "State Terrorism and Repression in the Third World: Parameters and Prospects." In *Government Violence and Repression: An Agenda for Research*, edited by Michael Stohl and George A. Lopez, 97–164. New York: Greenwood Press.

——. 1991. *America Insecure: Arms Transfers, Global Interventionism, and the Erosion of National Security*. Jefferson, NC: McFarland.

Wood, Pia Christina. 1997. "French Political Party Opposition to European Integration, 1981–1996: Myth or Reality?" In *Europe's Ambiguous Unity: Conflict and Consensus in the Post-Maastricht Era*, edited by Alan W. Cafruny and Carl Lankowski, 131–54. Boulder, CO: Lynne Rienner.

Wooldridge, Jeffrey M. 2000. *Introductory Econometrics: A Modern Approach*. Cincinnati: South-Western College.

Worcester, Robert M. and Roger Mortimore. 1999. *Explaining Labour's Landslide*. London: Politico's.

Wright, Robin. 2007. "Iran Is Critical as U.S. Unveils Arms Sales in the Middle East." *Washington Post*, July 31. Retrieved July 31, 2007, from http://www.washingtonpost.com.

Wroe, Ann. 1991. *Lives, Lies, and the Iran–Contra Affair*. New York: Tauris.

Wulf, Herbert. 1993. "Arms Industry Limited: The Turning-Point in the 1990s." In *Arms Industry Limited*, edited by Herbert Wulf, 3–26. New York: Oxford University Press.

——. 1996. "German Arms Export Policy." In *The European Arms Trade*, edited by Martin Navias and Susan Willett, 31–46. New York: Nova Science.

Wyatt, Charli. 2002. "The Forgotten Victims of Small Arms." *SAIS Review* 21 (1): 223–28.

Yanik, Lerna. 2006. "Guns and Human Rights: Major Powers, Global Arms Transfers, and Human Rights Violations." *Human Rights Quarterly* 28 (2): 357–88.

Young, Oran R. 1992. "The Effectiveness of International Institutions: Hard Cases and Critical Variables." In *Governance Without Government: Order and Change in World Politics*, edited by James N. Rosenau and Ernst-Otto Czempiel, 160–94. New York: Cambridge University Press.

Zarakol, Ayşe. 2011. *After Defeat: How the East Learned to Live with the West.* New York: Cambridge University Press.

Zürn, Michael and Jeffrey T. Checkel. 2005. "Getting Socialized to Build Bridges: Constructivism and Rationalism, Europe and the Nation-State." *International Organization* 59:1045–79.

INDEX